Returning To The Source

Osho taught philosophy at the University of Jabalpur before establishing the commune in Poona, India which has become famous all over the world as a mecca for seekers wanting to experience meditation and transformation. His teachings have influenced millions of people of all ages and from all walks of life. He has been described by *The Sunday Times* as one of the 1,000 Makers of the Twentieth Century, and by *The Sunday Mid-Day* (India) as one of the ten people – along with Gandhi, Nehru and Buddha – who have changed the destiny of India.

BY THE SAME AUTHOR

Finger Pointing to the Moon
Heartbeat of the Absolute
The Heart Sutra
Journey to the Heart
The Mustard Seed
No Water No Moon
The Psychology of the Esoteric
My Way: The Way of the White Clouds
Tantric Transformation
The Tantra Experience
The Zen Manifesto

and many more

Returning To The Source

OSHO

ELEMENT

Shaftesbury, Dorset • Rockport, Massachusetts
Brisbane, Queensland

This edition published in Great Britain in 1995 by
Element Books Limited
Shaftesbury, Dorset SP7 8BP

Published in the USA in 1995 by
Element Books, Inc.
PO Box 830, Rockport, MA 01966

Published in Australia in 1995 by
Element Books Limited for
Jacaranda Wiley Limited
33 Park Road, Milton, Brisbane 4064

Editing by Ma Yoga Sudha,
Swami Krishna Prabhu
Design and typesetting by Swami Bhaven
Cover design: Max Fairbrother
Production by Ma Deva Harito

Printed and bound in Great Britain by
Hartnolls, Bodmin, Cornwall

British Library Cataloguing in Publication
data available

Library of Congress Cataloging in Publication
data available

Second Edition

ISBN 1-85230-700-5

ACKNOWLEDGMENTS AND COPYRIGHT NOTICES

For permission to use the following material grateful acknowledgment is extended to:

Yu Nien Tze Chang for her kind permission to quote from "The Practice of Zen" by Chang Chen-chi. Harper & Brothers, New York, 1959 (further identified in footnote).

Doubleday, a division of Bantam Doubleday Dell Publishing Group. Inc., for permission to quote from "Zen: Poems, Prayers, Sermons, Anecdotes, Interviews" edited by Lucien Stryk and translated by Takashi Ikemoto, © copyright 1965 by Lucien Stryk and Takashi Ikemoto (further identified in footnote).

First Zen Institute of America for kind permission to quote from "The Three Types of Religious Method" from "The Cat's Yawn" by Sokei-an, First Zen Institute of America, New York, 1947 (further identified in footnote).

Hokuseido Press for permission to quote from "Oriental Humor" by R.H.Blyth, Hokuseido Press, Tokyo, 1959 (further identified in footnote).

John Murray Publishers Ltd., London, for kind permission to quote from "Wisdom of the East Series, The Book of Lieh-Tzu" translated by A.C.Graham (further identified in footnote).

Peter Pauper Press, Inc., for permission to quote from "Zen Buddhism" © copyright 1959 Peter Pauper Press, Inc. Reprinted with permission (further identified in footnote).

Charles E. Tuttle Co., Inc., Tokyo, for permission to quote from "One Note of Zen" from "Zen Flesh, Zen Bones" by Paul Reps, © copyright 1957 (further identified in footnote).

Spontaneous discourses
given by Osho
to disciples and friends
in Lao Tzu House,
Poona, India.

Contents

Introduction

The Zen in this book is no-nonsense Zen. It is not only the flesh and bones, it also carries the essence. It is not Zen explained, because Zen cannot be explained.

The essence is Osho.

Through the vehicle of Osho, Zen comes to life and hits home. If you try to figure out and analyze, the precious quality of this book will elude you. If you want to taste something of what Zen is, this book will help. Simplicity is often obscure, and Zen is the ultimate simplicity. Looking at a tree we see the tree; it is there, but we can only feel ourselves. We cannot see the most obvious thing, the thing that makes the tree be there...the place where we are standing.

So it is with Zen. It cannot be understood with mind but it can be felt. When the mind is at a loss to understand a statement such as "nothing is everything," or, for that matter, "everything is nothing," the heart that is open can immediately absorb the truth of this, the possibility.

And Osho is the Zen master who unveils the magic of Zen. His being is food, nourishment for the neglected being in ourselves.

In going inwards there are many rivers to cross, many source-wounds to heal. The journey back to the source is always new, full of wonder and discovery every moment, at each level. It can never grow old because the source is the beginning. It is like a house with layers of doors in layers on layers of rooms: there is the source, and the source, and the source. Entering is leaving behind, leaving behind is entering, and on and on in an infinite cosmic striptease. We never finish. But it's fun, so who wants to finish?

As we listen to the old Zen masters speak through Osho, his words are like bubbles; if your heart is open they bathe you in his silence as they burst.

In this book, if you let him in just a little, he will give you much food for thought. Then for you this book can be a wealth of knowledge. But if you let him enter you...between the lines... between the words...between the verses, then it can be an explosion of understanding. It could transform you.

The essence is ever available. The key is within, in how much we can receive.

Says Osho:

Listen to the music, don't listen to the logic.
It has no logic in it, it has only a melody.

Ma Yoga Sudha

一

Discourse 1

One Short Note

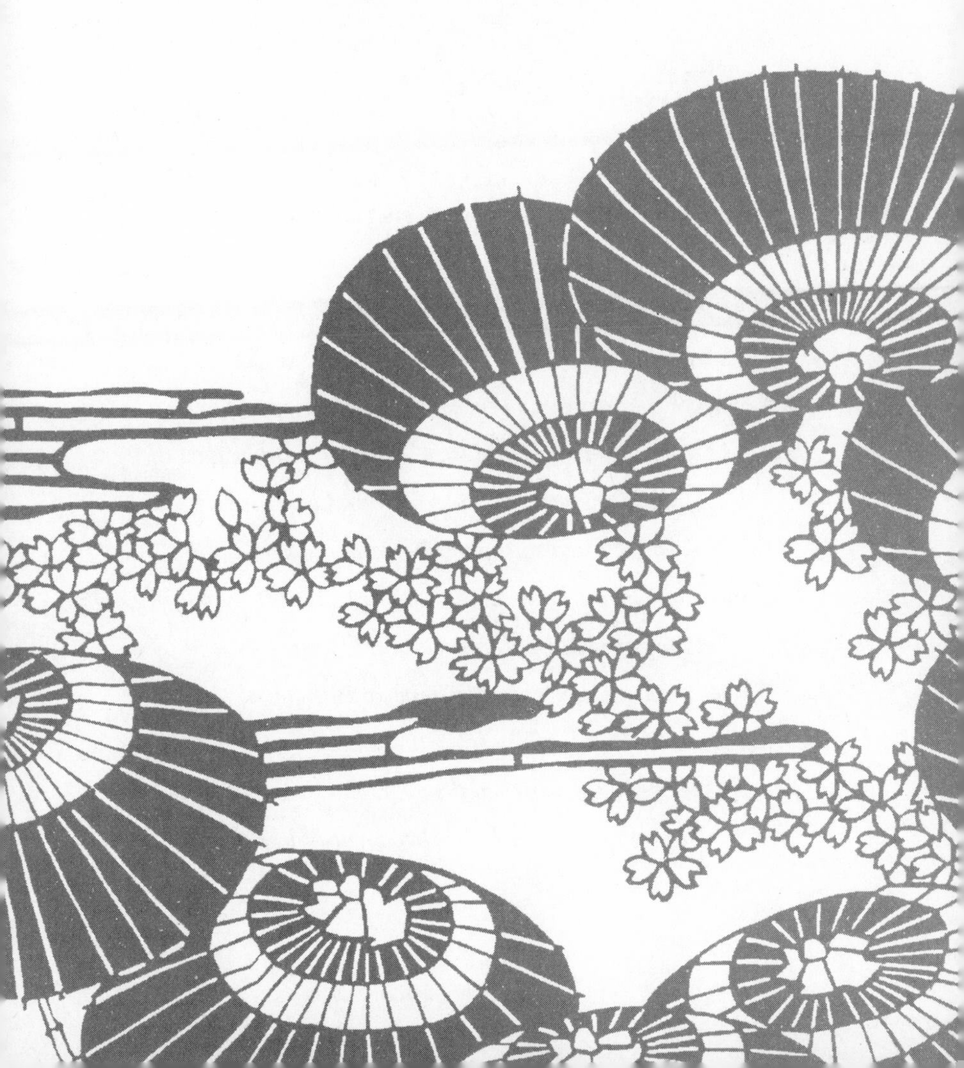

Kakua was the first Japanese to study Zen in China,
and while he was there he accepted the true teaching.
When he was in China he did not travel. He lived in a remote
part of a mountain and meditated constantly.
Whenever people found him and asked him to preach,
he would say a few words and then move to another part of
the mountain where he could be found less easily.
When Kakua returned to Japan, the emperor heard about
him and asked him to come to court to preach Zen
for the edification of himself and his subjects.
Kakua stood before the emperor in silence.
He then produced a flute from the folds of his robes,
blew one short note, bowed politely, and disappeared.
No one ever knew what became of him.

The real teaching cannot be taught but still it is called a teaching. It cannot be taught but it can be shown, indicated. There is no way to say it directly, but there are millions of ways to indicate it indirectly.

Lao Tzu says that the truth cannot be said, and the moment you say it you have already falsified it. The words, the language, the mind, are utterly incapable. It defies reason, it defies the head-oriented personality, it defies the ego. It cannot be manipulated. It is utterly impossible for reason to encounter it.

This is the first thing to be understood, and the more deeply you understand it, the more possibility will be available for me to indicate towards it. Whatsoever I am saying is not the truth; it cannot be. Through words only a situation can be created in which truth may be possible. But that too one can never be definite about. It is unpredictable. No cause can be produced for it to happen – it happens when it happens. The only thing that can be done is to become available to it. Your doors should be open. When it knocks at your door, you should be present there. If you are present, available, receptive, it can happen. But remember, through scriptures, through the words of the enlightened ones, you cannot attain it.

So the first thing is that it cannot be said. And every master has to create an indirect situation, has to push you towards the unknown. All that he is saying is just pushing you towards that which cannot be said.

The second thing, before we can understand Kakua and this beautiful Zen story: the real teaching defies words but it cannot defy the heart. If there were a language of the heart, it could be said through it. But the heart has no language; or, silence is the only language of the heart.

When the heart is silent it says something; when the mind is silent it says nothing. Words are the vehicle of the mind. No-words, silence, is the vehicle of the heart. Silence is a language without words, but one has to learn it. Just as one has to learn the languages of the mind, one has to learn the language of the heart: how to be silent, how to be wordless, how to be without a mind, how to be a no-mind.

When the mind stops functioning, immediately the whole energy moves towards the heart. When the mind is not functioning the heart functions; when the heart functions, only then can something be taught to you. The real teaching can be taught through the heart. You must be near the heart. The nearer you are, the more capable you become of understanding the silence.

Remember, silence is not emptiness. To the reason it may appear that silence is emptiness – it is not. Silence is the most fulfilled moment possible. It is not only fulfilled, it is overflowing. But it is of a felt significance. The heart is not empty; it is the only thing which is full. The mind is just empty because mind has nothing but words. And what are words? – ripples in emptiness. And what is silence? – silence is the total.

When you think you are separate from existence, when you don't think you are one...in a non-thinking moment you lose all boundaries. Suddenly you disappear, and still you are. And this felt moment of non-ego, of no-mind, of no-thought, is the situation in which it becomes possible for the truth to descend in you. When you are empty of yourself you will be filled by truth. So all that a master has to do is to kill you utterly and completely, to destroy your ego utterly and completely, is to cut off your head so that you can become the heart. Then the whole energy moves into the heart.

Can you be headless? If you can be, only then can you be a disciple. If you cling to the head then you cannot be a disciple. Can you live without the head? If you cannot live without the head then you are closed to the truth. Head is the barrier, heart is the opening.

So how can the real teaching be taught? It cannot be taught. It is not a learning, you cannot learn it from somebody; it is an inner discipline. You have to become a receptive vehicle, a medium. It is not something which you can learn remaining as you are. It cannot be an accumulation. You have to go through a transformation, you have to be different. You have to bring a different quality to your being.

Only then does communication become possible – not exactly communication but rather, communion. Through the head there is a communication, through the heart there is a communion; it is not a dialogue. In fact, it is a meeting of the master with the disciple. It is less a dialogue, more a merging, a melting, where the master and the disciple merge into each other just as lovers merge. But lovers merge in the body; at the most lovers can merge in the mind. But a disciple and a master is the greatest love affair in the world: they merge in the spirit, they become one.

Only when they are one can the truth be shown. It cannot be taught, it cannot be learned; nobody can teach you. You can get it from nobody. The whole effort of getting it from somebody, alive or dead, from scriptures or from teachings, is futile. And the sooner you understand it the better, because the time wasted will simply be wasted. Nothing can be achieved by it.

You have to pass through a transformation. You have to die and be reborn. You have to be completely new, totally new. Only with that 'new' – when the old has gone, when you have disappeared and a new being has taken place – then there is communion.

This beautiful Zen story says many things. Try to understand each word because each word is significant.

Kakua was the first Japanese to study Zen in China...

Zen is the most subtle teaching. The word 'zen' comes from *dhyana*. The teaching was born with Buddha in India, but then unfortunately India became non-receptive, and Buddha's disciples had to seek in China people who were more receptive to it.

Buddha has said many things, but he has never said a single word about truth. He talked his whole life; for forty years after his enlightenment he talked every day continually, but he has not said a single word about truth. Whenever somebody would ask, "What is truth?" he would remain silent.

Then one day it happened. He sat under a tree. Many people had gathered; all his disciples were present and they were waiting for him to say something. But he would not say anything, he simply sat there. He had a flower in his hand, a lotus flower. It is very significant, because in the East the lotus flower is the symbol of ultimate flowering. In the East, the highest peak of your being is thought to be like a lotus. It is. When your final peak comes, inside your being a flower starts opening. And then it goes on opening and opening and opening: from perfection to more perfection and still more perfection, there is no end to it. This lotus is called *sahasrar*, the one-thousand-petaled lotus.

Buddha came with a lotus; he sat under a tree and he looked at the lotus as if he had forgotten about the ten thousand people who had gathered there – who were there, and they were waiting impatiently. Moments passed, then hours started passing and people became very uneasy. It was as if Buddha had forgotten completely about them.

He is there, the flower is there, and he is so attentive to the flower that it seems that even the boundaries between Buddha and the flower are lost. Then suddenly one disciple – his name is Mahakashyapa – starts laughing loudly. It is unbelievable because this Mahakashyapa is such a silent one, nobody has ever seen him laughing; and such a belly laugh, as if he has gone mad. Everybody looks at him. Buddha calls him near, Mahakashyapa comes. Buddha gives the flower to Mahakashyapa and tells the assembly, "Whatsoever can be said I have told you, and whatsoever cannot be said I have given to Mahakashyapa – and this is the real teaching."

For thousands of years now Buddhists all over the world have been asking: What was given to Mahakashyapa? What was it? It became one of the most penetrating questions. Buddha told Mahakashyapa to find a man who could receive this lotus. Mahakashyapa found a man. For a few hundred years others could also, then others, but the sixth master, Bodhidharma, could not find a single man in the whole of India. He wandered around with a lotus. He went to every village, he knocked on every door; he couldn't find a man to commune with, to say that which cannot be said. Nobody was ready to receive the real teaching.

In India there were millions of scholars, men filled with knowledge – great pundits. Those were the peak days of the Indian mind. Never again has India reached to that peak of scholarship. But Bodhidharma could not find a single man who was able to receive Buddha's lotus. So Bodhidharma had to go to China to find a man there. Even there, he had to search for nine years continuously before he found one.

Zen is dhyana; in China it became *ch'an*. And then from China it had to be taken to Japan, because in China also it soon became impossible to find a man who was ready to receive it. This Kakua brought it from China to Japan. Just as Bodhidharma took it from India to China, Kakua brought it from China to Japan.

This man is very significant and very rare. Nobody knows anything about him; only this story exists. He is just exactly like Mahakashyapa – nobody knows anything about him. Only this story I told you about the giving of the lotus flower – only this story is known about him. About Kakua also only this story is known. No one ever knew what became of him. A man who becomes totally silent loses boundaries, loses definitions, loses autobiography. There is nothing to talk about, there is nobody to talk about.

Paramhansa Yogananda is the first yogi in the whole history of yoga who has written an autobiography. This is foolish because the yogi, by the very nature of his being, has no autobiography. Autobiographies exist around the ego. A yogi, by the very nature of his being, is nobody; that is his whole autobiography.

Nobody knows anything about Kakua except this small anecdote, but this is enough. Because this anecdote contains all the Vedas, all the Korans, and all the Bibles – all the Vedas that have existed and that will exist in the future – this small anecdote contains them all. So listen carefully.

Kakua was the first Japanese to study Zen in China, and while he was there he accepted the true teaching.

He accepted the true teaching... Look at the words. True teaching is always available. Somebody is needed to accept it. It is always available but you are not ready to accept it; you reject it. Whenever a master knocks at your door, you reject. This has been my experience working on so many people. It is rare that when I knock at their door, they accept me – it is very rare. They reject in millions of ways. Acceptance is difficult. Why? Because if you accept, your ego is lost. The ego decides whether to accept or not; the reason thinks whether this is true or not. The reason never loses control.

Just the other day I was talking to somebody and I told him, "Now you are ready, take a jump into sannyas." The man said, "I will think about it." How can you think about it? Thinking is possible only if you have known it before, because thinking moves into the realm of the known. If you had known in the past what sannyas is, if you had ever been a sannyasin, then you could think about it. But once you have been a sannyasin you can never be otherwise, because to be a sannyasin is such a transformation. You don't know what sannyas is and you say, "I will think about it." How will you think about it? What will you think about it?

Sannyas is a movement into the unknown. It is a trust. It is not your rational decision, it is an irrational jump. If you are fed up with your reason, only then. But you say, "I will decide." Who will decide? your mind? Are you not fed up with your mind? Have you not done everything the mind says to you to do? Where have you got through it? Where have you reached? What has happened? Look at your life; this is where your mind has got you to – it is a hell. Still you cling to it and you say, "I will think about it." And who are you, and who is saying, "I will think about it"? Who is this 'I'?

Sannyas is to drop the 'I', and if the 'I' decides then there can be no dropping, because in the very decision the 'I' has been saved. You cannot decide, that's why it is a trust. That's why I say it is an ultimate love affair. If you trust you trust a master. Then you don't say, "*I* will decide." You simply say, "I accept; I am here available, you do whatsoever you want to do with me. Don't ask, just do whatsoever you want to do with me." That is the meaning of acceptance – it is a trust, it is *shraddha,* it is faith; it is not a conviction.

...and while he was there he accepted the true teaching.

You cannot learn it, it cannot be taught. But it can be accepted and it can be given. Whenever you are ready to accept it, it can be given, just like the lotus flower of the Buddha. Don't think in literal terms. Don't think that Buddha really carried the lotus flower in his hand. His hand *is* the lotus flower; *he* is the lotus flower. It is possible that only Mahakashyapa could see it, nobody else.

Look at my hand – the lotus flower is there. If you accept, I can give it to you. But acceptance means a death. Acceptance means that you die as you are. Something new is born, disconnected, discontinuous with the past. When you are reborn you will not be able to connect it with who was there before, because the old man and the new man never meet. The old man goes out, the new man comes in, but in the innermost core of your being they never meet. The old goes out...only then the inner opens for the new to receive. They never meet.

Enlightenment is a discontinuity with the past. You will never become enlightened, remember; you will have to leave. Only when you leave, only when you are not in the way, does the new happen.

Kakua accepted the true teaching. Acceptance is one of the most beautiful words. Buddhists, the followers of Buddha, have a term for it which is even deeper than the English word 'acceptance'; it is *tathata.* Tathata means saying yes so totally that in your being there is no division. You become one in your yes. You say yes so totally that there exists no no inside you, no denial.

Tathata, or total acceptance, is not a majority decision. It is not parliamentary, it is total. It is not that the major part of your mind, the major part of your being decides, and the minor still goes on saying no. Then it is conflict. Then who knows, any day the majority may become a minority and the minority may become a majority. It is bound to be so, because sooner or later the majority will be tired of saying yes and will relax more and more, and the minority which says no without doing anything will gather force and momentum. By and by the majority will be exhausted and the minority will collect energy. Not doing anything, sooner or later it will become the majority. There is an inner politics.

Acceptance, total acceptance, tathata, means without any political decision – total. There is nobody who says no within you, not even a fragment, because even a fragment can be destructive. And even if part of you says no you cannot receive the true teaching.

People come to me. They say, "We surrender," and they don't do what they are saying. If I say to them. "Okay, change your dress to ochre," they say, "It is difficult, I am not ready for it." Just the dress, and you are not ready to change it! And you are thinking of changing your soul, your being! And just a moment before the person was saying, "I surrender to you."

He does not know what surrender means; he does not know what he is saying, he is fast asleep. In his sleep he may have used the word surrender, but the moment I say, "Change something, your dress, your name," he says, "It is difficult, I love my name. Let my name remain the same. My name is beautiful, don't change it." Even the name, which is nothing but a word.... And you don't come with a name when you are born, you come without a name, a nameless being; this is just a label attached to you – and you cannot even change the label. You are not ready for any change at all.

People ask me, "Why do you change people's name and dress?" That is just the beginning. That's how I start taking hold of you. That's how I feel whether you are ready to change anything or not.

You would like to receive the true teaching without any change. You would like to receive the true teaching as you are. That is not possible. It is not possible because of the very nature of the true teaching. I cannot do anything, nobody can do anything about it. It is in the very nature of the phenomenon: you receive it only when you accept it.

God is available, truth is available, light is available, but you are such a miser in receiving. You are not only a miser in giving, you are a miser in receiving also. A miser has to be a miser whatsoever he does. You cannot give, you cannot receive. What type of life have you got? Giving and receiving are two aspects of the same coin. If you can give you can also receive. Hence, so much insistence on giving – giving to people whatsoever you can give – giving in love. So much insistence from all the religions: Give. Give more and more. Why? – so that you can become capable of receiving more and more.

Remember, it is just like inhalation and exhalation: if you exhale deeply, automatically you will inhale deeply. If you want to inhale deeply you will have to exhale deeply – there is no other way. And life is a balance between exhalation and inhalation. If you are afraid of exhalation your breathing will become shallow. Then your inhalation cannot be very deep, it is impossible. Exhalation is giving, giving whatsoever you can give. And the more you give, the more you become capable of receiving. And when you give completely, utterly, totally, that is the moment of acceptance.

Kakua must have given to his master so totally that he became capable of accepting, receiving. He received the true teaching.

When he was in China he didn't travel. He lived in a remote part of a mountain and meditated constantly.

These are symbolic words: *When he was in China he didn't travel.* Mind is constantly traveling. Your outer traveling is just a manifestation of your inner turmoil. When people become so tense inside, so much movement, outside also they start traveling. Hence the American travelers; all over the world American tourists.

It is said: Chuang Tzu reports that he has heard that in the old days, people wouldn't even go to the other side of the river. Chuang Tzu said, "I have heard my grandfather say that in his time they knew that there existed a town on the other side of the river, because in the evening the smoke would rise in the sky, and in the night, in the silence of the night, dogs would bark in the other village."

They knew, but nobody would even ask who lived there. A different quality of people – why bother? They must have lived in total silence – why inquire? Why this curiosity? Somebody must be living there, so it is okay. Nobody went to the other shore of the river to see who was living there.

And just the opposite is happening in America. I have heard an anecdote. Near a Greek volcano an American tourist was standing with a guide. He looked deep into the volcano and he said, "Looks like hell." The guide said, "You Americans – you have been everywhere!"

Kakua did not travel at all, neither to hell nor to heaven. This is just symbolic: one has to be where one is. Non-traveling means not only in space but in time. There are two types of traveling: one traveling is in space – you go from New York to London, from London to Poona, from Poona to Singapore; this is a traveling in space. And then there is a traveling inside the mind, in time. You go into the past, you go into the future, and that is a greater traveling. Instantaneously you can go anywhere; no passports are needed, there is no visa problem. You can move into the past, you can go into the future, you can go anywhere. Mind constantly moves.

Remember, mind is never where you are, it is always somewhere else. You are never in the present moment, because to be in the present moment one has to learn how not to travel, not to go somewhere else, not to visit the past and not to dream the future. Past is no more, future is not yet. You are wasting your life, your energy. You are wasting your precious moment, that which is. It is here, now. The door opens in the present and you miss the door. That is your misery and anguish.

Why are you in such misery? – because you have been missing life itself. Your misery is just an indication that you have missed what life is. Life is in the present, and you go on either in the past or in the future. You are just like the pendulum of an old grandfather clock: you go from this to that...right, left, right, left. The pendulum goes on, it never stays in the middle. If the pendulum stays in the middle, immediately the clock stops.

Mind is just like a clock, and this traveling from past to future is the pendulum. If you stop in the moment, this very moment, if you are here listening to me...to the breeze that passes through the trees, to the airplane that is just now passing, to some bird, to the traffic noise, to all that is happening right now, open to it, receptive to it, the past dropped, the future not there...then you are in a non-traveling state of mind. And this is all that meditation is.

Kakua...did not travel. He lived in a remote part of a mountain and meditated constantly.

There are mountains outside and there are mountains inside. A whole parallel world exists on the inside also. That's why people used to move to the mountains, just to create an outer situation to move inwardly, to the inner mountains. Hindus even have a name for the inner mountain: they call it Sumeru. If you ask where it is, they say it is in heaven. If you think that there is a mountain like Sumeru in heaven you miss the point. They are saying that inside you there is a moment when you are on such a top peak of your being. That top peak of your being is Sumeru, the mountain that exists in heaven, because at that moment you are in heaven.

These are all symbols: Kakua lived on a remote part of a mountain.... He may have lived there outwardly also but that is not very significant. Inside you there are remote parts. Inside you there are parts which belong to the market, there are parts which belong to the family, there are parts which belong to the surface. And there are remote parts inside you which do not belong to the market, to the family or to anybody. Those remote mountains where nobody ever moves, where only you are, you have to seek. You have to sit silently and seek the remote parts within you.

You are a vast universe, remember. The surface that you have taken for granted that you are is just the beginning, the porch. If we are talking on the porch it is because of you. There are remote corners inside the house. Many people live their whole lives on the porch, just by the side of the road: market, family, things, prestige, politics. You live on the surface. Kakua moved inside to inner, remote, and still more remote places inside. How can you go inside? – first stop traveling.

There are two movements of energy, only two. Energy has only two dimensions: one is horizontal, the other is vertical, just like the Christian cross. And the Christian cross is really the symbol for that. One is horizontal: you go from one thought to another, from A to B, from B to C – horizontal. Then there is another movement of energy: you don't go from A to B, you go deeper into A – from A1 to A2, from A2 to A3; you go deeper, or vertical, or higher, because they all mean the same thing.

Look at the cross on which Christ was hung. It has two poles: one is horizontal on which his hands were nailed – that is ordinary time, that is living near the roadside, living in the market, living on the crossroads – and then the depth. His whole body is on the vertical pole. That is going deeper, deeper. When you go for a swim you swim on the surface; that is horizontal. Then you dive deep; that is vertical. A meditator dives deep, a thinker moves on the surface. Thinking is like swimming. Meditation is not like swimming, it is diving deep, going to the same point but on a deeper and deeper layer.

Stop traveling, because traveling is on the surface. Be still, don't travel, remain in the moment; then you start falling into the abyss. You may be afraid and that may be the reason why you go on thinking of the past and the future, because if you remain in the moment you will fall into an endless abyss. A depth opens and you are absorbed into it.

The ego cannot exist on the vertical, it can exist only on the horizontal. The mind cannot exist on the vertical, it can exist only on the horizontal. But the horizontal and vertical meet; that is the meeting of the two poles where they become a cross. They meet, they meet in the present moment – the present moment becomes the meeting point. Here, the horizontal crosses the vertical. From the present moment you can move in two directions: either from A to B, or from A1 to A2. Kakua was traveling from A1 to A2, from A2 to A3 – and it is an infinite depth, you can never reach to the end.

When he was in China he didn't travel. He lived in a remote part of a mountain. And the deeper you go into the vertical, the more remote you go, then the farther from the world you go. Then the family is left on the surface; the anxieties of the day-to-day existence are left on the surface. They belong to the road, the traffic, the market. You simply move inside and they disappear.

Remember, there are two ways to encounter worries: one is to try to solve them on the surface – nobody has ever solved; the other is to remove yourself to a remote corner of the mountain. The further you go away, the greater the distance, the better you can see, because distance gives perspective. And when you can see better the worries start dissolving. The further away you move, the more worries automatically dissolve, because now you are not feeding them by constantly remaining near them. Now you are not giving your attention to them, they wither away. And once you have reached the farthest corner of your being you simply don't know whether there are worries or not, whether they ever existed. You simply wonder.

This is the Eastern way to solve worries: to move inside to a remote corner. The Western way is to face the worries and try to solve them. And the West has been a failure. Nothing helps – neither psychoanalysis nor other trends in psychiatry, nothing helps – because everybody is trying to solve them on the surface. They may give you a little consolation or they may make you more adjusted to the society; they may give you a little more confidence, they may make you normal, that's all.

But 'normal' simply means normally-abnormal, nothing else. Normal simply means like everybody else. But how is everybody else? Everybody else is also neurotic, lukewarm neurotic. Psychiatry, psychoanalysis, and all trends in the West, can make you more adjusted, normal, that's all. The maladjustment disappears; you become adjusted. But what do you become adjusted to? – if the whole society is sick, you become adjusted to sickness. If the whole society is neurotic, you become adjusted to the neurosis.

The Eastern way is totally different. It is not to become more adjusted to society, no, because society itself is ignorant, ill, sick. To be adjusted to it is not the point. The point is to become more remote from the society so that you can find your own roots, your own grounding. Once you find your own grounding, worries will exist – they are part of life – but you are not worried by them. They exist and you tackle them on the surface, but you are not involved, you remain outside.

A real meditator becomes authentically an outsider. He remains outside. He remains at such a faraway distance that he can look at himself as if he is looking at somebody else. Worries will be there just like waves will be there on the surface of the ocean, but in the deeper layers of the ocean there are no waves. If you get identified with the waves then there is trouble. This identification is the root cause of all misery. The more remotely you move, the more the identification dissolves; it breaks, it falls. Suddenly you are in the world but not of the world. Suddenly you have transcended.

There is only one transcendence, and transcendence is the only way. And that transcendence is to go deeper and deeper within yourself. Just witness your mind and the deeper you will move. Just remember that you are not the mind and the deeper you will move. Just remember that you are not to fall into the old trap of going into the past or the future. Just remember that you are not here to travel but to be. You are not here to become something; you are already that which you can become. But just to know this being, what it is....

The West has been making vast, tremendous efforts to become something. And the East has been doing only one thing: relaxing and knowing who you are. The becoming is not the point because becoming is traveling; you have to become something. The point is first to know who you are. You may already be the thing you want to become. And those who have known, have known that it is already the case: you are already that which you can become. You just have to become acquainted with this fact.

This fact is hidden deep in you. More significant facts are always hidden deeper, they are not on the surface. They are not on the skin, they are in the heart. Be a witness to the mind and you will find remote corners of your being, unacquainted, unknown to you.

You don't know yourself. You know only a part, the porch of your house. You just move on the outside.

Kakua...lived in a remote part of a mountain and meditated constantly.

This has to be remembered: meditation cannot be a part. Either it is the whole or not. It is a twenty-four-hour thing. You cannot do it and leave it. It is not a fragment like your going to the church or your going to the temple, meditating for a few minutes and being finished with it. It is not an act that you can do and be finished with. It is not an act, it is *you*. How can you do it and be finished? It is for twenty-four hours. Meditation is a way of life. It is not an activity, it is your very being. It has to be constant, it has to be continuous, it *has* to be; whether you are walking, eating, or even when you are sleeping, it has to be there. It must become a crystallized continuity. Only then enlightenment happens, never before it.

Of course, in the beginning you have to start: you do it in the morning, sometimes you do it in the evening, then you forget about it. Even that helps. But it is not meditation yet, it is still an activity. It has not become part of your being. It is not yet like breathing. Can you do breathing in the morning and then leave it? It must become like breathing, continuously with you. And a moment comes when it becomes even deeper than breathing, because breathing is also not constant; it is not really constant. When you breathe in there is a moment when breathing stops. When you breathe out there is a moment, a fragment of a moment, when breathing stops. When you are very very silent, breathing stops – no breathing.

Meditation is deeper than breathing, because breathing belongs to the body. Meditation doesn't belong to the body; meditation belongs to the seed, to the very center around which body revolves. The body is just like the wheel. Breathing is necessary for the body and meditation is necessary, just as necessary, for the soul. Without breathing you will be dead; that means the body will be dead. Without meditation you will be dead; that is, the soul will be dead.

Gurdjieff used to say: Don't believe that you already have a soul. How can you have a soul already unless you meditate? – and he was right. When you meditate, for the first time the soul revives in you. It has been waiting for you. And when the soul starts breathing within you just like the body, when the soul starts beating within you just like the heart, then you have a different quality; that quality is the religiousness. It has nothing to do with rituals. Then you are a different, a totally different human being.

Desire disappears; instead of desire, contentment, deep contentment comes to you – because desire is discontent. Anger disappears, and instead of anger, compassion – the same energy becomes compassion. In anger you would like to destroy the other. In compassion, just the opposite: you would like to create, you would not like to destroy. Hate disappears without any trace, you simply cannot find it within you. You happen to be loving, and then love is not an affair; it is not falling in love with someone, it is simply the way you are. If you touch a leaf there is love, if you carry a rock there is love, if you look at the sun there is love. Whatsoever you do, it becomes a love-act.

Meditation is not part, it is the whole, so one has to be constantly remembering, constantly aware. You cannot afford to meditate in the morning and then forget about it.

He lived in a remote part of a mountain and meditated constantly.

Whenever people found him and asked him to preach, he would say a few words and then move to another part of the mountain where he could be found less easily.

He moved outwardly, and inwardly also. Sometimes, even if you go to a remote part inside yourself, you will find that a thought comes and visits you; those are the people inside. And outside also, even if you go to a very remote part of the Himalayas, somebody, someday – a hunter, a woodcutter, or a traveler who is going to Mansarovar Lake, or somebody who has forgotten his way – will visit you. And just the same happens inside: sometimes a vagrant thought that has forgotten the way will visit you.

Even in deeper meditations suddenly you will see one thought standing – but it will be one, it will not be a crowd. And when one thought visits it is beautiful, because you can see it so clearly. It has a personality of its own. Thoughts are people, but you live in such a crowd.... A crowd has no personality. You are so filled with thoughts that you cannot see the beauty, the face of a single thought. By the time you become aware the thought has gone, another is passing; it is a constant traffic.

In traffic, in a crowd, you don't look at faces, you don't feel people, you simply feel a mass all around you. In a crowd others are things, not people. Have you watched it? If you are traveling in a crowded train, many people around you touching from everywhere, even if you are a woman and somebody is touching your body, you don't feel bothered. Why not? – because he is not a person, they are not people, it is just a crowd. If you are standing alone under a tree and the same man comes and rubs against you then you will become angry; now he is a person.

In a crowd nobody has personality. It is just a crowd – with whom can you be angry? – and you shrink into yourself. In a crowded bus, in a crowded train, you shrink inside so you are not available on the surface of the skin, so if somebody touches you it is okay. It is not a touch, it is a dead thing. But alone with a single person, then it's different.

And the same happens within. You have lived in a crowd of thoughts, a mad crowd. You have never looked at a single thought. Thoughts are people and they are beautiful. When you can see a single thought against the sky, with a personality, its own being, its own energy, then that thought will ask you something. The mind has never asked you anything because you are so identified. When the identification breaks, by and by, even the mind starts asking you many things.

People would ask and inquire of Kakua. He would preach, he would say a few words, and then move to another part of the mountain, because this part had also become crowded; people were reaching. And this will happen every time you settle inside with your meditation: every time you settle a thought will visit. That shows that you are still available to thought, still not really removed to where nobody can reach. You have to change, you have to go still deeper. And you will feel a very very deep gratitude for the thought that visited you, because it showed you that you are still not very far away from the surface: a thought can reach, a wave can come. You will think the thought, take your belongings, and move on.

Kakua would preach a few words, he would have a good communication with the thought, and move further into the interior so that nobody could reach him. One has to find a place which is absolutely individual, nobody reaches you – that is your soul. Nobody reaches you, not even a thought – it is total aloneness.

You cannot imagine the silence, you cannot imagine the beauty, you cannot imagine the flavor of it when you are absolutely alone, when nobody can reach you, when nothing reaches. You cannot understand the benediction, the bliss that happens. Go on moving, go on moving inside yourself, and reach to the point where not even a single thought can come and visit you. Reach to the point where only the host remains, and no guest ever comes. Only then the real guest will knock at your door. Only then the God, only then the nirvana, the enlightenment, the supreme light, truth, or whatsoever name you would like to give it, knocks at your door. When you are not available to the world you become available to God. Until that happens, the total aloneness, you are not yet a right vehicle for the divine to descend.

A moment came in Kakua's life when he achieved, achieved the total aloneness, and then the supreme guest knocked at his door. Then he returned to Japan.

When Kakua returned to Japan, the emperor heard about him and asked him to come to court to preach Zen for the edification of himself and his subjects.

Kakua stood before the emperor in silence.

It must have been a very awkward moment for the emperor. Kakua simply stood there in silence. He would not say anything. He tried to commune, but the emperor was waiting for communication. In that world even emperors are beggars, because emperors also live where you live. They may be living in great palaces, but they live in words just like you. They think just like you, they imagine, they desire; they move to the past and the future just like you. As far as the ultimate reality is concerned, a beggar and an emperor are in the same boat. There is not a single bit of difference. Just their outer garments are different; their inner being is the same.

Kakua stood in silence, he would not speak a single word. The emperor waited, the court waited.... Then, feeling the impossibility – that silence will not be understood, that there is nobody who can laugh like Mahakashyapa and can understand his silence – Kakua did the next best thing. What did he do?

He then produced a flute from the folds of his robes, blew one short note, bowed politely, and disappeared. No one ever knew what became of him.

That is the next best thing. If silence cannot be understood, then the next best thing is music.

Something has to be understood about music: music is not language, and yet it is language; it does not say anything, and still it speaks. Music is not words, it is just sound. Sound is just in the middle of no-word and word. If no-word cannot be understood, then music. And if music also cannot be understood, then Kakua simply disappears.

I am talking to you – in fact it is nothing but music. The flute may not be apparent, but I am not really talking, I am singing something. It is not a philosophy, it is a poetry; hence all the contradictions of a poet. I say something today, I said something absolutely different yesterday, and you cannot predict me; tomorrow

I may say something else, because what I say is not the point, what I sing through it is the point. The words change, flutes can change, that is not the point – but the single note....

And I have been talking and talking, but have you observed the single note? The single note remains single. In different ways I sing the same song with different flutes, with different words. They may look contradictory, because sometimes I use a bamboo flute and sometimes a golden flute; sometimes with few holes, sometimes with many holes. Flutes are different, even the sounds may be different, but the basic note remains the same.

All buddhas have been singing the same note. Listeners go on changing; buddhas never change. I am singing the same song that Kakua sang before the emperor. *He produced a flute from the folds of his robes, blew one short note...* Just like a single flower in a big garden – a single note against the whole sky, a single note against the whole mind, the chattering of the mind. And then he...*bowed politely, and disappeared.*

No one ever knew what became of him.

He tried his best. First he tried silence. I have also tried silence first, but it was difficult; the listener could not hear anything. Now I am trying the single note with a flute. And if you don't listen, remember this story: Kakua disappears. Then nobody ever hears anything about him.

And Kakua tried with the best, the emperor and his court. And when he saw that even the emperor and the court could not understand, then what was the use? Who could understand? He simply didn't bother again. And this has been happening many many times, millions of times. Many Kakuas never even tried when they saw the whole absurdity. They simply looked at your faces; they found walls there. They simply never tried. But some Kakuas are very bold – they try. That is hoping against hope.

This story is a very beautiful indication. What will you do because of this story? First try silence...be silent with me. If you feel it impossible then listen to the music, not to the words I am saying to you. Words are just excuses – listen to the music. And don't argue, because what I am saying is not a logical statement, it is absurd. But that is not the point at all, the logic of it. The point is the music of it.

First try silence with me. If it happens, it is beautiful. If it cannot happen, then try music. These two are the only ways, there is no third way. Don't listen to what I say, just listen to the rhythm. Just listen to the harmony, the harmony of the opposites. And it is a single note, remember. I go on repeating the same thing every day in different ways. Sometimes a Zen story is the excuse, sometimes a Sufi story is the excuse, sometimes the Gita, sometimes Jesus or Mahavira; these are all excuses – but I go on repeating the same note. I go around you trying from everywhere, all the possibilities.

Listen to the music, don't listen to the logic. It has no logic in it, it has only a melody.

Enough for today.

二

Discourse 2

Throw It Out!

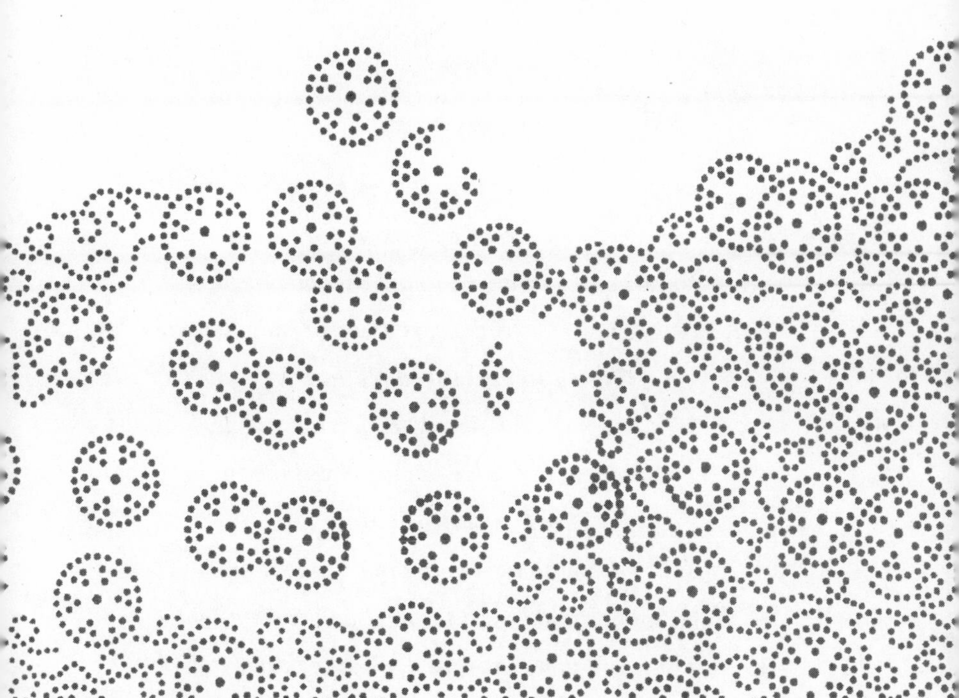

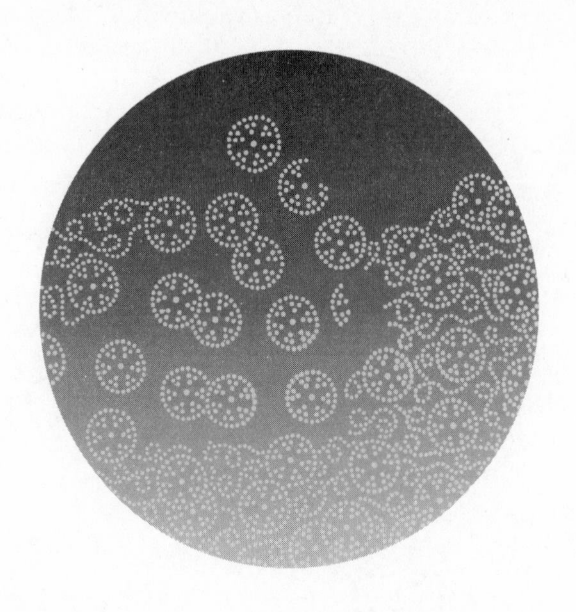

Joshu was a master who started to study Zen
when he was sixty.
When he was eighty he found enlightenment.
They say he taught for forty years after his enlightenment.
Once a student asked old Joshu,
"You teach that we should empty our minds.
I have nothing in my mind – now what should I do?"
"Throw it out!" said Joshu.
"But I have nothing – how can I throw it out?"
Joshu said, "If you can't throw it out, carry it out,
drive it out, empty it out – but don't stand there in front
of me with nothing in your mind!"

What is Joshu's single note? This is the single note – emptiness. This is the lotus flower that Buddha transmitted to Mahakashyapa. And this is what all the buddhas have been teaching through the ages: be empty. The ego wants to be all. The all happens, but it happens through emptiness, and therein lies the difficulty, the impossibility of it. You can become perfect, but if perfection is the ideal then you will miss it. You can become perfect through being totally empty. That seems inconceivable for the mind, because the mind says that to be perfect one has to make much effort, to be perfect one has to create an ideal in the future, and one has to make effort to reach that goal.

The goal happens. Perfection comes to man, man need not go there. The goal comes to you. Nobody has ever gone to the goal. It has always been otherwise: the goal comes to you when you are empty. And to be empty is just the opposite, just the opposite of all efforts towards perfection, because perfection means you would like to be God himself. Perfection means you would like yourself eternally, infinitely, spread all over. Emptiness is just the opposite: you have to destroy yourself utterly. Not even a trace should be left behind. When your house is empty the guest comes. When you are no more, the goal has been attained.

So don't make perfection your goal, the goal happens indirectly. Be empty and you have created the situation for it to come. Because nature abhors emptiness, nothing can remain empty. If you empty yourself completely you will be filled by the unknown. Suddenly, from all directions, the divine rushes towards you. You have created the situation; it has to be filled. When you are not, God is.

So remember, there cannot be any meeting between you and God. There has never been and there will never be. When you are not, God is; when you are, God is not. They cannot both be together. Here you disappear, and suddenly the total, the perfect, the whole appears. It has always been there, but you were filled by yourself so much that there was no space for it to come in. It was all around, but you were not empty.

You are just like a house without doors – just walls and walls and layers and layers of walls. And remember, a house is in fact not the walls but the doors. Lao Tzu says: What is a door? – a door is nothing, it is an emptiness, and from the door you enter. The wall is something, the door is nothing. And have you observed that the house is not the walls but the emptiness within? The very word 'room' means emptiness, space. You don't live in the walls, you live in the space, in the emptiness. All that exists, exists in emptiness. All that lives, lives in emptiness.

You are not your body. Within your body, just like within your house, space exists. That space is you. Your body is just the walls. Think of a person who has no eyes, no ears, no nose, no windows, no doors in the body – he will be dead. Eyes and ears and nose and mouth, they are the doors, they are emptinesses. And through that emptiness, existence enters into you; the outer and the inner meet, because the outer space and the inner space are not two things, they are one. And the division is not a real division.

It is just like...you can go to the river and you can fill an earthen pot with water. When the water is moving into the earthen pot, the river outside and the water inside the pot are the same. Only an earthen wall exists, and even that earthen wall is porous; water is continuously flowing out and in. Your body is also porous, existence is continuously flowing in and out. What is your breathing? – it is existence coming in and going out. And scientists say that millions of holes in the skin are continuously breathing in and out. You are porous. If your whole body is painted thickly and only the nose is allowed to remain open, you can go on breathing but within three hours you will be dead – because the whole body breathes, it is porous. Existence continuously renews you.

And inside who are you? Inside is an emptiness. When one realizes this emptiness, the ego simply disappears. It is a myth, it is a dream, it is a fallacy. Because you have never looked within, you have created a false ego.

There is a necessity, because no man can live without a center. And you don't know your own center, so the mind creates a false center: that false center is the ego. When you move inwards and look for the ego you will never find it there. The deeper you go the more you will laugh, because the ego is not there, *you* are not there. Sometimes, just close your eyes and look for the ego. Where are you? Who are you? An emptiness surrounds you from everywhere; nobody is there inside. And this moment is the most beautiful and ecstatic moment possible, when you feel that there is no ego.

When there is no ego, you are empty. And when you are empty, the divine rushes towards you. You have created the situation.

This was the single note of Kakua, and this is my single note also. This story is very beautiful. Try to understand every word of it.

Joshu was a master who started to study Zen when he was sixty...

Remember, your age is not relevant. You may be a child or you may be very very old. You may be young, you may be healthy, or you may be ill – it makes no difference, because the basic thing is to be empty within. It has nothing to do with your walls, young or old. A child can attain enlightenment, a man just on the verge of death can attain enlightenment, because enlightenment is not concerned with your body; it is concerned with something which is absolutely bodiless. It is concerned with the within which has no age. It is non-temporal. Time is not at all a problem. You may not have observed this because you live such an unconscious life, and observation needs consciousness, alertness, awareness.

If you look within can you feel the age, how old you are? If you close your eyes and look within, the emptiness within seems to be ageless, without age. Are you a child? Are you young? Are you old? The inner space seems to be non-temporal – it is! That's why you become old through others' eyes. You become old because of the mirror. If mirrors disappear and nobody talks about your age, and there is no calendar and no time measurement, you will remain young longer.

In the ancient days people stayed younger for a longer time. It is said that they lived for hundreds of years – sometimes even three, four, five hundred years. Now these things look like stories, myths, fictions. They are not fictions. They must have lived, but they had no time measurement; no mirrors existed, nobody talked about age, nobody knew when he was born, nobody knew his birthday. They couldn't count beyond ten fingers. And nobody ever asked, "How old are you?" People lived, they simply lived, not knowing how old they were. They lived very very long. It has happened many times.

Just a few days ago I was reading about a man, a Dutchman. A few years back he reached one hundred and sixty-five years. And he was working when he was one hundred and sixty-five, doing everything normally. He lived in a very very distant village. Then some newspaper got the news; his name was published, his picture, and then people started coming to see him. Then doctors became concerned and they also came to study him. They killed him within two years, because with everybody coming and asking, "How old are you?" suddenly for the first time that poor old man became aware that he was one hundred and sixty-five, which was unbelievable! He had never bothered, nobody had ever asked. He had simply lived, not conscious of time.

When you are conscious of time you are in the grip of death. When you are not conscious of time, death simply cannot enter. It enters through time. Death is time, and life is eternal, timeless. You are life, not death.

What did the doctors do to that poor old man? They suggested to him, "Now you don't work, you rest, because if you rest you can live even longer; you may live two centuries, and that will be a phenomenon for medical science!" So they helped him to rest. They put him on a bed and they started giving him injections and vitamins. He was dead within two years – he had become so conscious and worried.

If you are too concerned with the body you become the body. If you go on looking in the mirror you become the body. That's why women age faster than men – the mirror. And the miracle is, basically they live longer than men but they age faster. On average, all over the world, they live four years longer than men, but they age faster. They lose their beauty and their youth quickly. The mirror kills them – continuously meditating on the body.

Meditate on the inner being, not on the body. Find a mirror which reflects *you,* not the body. That mirror which reflects you is meditation. The more you meditate, the more ageless you become.

Joshu was a master who started to study Zen when he was sixty... So it is never too late. Don't be worried. Whenever you come, it is okay. It is never too late, it is always early, so don't think about it.

Many people come to me and they say, "Now we are very old...." And the mind is so cunning. Young people come to me and they say, "Now how can we meditate? We are too young." And old people come and they say, "How can we meditate? We are too old." Others come to me and they say, "Don't initiate children. They are just children – don't give them sannyas, don't initiate them." So who am I to initiate? – dead men? Nobody is left. Some are children, some are young, some are old.

Mind is cunning. When you are a child, you say you are a child. When you are young, you say you are young, you have to live life a little more. By the time you are old, you feel exhausted, energy gone, tired. You say, "Now what can I do? Nothing is left. I can simply wait helplessly for death."

Never in the history of man has man been as helpless before death as he is now – and with such tremendous advances in medical science! Never before has man been so helpless before death. Never has man worried about death as much as he worries now.

Why such a helplessness? – because you are not in contact with the eternal, your roots are not in the eternal. You have lived a temporal life, and death is the end of time, not of you. Remember, death ends time, not you. And if you have lived in time, with time, only with temporal goals, then death is a problem. But if you have lived deeper within yourself, in the remoter mountains where

Kakua moved, inside, where nobody can visit you, totally alone, then death is not a problem – because you know the deathless. It is hidden there.

On the surface is time, at the center is eternity. Remember, eternity is not a long, long time, no. Eternity is not time at all. Eternity means 'no-time'.

At the age of sixty, Joshu started. You can start anytime, and this has always been my feeling. Joshu lived so long – he lived one hundred and twenty years. He *must* have lived one hundred and twenty years, because he started at the age of sixty. And when you start meditating you become so fresh and young, you can simply live long without any effort.

A person who is ready to learn always becomes a child. Joshu again became a child at the age of sixty. You cannot start at sixty because you already know too much. You cannot learn, you cannot become a disciple – you are so knowledgeable; you are already wise. You have known so much, experienced so much, collected such rubbish. You are a junkyard, but you think you are very very experienced. What is your experience? What have you known exactly? – nothing. I see your hands are empty, I see your being is just poor. You have not attained any inner experience which gives you richness, which gives you significance.

But just by being old you have passed through many things of course, traveled on many many paths. Frustrated, hopeless, helpless, you stand before death trembling, just waiting, not knowing what to do. In the West particularly, the old man has become such a helpless phenomenon, just waiting for death with nothing to do. You cannot imagine....

In the past only a few people had to wait for death, those who were sentenced to die. They had to wait in the prisons for a few days, just waiting – it was terrible agony. But now, everybody. Retired, you are sentenced to death. Nothing else to do, just waiting...any moment death will come. And the agony is increased still more by medical science because they go on prolonging you, they go on giving you injections and vitamins. For what? – to wait still more, a little longer? They go on pushing you back in the queue, but you *are* in the queue. What difference does it make when one has lost everything? And just waiting, just waiting, waiting to die. Never before! That's why I say that man is so helpless before death.

In the East, when death started approaching, when death knocked for the first time on the door, people became very very happy. Death was a door, it was not the end. Something new was going to start. And it was not the enemy, it was God coming in the garb of death. They had come to know that they are not the body, they are not going to die. The bodies will be left behind and they will go on an eternal journey. Death was not the end; death was a meeting, a meeting with the unknown. Death was a long, long-awaited moment – desired, dreamed, hoped for. It was the last desire: to leave the body and to meet the divine, to merge into it so totally that not even a trace of you is left behind. The body looked like a barrier, so when it was dropped you were completely free. Death was freedom and the culmination of life, it was not just the end.

If death is just the end and you simply finish, life cannot be meaningful. How can life be meaningful when it just ends? Then the whole life becomes gloomy; the shadow of death makes it sad. Whatsoever you do is meaningless, because you are going to end. Whatsoever you create is meaningless, because you are going to end. Whatsoever you do is just fooling yourself, because you are going to end.

If death is a new beginning, if death is a rebirth, if death is a meeting with the divine, then life has a significance. Then whatsoever you do is meaningful. Then you are something significant, and the existence hopes for many many things through you.

At the age of sixty Joshu was again beginning a new childhood; he started learning Zen. Remember, if you can learn to the very end you will never become old. A man who can learn is never old. A man who cannot learn anymore is already old. A man who cannot learn anymore is already dead; now there is no purpose for him to be here. Life is a school, a discipline; it is a learning process.

If you have stopped learning you are already dead. Sufis say that ordinarily people die at thirty and are buried at sixty. When you stop learning you are dead.

Joshu started at the age of sixty, and when he was eighty he found enlightenment.

Remember, enlightenment is not a game. Everything else is a game except enlightenment. It is not a game, you have to be patient about it – and Joshu must have been a man of infinite patience. Beginning at the age of sixty, it is difficult to wait: one thinks of death. One thinks: If death comes before enlightenment, what then? Then one must be in a hurry. But Joshu was not in a hurry. Remember, the more you are in a hurry, the less is there a possibility for you to reach. The more you are patient, the more is the possibility.

I will tell you one small Hindu anecdote.

It happened that a messenger was going to God, and he passed one very ancient ascetic, an old man, very old, just sitting under a tree, meditating. He looked at the messenger and said, "Wait – are you going to God? Then just ask about me. It is already too long. I have been making thousands of efforts, and it is now already three lives that I have been making them, so just ask how much longer have I to wait."

When you ask, "How much more do I have to wait?" you are not patient. You are in a hurry. And with God nothing is possible in a hurry, because he is not in a hurry. He has no time problem, he is eternity.

The messenger said, "Yes, I will ask." And just jokingly he asked another young man who was dancing under another tree and singing praises to God. He asked, "Are you also interested in knowing how much time it will take for you to become enlightened?" The young man didn't bother. He wouldn't even stop, he continued his dance.

The messenger returned. He said to the old man, "I asked and God said, 'Three lives more.'"

The old man threw his rosary and said, "Enough is enough! Is this justice? I have been wasting my life continuously for three lives – and three lives more?...this is too much!"

The messenger went to the other tree where the young man was still dancing ecstatically. He said, "Even if you have not asked, I have asked. And God has said, 'That young man? It is very very long before he will attain enlightenment, the same number of lives as there are leaves on the tree under which he is dancing.'" Hearing this the young man became more ecstatic, mad, and he started dancing faster and faster. And he said, "Then it is not too long, because on the whole earth, how many leaves are there and how many trees? And this tree, *only* this tree? And these leaves? Then it is not too long, I have already achieved!" And it is said that in that very instant that young man became enlightened.

Infinite patience can bring it this very moment, because infinite patience changes your total being. When you have infinite patience you have no tension inside, because all tensions are for the future. All tensions are: when, how, how much more time, will I achieve or not, am I going to miss? All tensions are concerned with your impatience. If you are patient, tensions cannot exist within you. Patience is the only relaxation. You cannot relax with tensions inside the mind. A goal-oriented mind cannot relax; the tomorrow is too heavy, and you are so worried about it.

Passing by a garden, Jesus said to his disciples: Look at the lilies, they don't worry about the future; that's why they are so beautiful. Even Solomon in his glory was not so beautiful. Look at these lilies; they are so beautiful, so graceful, because they don't worry about tomorrow, about what is going to happen. They are not worried at all, they are simply here and now.

Twenty years is too much when a man is sixty. I have come across young men who come to me and they say, "Three days have passed. I have been meditating for three days, and yet nothing has happened." How many lives will these people have to wait? You calculate: how many trees and how many leaves there are on the whole earth, and all the trees on this earth and all the leaves – no, that number won't do. "Three days," they say.

I have come across one woman, and no *ordinary* woman, a professor in a university. She had just meditated once and she came and told me, "I have not realized God yet." One meditation! How much you oblige God! Just by sitting foolishly for forty minutes – and you will be sitting foolishly because a fool cannot sit otherwise. You may look like a buddha, but that is just on the surface. Inside the fool travels, chatters. Inside you are a monkey. You can control the body, but the monkey inside goes on jumping from one branch to another and chattering continuously.

That's why I always feel that Darwin must be right. I don't know whether scientifically he is right or not, but spiritually, the more I observe you, the more I am convinced that he must be right. Man must have come from the monkey – because deep inside he still remains a monkey. Only the surface has changed; it is just the body that is a little different, but the mind is the same. And just by sitting once, you start hoping for the infinite?

Joshu, at the age of sixty, could wait for twenty years. A rare man. At the age of eighty he found enlightenment, and they say that he taught for forty years after his enlightenment. Not in a hurry, he waited for twenty years. It is said that he never asked his master when it would happen. It is said that even the master was a little worried about it, because this man was so old. But Joshu, never; he never asked his master, "When?" He simply waited and meditated, and waited and meditated. He attained. When he attained, the master said, "Even I was worried a little, because this man is so old." And after his attainment, for forty years he continued teaching. But the note is one, the same as Kakua's. The note is emptiness. He was teaching for forty years on how to be empty. And this is the whole teaching of all the religions. If something else is taught to you, know well that it is not religion. Then something else it may be, but not religion.

Religion is concerned with making you empty so that God can enter into you, to create space within you. Very shattering. You would like to be somebody, not nobody. How subtly you try to be somebody; how subtle are the techniques you employ to be somebody – somebody in this world or somebody in that world, but somebody.

On the last night, when Jesus was to depart and it was almost destined that the next day he would be killed, the disciples were asking him, "In the kingdom of God you will be sitting just on the right side of God. Where will we be sitting? – where?" They were not worried about Jesus, they were not worried about his death the next day – they were not worried about it. They were worried about their positions: twelve disciples – in what hierarchy? Jesus would be sitting there of course – that much they could tolerate – by the right side of God, but then who would be next, then who, and then who?

Politics follows you to the very end. This mind is political, not religious. Politics is concerned with who you are in the hierarchy. Religion is not concerned with who you are; religion has no hierarchy, because in religion only one enters who is nobody. Then how can a hierarchy exist? Only one enters who has left himself behind.

There is an old poem about a small sect that existed in Bengal known as Bauls. Baul means madman; the word *baul* means mad. They were one of the most beautiful, a small sect. They were really mad, mad after God. They had a small story, and they sang this story in their songs. They said: A poor man, a very deep ascetic who had renounced everything, reached the gate of heaven. He had nothing with him, he was naked. He had remained a naked fakir for many lives. He had not touched gold for many lives, he had not accumulated anything for many lives. He was a perfect ascetic. He knocked at the door of heaven; the door was opened. The man who opened the door looked at this ascetic and told him, "You can enter only when you have left all your possessions behind." He was naked and with no possessions. The naked fakir started laughing. He said, "Are you a fool? I have got nothing. Can't you see? Are you blind? I am completely naked, without any possessions."

The man started laughing and said, "Yes, that I can see, but I can see deeper also. Inside you are carrying yourself, and that is the only possession which is the barrier. We are not concerned about what clothes you are wearing, or no clothes; that is not the point. Whether or not you are carrying yourself, that is the only thing. You have to throw it out, then you can enter."

The ascetic became very angry. He was in a rage. He said, "I am a great ascetic, and I have thousands of followers on the earth!"

Said the man, the doorkeeper, "That is precisely the problem, that you have thousands of followers and you are a great ascetic. Throw this out! Otherwise I will be forced to close this door." And he had to close that door. The ascetic had to come back. Remember, only you are the barrier; that is why emptiness is the door.

Once a student asked old Joshu, "You teach that we should empty our minds. I have nothing in my mind – now what should I do?"

Listen with attention, because this moment is also bound to come to you someday or other. A student asked Joshu, "*You teach that we should empty our minds. I have nothing in my mind – now what should I do?*" Remember this well, then when a real emptiness happens this question cannot arise: "What should I do now?" – because in a real emptiness there is no 'I'.

You become a vehicle, you become a flute. And God goes on singing, or not singing; that is up to him now. If he wants to do something he will do it through you, if he doesn't want he will not do it through you, but you are no longer the chooser. You are no longer the decision-maker. You are no longer the doer. This is what emptiness means, that the doer has disappeared. Now you are only a medium. If he chooses, that is his problem. Then it is not for you to ask and inquire.

Joshu used to say: When he feels hungry within me, I eat. When he feels sleepy within me, I go to sleep. I don't do anything now.

Sometimes he sleeps a little longer, then who am I to wake him up with an alarm clock? Sometimes he doesn't feel like eating; then who am I to force him to eat? – then a fast happens. Sometimes he wants to go for a walk in the hills, then I have to follow. Now he is the doer. This is the transformation.

You are the doer – then you are not empty. When he is the doer, the total, when existence is the doer and you are just a wave on the ocean and the ocean waves, not you, then you simply enjoy. Whatsoever happens, you simply watch. And when the doer disappears within you the watcher comes in. He is the doer, and you are just a watcher, a witness.

Right now just the opposite is the case: you are the doer and he is the witness. He is the watcher and you are the doer. This is a wrong situation. Everything is upside-down. You should be the witness and he should be the doer. When you are a witness, how can you accumulate ego? A witness is simply a witness – he cannot say 'I'. When you are a witness, 'I' disappears. You simply look. And when you have a simple look, there is no one inside; just the look exists.

This student came to Joshu and said: "*You teach that we should empty our minds.*" The very question, the very wording of it, is absolutely wrong.

Joshu is not teaching that 'you should', because if 'you should' you can never be empty. It is not a 'should', it is not something to be done. If you do, how will the doer disappear? Only in your non-doing can it disappear. Only when you are effortless can it go. If you do something, it can never go. So there is no 'should'.

And this is the difference between morality and religion. Morality exists around the 'should': this should be done, that should not be done. But the emphasis is on doing, and that is the difference. Religion is not concerned with 'should' at all. Religion says 'should' or 'should not' is not the point, because doing is not the point. You be a watcher. You simply watch, don't choose. And when you watch, he chooses, and when he chooses there is no repentance. When he chooses there is no looking backward. When he chooses, then there is no fault. When he chooses, then everything is always okay. It is always absolutely okay. Then you are never in error. It is human to err, it is divine not to err. Leave everything to the total – you may call it God. Leave it to the total and you simply become a shadow, and whatsoever he wills, let him will. Don't bring yourself in – you watch. So there is no question of 'should'.

This student said: *"You teach that we should empty our minds."*

This is how when a master says something it is misunderstood. Joshu never taught that you should do this or that. But our mind always transforms everything into the terms of action. Action is our language.

I say to people, be meditative – and what do they hear? They hear that I teach that you should meditate. There is a vast difference. When I say be meditative, I am not saying that you should meditate, because meditation is not an act; you cannot do it. You can be in it, you cannot do it; it is a state, not an act. I say, be love – and what do you hear? You hear that I teach that you should love. You have changed the whole thing. Now, whatsoever you will be doing, I am not responsible for it, because you have not heard at all what was said. Love is not an act, it is a state of being. You can be loving, you can be love, but you cannot do it. How can you do it? Have you ever observed? How can you 'do' love? How can you force? Of course, you can act. That's why there are so many actors who are acting love, and so many actors who are acting meditation. You have missed the point; it is a state of being. But you will again ask, "Then what is to be done? If it is a state of being, then what is to be done? Then what should we do?" You again go on missing.

No, just try to understand; just try to understand, and the very understanding becomes meditation. Just try to understand the nature of the mind, that it goes right and left, past and future, moves from one thought to another. It is a monkey. Just try to understand, just try to watch what mind is. And just in watching what mind is, suddenly one day you will feel something has clicked, something has changed gear, you are no longer the same. Something unknown has entered into you – there is no mind. Meditation has come in, just by trying to understand.

In anger, try to understand what is happening. In hate, in love, in relationship, try to understand what is happening. When you feel sad, try to understand what is happening and you will simply be wonderstruck! If you try to understand what is happening in anger, you will immediately feel a change of quality. Something is already changing through your watching: the anger is no longer the same, the violence of it has disappeared. It is still a cloud hanging around, but there is no aggression in it. Go on watching, and you will feel that even that cloud is disappearing; rays of the sun are entering.

Watching anger, anger disappears. Watching hate, hate disappears. If you can watch anything, immediately a new dimension has penetrated into it. The watcher has come in, and the watcher is the greatest phenomenon in the world. God comes through your watching, not through your actions.

What you should do or should not do is not the way. Just watch, be alert, and sometimes if you lose alertness then be alert to this non-alertness. Don't create a problem. Sometimes you will miss. Sometimes you will forget completely that you were to be watchful, so be watchful of this non-alertness. It is okay – you missed the point, you missed; don't create a problem about it, again watch it.

You watch anger, sometimes you forget. You become angry, then you remember – watch again. Don't create a problem out of missing the point, out of forgetting again, out of getting identified with the anger. Don't feel miserable, don't pity yourself and don't repent. When you have forgotten you have forgotten; now be watchful about this forgetfulness and remember, because the only point is to remember whatsoever is happening. Inattentiveness is happening – watch it. Simply go on watching, and soon you will understand a new dimension within you, and that dimension comes through watching. Problems start disappearing.

Nobody can control anger. Through controlling you become miserable. This whole sad lot of humanity is so because of controlling. Nobody can control. If you control, the poison enters into every fiber of your being. Just watch, and observation becomes transformation. And when you observe, it is not a question of 'should' or 'should not'.

This disciple simply missed. He said, "You teach that we should empty our minds." Nobody has ever taught that. Everybody who knows has taught that if you watch, the mind will empty itself. If you watch, mind becomes empty. Watching is emptiness; it is the door through which emptiness enters into you.

"I have nothing in my mind," said the disciple. "Now what should I do?"

Remember, the emptiness that Buddha gave to Mahakashyapa, the emptiness that Kakua sang through the flute, the emptiness that Joshu was teaching for forty years, and the emptiness which I am here just before you, is not a negative state. It is not really emptiness. It is called emptiness because the ego doesn't exist there. It is called emptiness because the mind doesn't exist there. It is called emptiness because *you* don't exist there. It is because of you – you are no longer there, that's why it is called emptiness. Otherwise, it is the greatest, the most positive state. It is full, overflowing with the divine, with the total, with the whole. From your side, it is emptiness.

Just look: a man is ill, there are many diseases around him, but he knows only illness. He has never known health, what health is. He has never known that well-being. He has always been ill. And he asks, "What is health?" How will you answer him? How will you define it? You will say, "It is an emptiness, because all your diseases will not be there. It is an emptiness, because you with your ill feeling, your ill-being, will not be there."

But is it emptiness? Is health emptiness? Yes, it is emptiness if you look through the disease. But if you look through the standpoint of health itself, the intrinsic standpoint, then it is a whole, overflowing whole – not empty, but the most positive thing in the world.

So don't mistake absent-mindedness for emptiness. There are

moments when you are absent-minded, nothing on your mind. Don't think that this is what Buddha gave to Mahakashyapa – not absent-mindedness. There are moments when you are so dull that there is nothing on your mind. We are not talking about that dullness. Idiots have nothing on their minds, that's why they are idiots. Stupid people have nothing on their minds; they simply don't have that kind of energy. They are so low, the mind doesn't function; they are still like animals. That is not the no-mind of Zen, that is a negative state: even thoughts are not there.

And those moments come in your life also. Sometimes when you are shocked, somebody has died, and the shock is so much that a little gap will be there before the mind starts functioning again. In that gap you are absent, not empty, because the whole turmoil is in the unconscious. Through shock, the conscious mind has become empty, because mind always becomes empty through shock if something happens which it cannot control, cannot understand. But sooner or later it takes control again, it starts functioning.

Somebody has died or is in an accident, in a car accident. You are driving; suddenly you feel that the accident is going to happen. The brakes are not working, you are going downhill, and a bus is coming or the steering wheel has gone wrong. Whatsoever you do you cannot move anything, and you know that the accident is just about to happen. Just a moment more...in that moment the mind stops, because this is something unknown. The shock is so much that the mind cannot think. That's why shock treatment is used for mad people. Electric shock can help, but whenever shock treatment is used the person will become more stupid than he was before, because through electric shock the energy is being forced to become low, so he cannot think.

So there are two poles of emptiness: one is the negative pole, and one is the positive pole. The negative pole can be achieved through shock, through electric shock. The positive pole is achieved through meditation and observation. If too many thoughts are there and you cannot meditate, you will go mad. And then there is only one way: some type of deep shock so your mind loses energy

– shattered. Then you will not go mad, but you will not become enlightened. You will remain on a low energy-level. You will remain absent-minded. That's why a stupid person or an imbecile or an idiot can sit not doing anything, can keep his head hanging low – because if you think then the head is needed, upright. If you are not thinking there is no need for it to be upright – it hangs. Go to a madhouse and look at imbeciles or idiots: they are absent-minded; nothing is on their minds.

This disciple of Joshu says, *"I have nothing in my mind – now what should I do?"* This state can come even to you. Thinking too much about the state of no-mind you can create a state of absent-mindedness, and that is easier. And that has happened to many people, particularly in India. Soon those people will be in the West also, because many Indians are teaching nonsense there.

In India you go to the ashrams and monasteries and you will feel that the people there are not bad, not bad in any way, moral, puritan – but stupid. You look at their faces and you will not see any energy, any vitality. You will not see any freshness, they are dull. Look at the Jaina monks; almost always they are dull. Their faces have no energy, no radiance, no life – just dull. They don't create any trouble, that's good. They don't do anything wrong – that's good – but they have dulled themselves.

There are methods to dull yourself, your sensitivity. If you take less food, then by and by sex will disappear, because sex needs energy. If you take enough food so that only a small amount of energy is created which is used in day-to-day activity, then there will be no sex. But then you are not beyond sex, you are simply below sex. If you fast for twenty-one days, sex will disappear completely. Even if the most beautiful woman passes you won't be interested in looking at her. Not that you are transformed; there is no energy even to look. And when the energy is not there you cannot do wrong, that's right. But this is a negative type of man – he cannot do bad. So it is better to die, because dead men never do anything bad; dead men are always good. That's why whenever a person dies, nobody says anything bad about him. A dead man is always good.

I have heard that one friend of Mulla Nasruddin phoned him and asked, "What is the matter? Are you dead?"

Mulla Nasruddin said, "Who told you that I am dead?"

The friend said, "In the town everybody is talking in such good terms about you that I thought you must be dead!"

It is easier to deaden your sensitivity, your energy: you become dull. India has many techniques for dulling yourself. When you are dull you have nothing on your mind, but this is not enlightenment. It is simply that you have no energy for the mind to function. If energy becomes available it will function again. So feed your monks well and see: they will be afraid. That's why Jaina monks are afraid of eating anything that can give vitality. They eat things which are non-vital so they remain on a low energy-level. But that is not *brahmacharya,* that is not celibacy; that is just suicide. You are killing yourself – of course, in installments, slowly, not taking a jump, because you are not even that courageous. Otherwise go and be finished. Why this long, gradual suicide?

This disciple must have been at that negative point of emptiness. He said, *"I have nothing in my mind – now what should I do?"* Joshu is beautiful. He says, *"Throw it out!"* Even nothingness, even emptiness is something; throw it out. Because if you think that you are empty, you are not; the very thinking that you are empty is there. The idea is there, the thought is there, the mind is there. If you say, "I am empty," you are not, because never can you say that you are empty. That cannot be said. Who will say it? And the one who says it inside is still there. Before it possessed other things, now it possesses emptiness.

Said Joshu, "Throw it out!"

You cannot deceive a master – it is impossible, because he looks through you, you are transparent to him. He knows more about you than you can know right now, because inside you there are deeper layers. He can penetrate them also.

"Throw it out!" said Joshu.
"But I have nothing – how can I throw it out?"

If the man was simply empty, at that moment he would have laughed. At that moment a *satori* would have happened. At that moment, when the master says, "Throw it out!" he would understand the idea. What is the idea? The idea is: don't carry emptiness. Just *be* empty, don't carry it as a thought, because the very thought will fill you and then you are not empty. Even a single thought is enough to fill your mind. There is no need for millions of thoughts; even a single thought is enough, and you still possess something. You are still not in that state which Jesus calls 'poor in spirit' – you are still rich. Now, a new richness: that you are meditative, that you are empty, that now your mind has no thoughts. A new possession, a new disease has entered into you, and this is the last disease.

If the disciple had really been empty he would have understood. And in the very understanding the thought is thrown. You cannot throw emptiness, of course; that Joshu knows. Nobody can throw emptiness. But the idea that "I am empty" can be thrown.

But the disciple missed completely because he was just at a low energy-level. He had just touched the negative pole of emptiness, absent-mindedness. *"But I have nothing – how can I throw it out?"* The very question, "How can I throw it out?" and he has missed.

Joshu said, "If you can't throw it out, carry it out, drive it out, empty it out – but don't stand there in front of me with nothing in your mind!"

Do something! The last barrier is the idea that "I am empty: I am enlightened, I have achieved, I have reached, I have known, I have realized God" – the last barrier. Because with this realization, the 'I' is still clinging. Only the objects have changed but not you. First you were clinging to riches, to your prestige, to your power, domination, your house, your car. Now they have changed; now it is emptiness, now it is enlightenment, now it is God. But your hands are still not open, you are carrying something within them. Your hands are closed. The very word 'emptiness' means that now you have nothing, not even the one who can declare. That's why Joshu says: Do something, but be finished with this idea.

"If you can't throw it out, then carry it out, drive it out, empty it out – but don't stand there in front of me with nothing in your mind!"

It happened that one Sufi mystic, Bayazid of Bistam, reached his master and told him, "I have realized!" The master didn't look at him, as if he had not heard. He didn't pay any attention to him, as if he were not there. And he had brought such great news: "I have attained." The master did not pay any attention at all. He continued talking with others.

Bayazid thought that the master had not heard him, so he told him again, "I have attained, I have reached the goal."

The master said, "Keep silent, keep silent. When there is nobody, then tell me." So he had to wait.

It was too long, because the ego is always impatient. And people went on coming and going. By the evening, just for a few moments there were no people, so Bayazid said, "Listen now, I have attained!"

The master said, "Are you still here? When there is nobody, then tell me."

If you are there, how can you attain? With you there, everything in a subtle way remains the same. Unless you drop completely, it cannot happen.

It happened, one king came to Buddha, in one hand precious diamonds and in the other hand beautiful flowers. He thought: Maybe Buddha may not like diamonds, so just as an alternative he also brought a few flowers – rare roses. When he came to Buddha, Buddha looked at him. In his right hand he was carrying the diamonds; he was just about to put them at Buddha's feet, and Buddha said, "Drop them!" So he thought he had been right; Buddha would not like diamonds, so he dropped them.

Then he was about to put the flowers at Buddha's feet, and Buddha said, "Drop them!" He was a little worried; he dropped them because Buddha said so. There was nothing else to do, so he dropped the flowers also.

Then with empty hands he stood there. Buddha said, "Drop it!" The king thought, "This man is mad. Now there is nothing to drop." He looked around for some clue. Now what to drop?

One disciple, Sariputra, said, "Buddha never meant the diamonds, he never meant the roses. Drop the dropper – drop yourself!" That man must have been of a rare understanding. He was not like Joshu's disciple. Immediately, as if a light dawned upon him, he felt it; he dropped himself, really dropped himself. And it is said, in that moment he attained enlightenment with no effort. He had done nothing to attain it, he simply dropped himself...a man of rare understanding.

It depends on your understanding. If you bring your total understanding to this moment, and I say to you, "Drop it!" and you drop it without thinking about it a single moment, the enlightenment can happen right now. But if you think, you have missed. If you think, you are there. And if you decide that "Okay, I will drop," then the 'I' will remain behind. "Drop it!" simply means drop it. Don't decide. Don't think about it.

This was what Joshu was saying to him:

"Throw it out, drive it out, carry it out, empty it out – do something immediately! – but don't stand there in front of me with nothing in your mind."

The disciple missed. Many disciples miss. He must have looked puzzled. He must have thought, "This man has gone crazy. This old Joshu is no longer in his mind. I am saying I have got nothing in my mind, and first he says throw it! How can nothing be thrown?"

The disciple must have been very logical: "How to drop it? And when I say I cannot drop it – because how can nothing be dropped or thrown? – this old man says: *Drive it out, empty it out, throw it out...* But how can nothing be thrown?" And the disciple must have left this old man thinking that he had gone crazy or mad. Absurd – Joshu looked absurd.

But if you understand, Joshu was giving him a possibility. He had opened a door. In that moment, just like the king who dropped himself before Buddha, if he had dropped himself he would have said, "Right, I understand!" He would have dropped, he would have laughed. But he must have gone away. The story says nothing more about him. He must have left Joshu.

One of the most penetrating thinkers in the West is Arthur Koestler. He came to the East to understand Zen. He went to Japan, and he went back thinking that these people are absolutely absurd and mad. If you were to show this story about Joshu to Koestler, he would be convinced by the disciple and not by Joshu. He would say, "He is so right! And what is wrong? The disciple is asking how nothing can be thrown. How can you throw nothing? If it is something, you can throw it."

But in the deeper realms of being, even nothing is something – it can be thrown. It has been thrown. And unless you throw it you are not available for the whole, for the total to descend into you.

Enough for today.

Discourse 3

THE ABBOT OF NANSEN

Nansen, the famous Chinese Zen master,
was in the woods one day, near the temple,
cutting down trees with a huge ax.
A monk, who had come from a distance to pay homage to the master, passed through the woods and came close to the woodcutter. "Is the abbot of Nansen at home?" he asked the woodcutter. The woodcutter replied to the monk, "I bought this ax for two pieces of copper." And lifting the ax above the astonished monk's head he added, "It is very sharp." The monk fled in dismay – to discover later that the woodcutter was Nansen himself.

The first thing to be understood, and understood as deeply as possible, is that Zen is nothing special. It is nothing extraordinary. The people who are in search of religion are always, almost always, very egoistic. Their very search starts because their egos are not satisfied with this world. They would like something more precious, to be more of the divine – something extraordinary. Egoists are attracted towards religion more easily – and this is the problem, because religion says that if the ego is there, there can be no growth. And egoists are easily attracted towards religion, but religion starts only when you drop the ego.

But this world is temporary; nothing is permanent here, and the ego would like something permanent, eternal. Everything in this world is made of the same stuff as dreams, and the ego is not content. The ego would like things made of solid rock. So the ego condemns this world and starts a journey towards the eternal. But the eternal has its own conditions, and this is the first condition: if you don't drop the ego you cannot enter the gate.

Religion basically is the understanding that all the trips of the ego are materialistic. Even the trip towards God is materialistic. It is not a question of what you seek, it is a question of who the seeker is. If the ego is the seeker then whatsoever you seek is material, is of this world. You may call it God, you may call it *moksha,* you may call it anything you like: the truth, the absolute, the Brahman – it doesn't matter. If the ego is the seeker, then whatsoever you seek is of this world. When the ego is not the seeker then everything, everything, I say, is of that world.

Even if you chop wood, even if you are a small shopkeeper, a clerk, a sweeper, nobody in particular, just ordinary – nobody knows about you, nobody ever thinks that you are a chosen one, nobody will ever hear about you – that doesn't matter. If the ego has dropped within, whatsoever you do is divine. Otherwise the ego poisons everything, and whatsoever you do is of the devil and not of the divine.

Zen is just being ordinary. And Zen is the essence of all religion, just to be ordinary. Realizing the fact that ego creates a hell around it, that ego is the source of all hell, that it has all the seeds of misery, anguish, one simply drops it without a second thought. Once one simply realizes the fact that one is suffering because of the ego, one simply drops it – but not in search of something.

You can drop the ego in search of something. Then you have not really dropped it, you are bargaining. Realizing the fact that ego is ugly, the source of all misery and illness, you simply drop it. You don't ask, "What will I gain out of it if I drop my ego?" – because all gain is the subtle search of the ego. You simply drop it because it is useless, harmful, poisonous.

You are passing through the woods, you come across a snake – you simply jump out of the way. You don't ask, "What will I gain out of it? I will not jump out of the way unless I am certain of what I am going to gain out of it." You simply jump without a second thought, because if you have a second thought about it, by that time the snake may have attacked you. You simply jump. Realizing the fact that the snake is there, death is there, you simply jump out of it.

The house is on fire. You don't ask, "What will I gain if I run out of it?" You simply run out of it without a second thought. You think about it when you are out of it; in fact, you run without thinking. When you are out of danger, then you sit under a tree and you have a look; then you think over all that has happened – why did you run away? You realize it, and the realization becomes a change, a transformation, a revolution.

If you realize that the ego is your house on fire you drop it. You don't ask, "What will I gain out of it?" You simply become a nobody, an ordinary being. And once you are ordinary, everything starts happening.

Zen is ordinary, it makes people just nobodies, and this is the beauty of it. When you become a nobody, when you are ordinary, this is the most extraordinary phenomenon possible. Listen: everybody wants to be extraordinary, so the longing to be extraordinary is very ordinary, because everybody wants it. And to become ordinary is absolutely extraordinary because nobody wants it, nobody longs for it. Remember this; only then can you understand Zen masters.

Because of this the seed, the seed of silence, the seed of inner emptiness that Buddha gave to Mahakashyapa, had to be taken to China, because in India a very great accident happened in the past, and that accident was the *brahmins*.

You cannot find more egoistic people than brahmins; they created the whole hierarchy in India. They were the most extraordinary, the chosen few, the head-people. They even divided the castes just like they do the body. They said: Those who are ordinary, workers who work with their hands, they are just like the feet – the lowest. Those who are business people, they are just like the belly; they help the body, they are the center of the body, the physical, just like the belly. Then the warriors, the soldiers, the *kshatriyas,* they are just like the arms – to defend, to protect. And brahmins, they are like the head – the thinkers, the philosophers – and the head is the highest. The whole body exists for the head; the head doesn't exist for anybody, it exists for itself. The head is there to order the body, discipline it. The whole body has to follow the head, and if a leg says 'no' it has to be cut off and thrown away.

These brahmins are the most egoistic. And it was not a coincidence that Adolf Hitler chose the name that the brahmins gave to the Hindus, the Aryans. Hitler chose that name for his own people – the Aryans; 'aryan' means the noblest, the best. So brahmins are the source of all fascism in the world; Adolf Hitler is just a by-product, an offshoot. Adolf Hitler's master, Friedrich Nietzsche, praised the brahmins very much. And the greatest brahmin, and the most mad of course, completely neurotic, was Manu. He gave the code, the hierarchy and the division of the society to the Hindus. Friedrich Nietzsche praised Manu, and he said Manu is the greatest thinker ever born in the world. And he was one of the most mad – he was the source of all fascism.

So it was very difficult for Buddha to teach people not to be special – it was almost impossible. Buddha was surrounded by brahmins. The idea of being special is so ordinary that it is in everybody's blood, and the brahmins are very very mad about their egos; they wouldn't think of being ordinary. One cannot imagine that a brahmin would be ready to do something manual. It is dirty, and the people who do it are dirty; they are untouchable, *sudras,* they cannot be touched. Not only can those people not be touched, even their shadows are untouchable.

Even now, in this twentieth century, there are villages in India where, whenever a sweeper or a shoemaker passes through the street, he has to declare loudly, "I am a sudra, an untouchable – I am passing through this street." So that if some brahmin is ready to go out of his house or something, he can stop, because an untouchable is passing through the street. The whole street is dirty at that moment. And if an untouchable passes and his shadow falls on a brahmin, it is a crime against him. He can be punished for it – punished! Even sentenced to death! They have killed many people in the past. The crime was only that a brahmin would be sitting and an untouchable would pass and his shadow – not he, just his shadow – would touch, would pass over.

It was almost impossible for Buddha to make people realize the beauty of being ordinary. He was born amidst people who were absolute egoists. That's why Buddhism couldn't survive in India. It was because of Buddha's influence, his personality, his force, his being, that it survived a little. But the moment Buddha disappeared...soon everything disappeared. Hence, Bodhidharma had to go to China. But why to China? – he could have gone to Burma, he could have gone to Ceylon, he could have gone to Afghanistan, he could have gone anywhere in the world. Why China particularly?

There was a particular reason: China had the right soil at that moment. Lao Tzu and Chuang Tzu had made the soil there. They had created a particular atmosphere, a milieu, because they lived like ordinary people. If you had come across Chuang Tzu you would not have been able to recognize him unless you had a very deep understanding, unless you had passed through a *satori,* a glimpse of the eternal. Only then would you have been able to realize that a Chuang Tzu or a Lao Tzu was there, otherwise not. They didn't have any outward show.

You can recognize a pope; he has the outward paraphernalia all around him. Nothing inside, everything outward. If a pope comes into a room in ordinary dress, nobody will be able to recognize him. If a Chuang Tzu comes, only the few people who have a certain depth of understanding will be able to recognize him. Chuang Tzu moves just like an ordinary man: fishing, cutting wood, doing this and that. Whatsoever life needs, he will do it. He is nobody special.

Buddha's teaching flowered in China, it came to perfection. Nansen is a meeting of Buddha and Lao Tzu, the meeting of Buddhism and Taoism, and Zen is the meeting of all that is beautiful in Buddha and all that is beautiful in Lao Tzu. That's why there is nothing like Zen, because two streams, tremendously powerful, tremendously beautiful, utterly of the unknown, came to a meeting. There has never been such a meeting. Other religions have met but they have met as enemies. They have conflicted, clashed with each other. Something has happened even out of that clash, but it cannot be so beautiful. It has not been a natural growth.

For example, in India it happened that Hindus and Mohammedans met – they clashed. The offshoot was Sufism; Sufis were born – very beautiful people. But it seems as if a child was born out of a rape, not out of love – a beautiful child is possible even out of rape – but not out of love. This meeting of Buddha's teaching with Taoism is out of love. They simply fell in love; there has been no clash, as if they suited each other perfectly. Something was lacking in Taoism and something was lacking in Buddhism. They simply complemented each other, they became a new being. The two disappeared and something new was born. The new was this man Nansen. Now try to understand this parable.

Nansen, the famous Chinese Zen master, was in the woods one day near the temple, cutting down trees with a huge ax.

You cannot believe, you cannot conceive! You cannot even conceive of Buddha chopping wood or cutting down a tree. He sits under a tree, right, never cuts it. You cannot imagine Buddha doing anything. You have seen his images. He has millions of images in the world, but always sitting silently with closed eyes: images of inactivity, images of meditation, but not images of meditation in action, no. And you cannot find an image of any Zen master just sitting with closed eyes, he is always doing something. That was the thing missing in Buddhism which was supplied by Taoism.

Life should be a balance between inactivity and activity. If you are completely active you miss something, you miss the inner. If you are completely inactive you again miss something, the outer. And the outer has its own beauty; nothing is wrong with it. In the West they tried to be active, more and more active. Activity became the whole pattern of life. They did many things – miracles – but the inner core was completely lost, forgotten. In the East they have been too inactive. When you look outside, everything has gone ugly. To look, to open your eyes in India, is really to pass through a very painful experience.

So I know why Buddha closed his eyes. Why do you always find him with closed eyes sitting under a tree, afraid to open his eyes? – all over, poverty, misery. But it is a vicious circle. If you close your eyes...the misery is not going to change just by closing your eyes. Something has to be done about it.

The East has become inward and has lost all contact with the outward existence. This is an imbalance. Zen is a perfect balance. A Zen master meditates, but then he also goes to the woods to cut wood because winter is approaching. He does many things just like an ordinary man. He is nothing special. Nansen is one of the very few, rare human beings who attained to the highest, like a Buddha, Mohammed, Jesus, and continued cutting wood.

When Nansen was very old somebody asked, "How are you?" He said, "Perfect. Cutting wood, carrying water to the ashram, preparing food, working in the garden...it is so beautiful."

Look: cutting wood he remains himself. Activity is there, but the mind is absolutely silent. Carrying water to the ashram he carries water, but there is nobody inside.

If you can act without somebody there inside you will enter a realm of tremendous beauty, because activity releases energy and silence enjoys the release. With activity you spread out, you become a vast sky; and deep inside, nobody, a silence. The silence spreads with your activity. Nansen carrying water to the ashram is silence carrying water to the ashram. Nansen cutting wood is silence cutting wood.

You cannot imagine what bliss is possible if you can act without the actor being inside, without the ego. If you can simply act and move from act to act without accumulating any identification – "This is me doing it, this is I; I have done this and I have done that" – without accumulating any 'I' through the activities; if you can move from one activity to another activity as a silence, as an emptiness, unimaginable benediction, unimaginable blessings shower upon you. You feel that the whole existence shares its secrets with you, because through activity you are connected with it and through silence you are capable of seeing, of looking, of enjoying, of touching.

Through silence you are sensitive, and through activity you are in contact. Sensitivity inside and contact outside – this is the balance. Then you have two wings. Otherwise you will be flying with one wing – either activity or silence. But one wing is not enough. You may flutter a little here and there, but one wing cannot lead you to the heights. You cannot move into the sky, you cannot go far away. Two wings are needed. And they balance – activity-inactivity, they balance.

Nansen cutting wood – remember it. And whenever your mind moves to the extreme, just pull it back to the middle. Either the mind wants to be active or it wants to be inactive, because with the extreme the mind can exist. In the middle, exactly in the middle, when activity and inactivity cancel each other, negate each other, mind disappears.

Nansen was cutting wood near his temple.

A monk, who had come from a distance to pay homage to the

master, passed through the woods and came close to the woodcutter. "Is the abbot of Nansen...?"

His ashram, his monastery was also called Nansen Monastery. Really, Nansen was not his name; it was basically the name of the monastery, and nobody knew Nansen's name. The abbot of Nansen ...he was just the abbot of Nansen; then by and by he became 'Nansen'. Nobody knew his name. And this was good, because nobody has a name. All names are false, so any will do. All names are meaningless, because you come into the world without a name and when you leave the world you go without a name. The name is just a tag attached to you for utilitarian purposes. Without a name it would be difficult – difficult for others – but you are without a name.

Nansen has no name; he was known by the name of the temple, the monastery. So the disciple asked, "Is the abbot of Nansen at home?" He asked the woodcutter this. If he was really a disciple he would have recognized the woodcutter; there was no need to ask, because a man who is enlightened is a light unto darkness. Can't you recognize light unto darkness? If you can't recognize light unto darkness you are blind.

The very thing that he asked this woodcutter – is the master at home? – is foolish. It is okay for a visitor but not good for a disciple. And he had come from a long distance to pay his homage. He might have known Nansen before, he might have seen him before – he was a disciple, he must have seen him – but he couldn't think of Nansen cutting wood. He must have seen him with eyes closed sitting under a tree; he must have seen him in silence or he must have seen him preaching. He must have seen him worshipping in the temple. He could not imagine that Nansen would be cutting wood, because he could not recognize....

Otherwise you would recognize an enlightened man wherever he is. He may be in a beggar – you will recognize him if you have the eyes, if you have the vision. If you have had even a single glimpse of what a realized man is you would recognize him anywhere. He cannot hide. How can you hide a light? – it cannot be hidden. It is such a tremendous phenomenon, you cannot hide it. In a thousand ways it is coming out. The whole forest was filled that day with Nansen, and this disciple could not recognize.

Disciples also recognize through the outside. Would you be able to recognize me if I were cutting wood somewhere? – difficult. Would you be able to recognize me if I were a beggar that had come to knock on your door? – impossible. Because you have not attained to your own inner realization, how can you recognize me? You can recognize me only to that extent which is your own span of inner realization. You can see a master only up to the same extent to which you can see within yourself, because the master is nothing but your within standing without. A master is nothing but your future standing in the present. A master is nothing but your fulfilled form. What will you be when you are fulfilled? – that's what a master is right now.

So if you have no inner vision you will miss. If you recognize only through outward forms, then you will be able to recognize Nansen in the temple, not because of Nansen but because of the temple. You will recognize him while he is sitting in meditation, not because of meditation but because of the posture. But have you ever heard of an enlightened man cutting wood? – you will miss.

It once happened: An enlightened man was here in India just a few years ago, Sai Baba. He lived just near Poona. He had a great disciple; he himself was a Mohammedan, the disciple was a Hindu. The disciple used to come every day to Sai Baba, and when Sai Baba would eat his food, only then would the disciple go and eat his own food. When the master had not eaten, how could he eat? And you could not find a more irregular man than Sai Baba. Sometimes in the morning the first thing he would do was to eat his food, and sometimes something late at night. On some days he would not eat the whole day, and this Hindu disciple had to wait sometimes far into the night. The master would eat, then he would go and prepare his own food. Because he was a brahmin he would not allow anybody else to touch his food; only then would he eat.

One day Sai Baba said to him, "Narayan" – Narayan Swami was his name – "you need not bother about this. If you are a real disciple you need not come, I will come to you. Whenever your food is ready I will come and give you my darshan there at your hut. You need not bother to come here, because you have to come five miles and then you have to go back. Now, I will do this."

Narayan was very happy because the master cared so much for him. He went back dancing. The moment he was stepping down from the mosque where Sai Baba lived, Sai Baba said, "But remember to recognize!"

Narayan said, "Of course! What a thing to say – how can I miss?"

The next morning Narayan was very happy. He took his bath, did his worship, prepared food – the master was to come. And the master came, but Narayan chased him out of the house, because it was no master, it was a dog. He was very worried...nobody came. The whole day he waited and waited, but except for that dog nobody came. So he ran to the mosque and said, "Sai Baba, have you forgotten? I have been waiting and waiting."

Sai Baba laughed and he said, "No, I have not forgotten. I cannot forget anything. I came, but you chased me out."

Then Narayan became aware. He said, "But it was a dog!"

Sai Baba said, "If you recognized me, you would have recognized me even in a dog. What difference does it make? If you recognize light you would recognize it in any form. The shape of the lamp is irrelevant. Or is it relevant, the shape of the lamp? It is irrelevant, because light is light whatsoever the shape of the lamp. But you recognize the shape of the lamp, not the light."

This disciple asked Nansen himself, *"Is the abbot of Nansen at home?"* And what a question to ask, because a master is always at home! Wherever he is, a master is always at home. That is the quality of being a master, that he is always at home. What a question to ask! You are never at home, that's right; even in your home you are never at home, because at-homeness is an inner quality. Even in your home you feel a stranger, even in your home you feel something is missing.

You are missing! You can change the home, you can have a better home, but the missing will continue. You will miss something in a better home also. You go on piling new furniture, new paintings, decorations, but again and again you find something is missing. You are missing. You are not at home. And the furniture cannot do it. Nothing can be of any help unless you come home; coming home is the whole point. Returning to the source is coming home. A master is always at home.

This disciple asked:

"Is the abbot of Nansen at home?"

The woodcutter replied to the monk, "I bought this ax for two pieces of copper."

He raised his ax and said, *"I bought this ax for two pieces of copper."* What is he doing, this man Nansen? Is he mad? But he was showing the quality of being at home. This is the quality of being at home, to be in the present. He was bringing this man to the moment, and at that moment the master happened to be cutting wood, at that moment the master was a woodcutter, at that moment the ax was the only reality, at that moment the master was in the ax, in the activity. The ax falls on the tree, the wood is being cut – the master is at home. He was in the ax right then, in the activity. That's why he raised the ax.

If the disciple had had even a little understanding he would have seen what the master was trying to show. There are things which cannot be said but only shown. And the master was telling him, "Come nearer, come closer. I am here. Look at this ax. Don't allow your mind to wander, don't go anywhere. This moment is enough. I am here, right now, this very moment. Look at this ax and come closer, nearer to the present."

So he says: *"I bought this axe for two pieces of copper."*

And only a Zen master can be so absurd. What an answer! The

disciple is asking something, he is answering something else. That's why Arthur Koestler goes back and says to the West that these Zen people are completely crazy, mad; don't fall into their trap, they are mad. For an Aristotelian mind, they are; for a logical mind, they are. You ask about A and they talk about B. But what they say is not the important thing. They are showing something, not saying something. Don't listen to what they say, just look at what they are doing.

What is this Nansen doing to this disciple? He is giving him a shock. The disciple has asked a question, he is not answering that question, because if that question is answered the mind continues. If the question is answered in a logical way – relevant, relevant to the question – the mind continues. The master is completely cutting. He is not only cutting the tree with the ax, he is trying to cut the mind with that ax also. Bringing down the ax, he is giving a shock. For a moment the disciple is at a loss: What to do? To whom have I asked? At least for a single moment there will be no thought. In that moment, the recognition is possible.

But you can miss, because the recognition cannot be forced upon you. You have to take it or leave it – it is up to you. A master can only create a situation: it is up to you whether you grow through that situation or not. You may not take it, you may try to escape. This is what the disciple did.

"I bought this ax for two pieces of copper."

He is bringing him from his mind to the reality. Zen is absolutely earthbound. Buddha is like the sky and Lao Tzu is like the earth, and where earth and sky meet there is Zen. This Nansen is the meeting of the earth and the sky. Buddha is like wings and Lao Tzu is like roots, and this Nansen is like a tree with both roots and wings. Rare reality – the earth, the solid earth, meets the inner sky. That can be recognized only if you use the situation.

I go on creating thousands of situations for you, and you go on missing. But remember, you are not going to win! You can miss a thousand times, I will create situations a thousand and one times. You can escape this way and that, but you cannot escape. Once a man is in the trap of an enlightened man his efforts are futile, because you cannot exhaust him and you cannot exhaust his patience.

"I bought this ax for two pieces of copper."

An infinite opportunity was given in that moment – Nansen with a raised ax talking nonsense to this man to bring him to his senses. *And lifting the ax above the monk's head he added...* But seeing that he has missed – this won't do, this disciple is a little thick.... I know those thick disciples!

And lifting the ax above the astonished monk's head he added, "It is very sharp."

The monk fled in dismay – to discover later that the woodcutter was Nansen himself.

The second opportunity. But the ax was over his head, it could fall at any moment...and this man looks mad! You could have recognized the moment, you could have become aware of the situation, because in danger even a stupid person becomes aware. In danger, the ax hanging over you in a madman's hand...and Nansen says, "This is very sharp."

But the disciple did what you have been doing: he escaped in dismay. That was the moment to be there. That was the moment to be there completely. If he had remained there for a single moment without escaping, then the mind would have disappeared, because in such a moment there is nothing for the mind to do. What can it do? It was a death situation; any moment the disciple could die. If he had remained there just a single moment, had not escaped, the mind would have disappeared...nothing to do. Facing death, mind disappears.

This situation comes to everybody that enters into deep meditation: a moment comes when the ax comes just over your head, and it is always sharp. A moment comes when you go deeper – you face death. That is the boundary between the ego and your inner being, where you face death inside. Because when you go deeper, a moment comes when the boundary of the ego has to be crossed – you go beyond it. And you are so identified with the ego that you feel it like a death.

My own disciples come to me and they say, "Now it is difficult. We have come to a terrain inside where it feels like death, and we have come here to know life, not to die; we have come to be more alive, not to be dead; we have come in search of life abundant, not to disappear."

But you have to disappear; only then life in abundance happens to you. A moment comes inside when, if meditation is really growing, you will feel like you are dying. Don't escape in dismay. There, my ax is over your head, and it is very sharp. If you escape from there, the mind functions again; the mind starts thinking a thousand things. And once you escape, then the mind won't allow you to go to that point again, because you will always start an inner trembling. Whenever that point is near you will become suspicious about whether to take a step more or not – or to escape. And only later on will you recognize that at that moment when you were dying the master was there; he was Nansen himself – only later on. But then you will repent, because later on you will recognize the moment.

Mind has a tremendous capacity to understand things when they are not. When you have missed, then the mind goes on repenting about it, thinking about what should have been. The mind has a tremendous capacity to think about the past, to think about the future. It has no capacity to be here and now. And that was the moment: an ax on your head... *"It is very sharp."*

The monk fled in dismay – to discover later that the woodcutter was Nansen himself.

...But he had missed a great opportunity. You can also miss – that is more possible – and later on you will repent. But what can you do about the past? You cannot undo it, you cannot go back. And even if you go back, remember, the same situation will not be given to you again.

If this man comes again, he will not find Nansen cutting wood. Even if he finds Nansen cutting wood, Nansen is not going to talk about the ax, that he has purchased it for two pieces of copper. A master never repeats the situation, because it is useless. A repeated situation will not help, because the mind knows about it and it will not be a shock; the mind can think about it.

Think: the monk comes again, realizing that the woodcutter was Nansen himself, goes to the tree, because he knows where he will be cutting wood and waiting for him. Nansen is cutting wood and the monk asks, "Is the master at home?" Now the whole thing is absolutely foolish because it is a repetition, and he knows that the woodcutter is Nansen. But he asks, "Is the abbot of Nansen at home?" And the master says, "This ax I have purchased for two coppers." The disciple knows that now the second thing will be that he will raise the ax over his head and he will say, "It is sharp," and he is not to escape this time. He will stand there and see what happens. Nothing will happen, because the whole point is lost.

A mind, when it knows what is going to happen, continues. That's why every master has to go on inventing different situations. Once a situation has been known, the mind becomes the master of it. The mind is the master of the known. Only the unknown can destroy it; the known, never. The known can always be manipulated. A situation cannot be repeated. That's why, in the ancient days, masters insisted that whatsoever was being done should not be written, because if it was written, that situation would be forever closed for future disciples as well as for future masters. It is written and people will read it and they will know what to do. And if you know what to do, if you are already prepared, it is useless. You have to be caught in a moment when you are not prepared. Unprepared you have to be caught! In that unprepared moment the mind is not there, because all preparations are in the mind.

So whenever I ask a person to take a jump into sannyas and he says, "I will think," he has missed that opportunity. He will take sannyas, but I will have to find something else for him. If I were to say, "Take sannyas," and he were to say without a single thought, "Yes," not even asking what sannyas is, not even asking, "Where are you leading me?" – not even asking, "What can clothes do? What will a new name do?" not asking anything.... If I say, "Take sannyas," and he were to say, "Okay, I am prepared"; if he were to take the jump, he has used an opportunity – a door is open at that moment.

If he says, "I will think about it and I will come later on," he will think, and he may come or he may not come, it doesn't matter; that opportunity is lost. He may come prepared. After a few days he may come and say, "Now I have thought it over and I am convinced of the utility of it." It is not a utilitarian thing. It has no utility – none. "I have thought about it and I have talked to many sannyasins and they say it helps, so I am ready. Now give me sannyas." I will give it to him also, but the opportunity is lost; I will have to find some other.

Your mind is your preparedness. What is Nansen doing? He is bringing this man to a moment of unpreparedness – and he escaped, he missed. He realized later on, but then nothing could be done. Remember this: while you are with me, remember that only through situations will you grow, not through teachings. Whatsoever I say will not be of much help; whatsoever I create around you will be the real thing. Talking simply helps you to hang around me, that's all. I go on talking to you; that is just like giving sweets to children, so they hang around.

And suddenly, in an unprepared moment, I will take the ax and I will say to you, "It is very sharp!" Don't escape in that moment. Later on you may recognize, but I may not be here. Later on you may recognize and come back, but the same situation cannot be repeated. And if you become habitual escapists, you may be ready for the old situation but from the new situation you will escape again. And if it happens many times, you will become addicted to escape. Then you don't know....

Whenever you feel unprepared you simply find yourself running away. Whenever you are prepared you feel at ease, secure. But you are not here in search of security, and I am not here to give you security. I am here to take all securities from you. All the earth beneath your feet I have to take away. I have to throw you into the abyss. Only in falling into that abyss will your ego disappear. And for the first time, through insecurity, you will attain to the eternal security – but the path goes through insecurity. The path towards life goes through death. Dying, you will achieve. Clinging to life, you will miss.

What does this story say? It says that Nansen created a death situation. And whenever there is a death situation you escape; you say it is insecure.

Mind is always afraid of dying. It clings – it clings to anything. In India they say that a dying man clings even to a straw. He knows well that it cannot save; he knows well that a straw cannot become a boat – there is no safety in it, but just clinging..."Maybe some miracle will happen and I may be saved."

When you cling to money you are clinging to a straw; when you cling to power and prestige you are clinging to a straw. When you cling to name, family, bank balance, you are clinging to a straw, because nothing can save you. Death is coming. Death is rushing towards you. Whatsoever you do is useless, it will not save you.

And what does a master do? He says: Before death overtakes you, you overtake death. Why wait for it? Waiting, you will be a victim. Going through it you become a conqueror, because one who is ready to die suddenly realizes that death is impossible. One who is ready to die suddenly realizes: the mind will die, the body will die, the ego will die, but the being – the being has been before the mind came in. The being has been before the body came in. The being has been before your birth, and the being will be after your death.

When in meditation the ax is raised over your head and you feel a death moment, don't escape. Let the ax fall on you. It is sharp. It is good, it is good that it is sharp. Let your head be chopped completely off. Once you are headless...and that is the meaning of being nobody, because the ego exists in the head, the mind exists in the head, the brain, the ego exists in the head. And you go on condemning everybody – you have to. A head-oriented person has to condemn everybody, because that is how he feels special.

I have heard that it happened in a small village: the community decided to change the old priest. They fired him and they brought a new priest. The first day, the priest gave his first sermon. The whole community had gathered. There was also one guest from another village. He asked the chief after the sermon was over, "Why? Why have you changed the old priest? What was the need?"

So the chief of the community said, "The old priest had been talking every day and he would say the same thing: 'You mend your ways, otherwise you will go to hell!'"

The visitor was amazed. He said, "What are you saying? The sermon was the same this morning – this man was also saying that you will go to hell if you don't mend your ways."

The chief said, "Yes, he was. But the old one always acted as if he was glad that we will all go to hell. That is the difference, and that was too heavy."

The brahmins are always glad that you will be in hell and they will be in heaven. The priests are always glad that you will be in the fires of hell.

I have heard that one preacher was talking to his congregation and he was saying, "You don't know what is going to happen in hell – there will be fire, there will be cold, freezing days. Your body will shake and your teeth will chatter."

One man raised a hand and he said, "But I have got no teeth."

So the priest said, "Don't worry, false teeth will be provided."

They make every arrangement for you in hell. The ego, the brahmin, the head is always condemning everybody; everybody is ordinary, only you are extraordinary. Only you are going to be saved, nobody else. That's why Christians go on preaching, "Come and follow Jesus. Only those who follow Jesus will be saved – everybody else is lost." That's what Mohammedans go on saying, and Hindus go on saying. There seems to be a very deep politics in existence: if you follow somebody and if you go to this church you will be saved; if you follow somebody else and go to another church you will be destroyed. And the same is the claim of the other church also. And God must be in a puzzle: what to do?

This whole condemnation comes from the head, the ego. A very subtle ego colors whatsoever you say and believe: your convictions, your philosophy, everything is colored by the ego. And Zen is a simple life.

And that is my teaching also: be simple and nobody. Don't condemn anybody. Don't put yourself in a situation where you can feel holier than thou – never. Just be ordinary. And when you are ordinary, all anxiety disappears. When you are ordinary, then your whole perception is totally different. Then the birds singing in the trees are a message from the divine. Then the breeze passing through the trees and a leaf dancing in the breeze is his hand, his indication. Then the sky, and the earth, everything is beautiful, and everything comes from him.

When you are ordinary, when you are nobody, all the doors are open. When you are somebody all the doors are closed. Be ordinary and live life silently. Don't be a politician. That is the only misfortune that can happen to a man. And politics and religion are opposite poles. Politics is the effort to be somebody in the hierarchy, somewhere at the top, and religion is the search to stand just at the very end of the queue, just to be nobody.

Says Lao Tzu: Nobody can insult me, nobody can bring me down, because I am already there. Nobody can defeat me – not that I am very strong, but that I am already defeated. Nobody can defeat me.

The ordinary person is the most beautiful phenomenon in the world, just living moment to moment, not expecting, not asking. Whatsoever comes, accepting. Whatsoever comes, not only accepting, but accepting with a deep thankfulness, a gratitude.

When you are ordinary, whatsoever comes is more than you ever expected. When you are extraordinary, when you think extraordinarily, something very great – a Napoleon, a Hitler – then everything is always something unfulfilling. Everything is lower than your expectations. You are such a great man; whatsoever happens is always below you. When you are ordinary, everything is more than you ever expected; and when this feeling comes, that it is more than you ever expected, you feel a gratitude. That gratitude is the inner shrine. In that gratitude, for the first time the light from the beyond descends.

Create this shrine of gratitude inside and soon you will find a light has come into it. The shrine is not dark, and this light doesn't belong to this world. It comes from the eternal.

Enough for today.

Discourse 4

The Good Wife

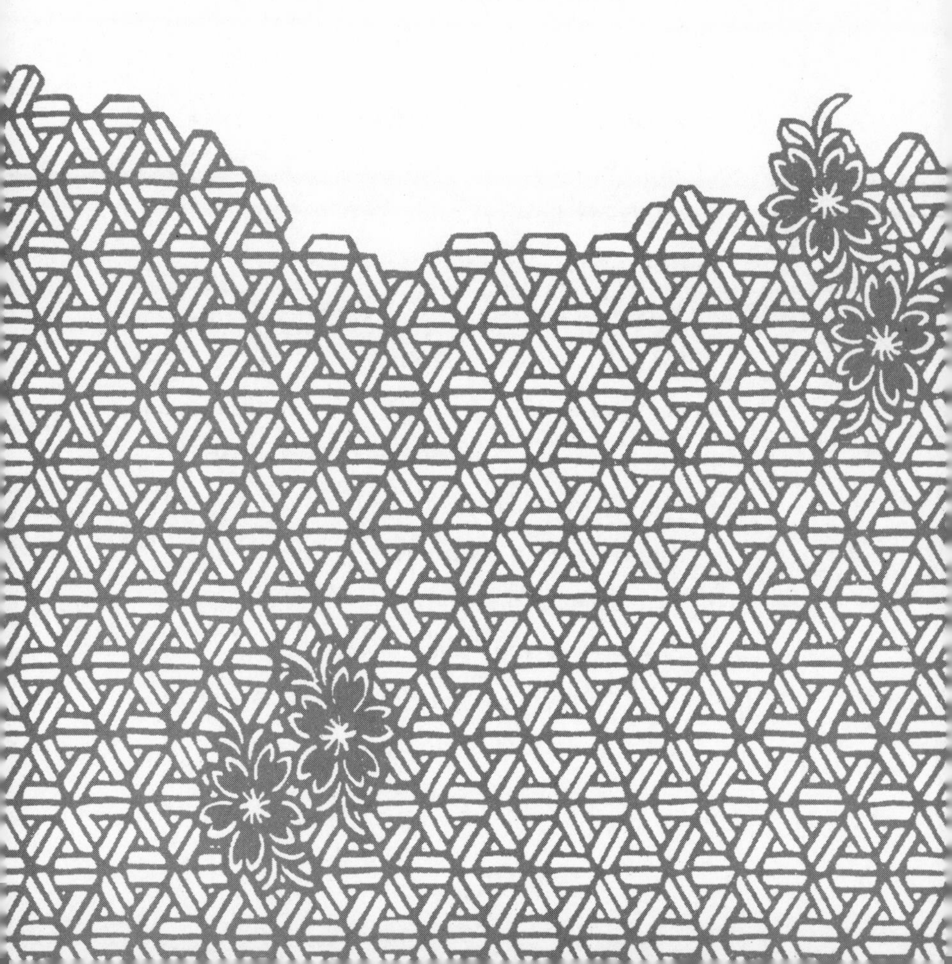

Mokusen Hiki was living in a temple in the province of Tamba. One of his adherents complained of the stinginess of his wife. Mokusen visited the adherent's wife and held his clenched fist before her face.

"What do you mean by that?" asked the surprised woman.

"Suppose my hand were always like that, what would you call it?" "Deformed," replied the woman.

Then he opened his hand flat in her face and asked, "Suppose it were always like that – what then?"

"Another kind of deformity," said the wife.

"If you understand that much," finished Mokusen, "you are a good wife." Then he left.

After his visit this wife helped her husband to distribute as well as to save.

The greatest art is to attain a balance, a balance between all opposites, a balance between all polarities. Imbalance is the disease and balance is health. Imbalance is neurosis, and balance is well-being.

I have heard: Mulla Nasruddin went to his psychiatrist. He rambled upon his miseries, troubles, and finally he concluded, "I am afraid. It seems that I am getting neurotic."

The psychiatrist smiled and said, "Nasruddin, if that is true, then you must be happy and grateful that you are neurotic."

Nasruddin was shocked. He said, "What? Happy that I am neurotic? Why?"

Said the psychiatrist, "Because that is the only normal thing about you."

Neurosis is the only normal thing, not only about Nasruddin but about everybody else also. Mind has to be neurotic. Neurosis is not a disease; neurosis is mind itself, so neurosis cannot be cured. With mind remaining there, neurosis is bound to follow it like a shadow. Hence all psychiatry fails. At the most it can make you normal, but to be normal is nothing but to be normally neurotic – neurotic like everybody else, not in your own way; just following the highway, not an individual path. People who are in madhouses have private neuroses, you have a mass neurosis. That's why you cannot be detected – you are just like everybody else. And people are in the madhouses who have tried to attain their own style of neurosis. They are individualists. That's the only difference. And this has to be so, because mind itself, the very functioning of the mind, is neurotic. Try to understand this.

Mind is never in the middle – cannot be. When you are in the middle, the mind simply disappears. Mind is always at the extreme – either this or that. That's why mind divides the world into white and black, into life and death, into hate and love, into friend and foe. The world is neither white nor black; the world is some sort of grey. One pole is white, another pole is black. Just in the middle, where black and white merge and meet and become one, is the reality. But mind sees in polarities. It says: Either this is true or this is untrue.

I have not come across a truth which has not got some lie in it. Neither have I come across a lie which is not true in a certain sense. Lies have fragments of truth in them, that's why they work; otherwise, how can a lie work? Why are people such liars? A lie has a fragment of truth in it. You cannot invent an absolute lie, impossible. And you cannot talk about the absolute truth – that too is impossible. That's why a Lao Tzu goes on saying: If you speak, you have already entered into the world of lies. The truth cannot be said. The moment you say it, a fragment of it is bound to be a lie.

Existence is not divided into either-or. It has no duality; it is one energy flowing from this end to that. Both banks of the river are joined together underneath; they are part of one land. They appear to you to be two because you have not entered the river and you have never gone to the very bottom. The banks are not two, they belong to one land. But for the river to flow, they *appear* to be two. Existence is just like the two banks meeting underneath, and mind is just looking at the surface. So mind says, "I am at this bank and you are at that. You are against me. If you are a friend then you are on this bank with me; you are an enemy if you are on that bank." But both banks belong to one earth.

The mind cannot see so deeply. The mind is the phenomenon on the surface – hence dualities. Existence is one, it cannot be otherwise. There are not two existences, only one exists, but because of the rhythm you are alive.

You inhale and exhale: that inhalation and exhalation becomes like two banks for your river to flow – but you are neither. The breath comes in, the breath goes out; it gives a rhythm – two banks. And that rhythm is beautiful if you are not stuck to some extreme. Even in breathing, the mind is always choosing. Rarely does it happen that you can see a person who exhales and inhales equally – rarely. If you come to a point where you can exhale and inhale and remain just in the middle, you will attain to enlightenment. As you are you only inhale, you never exhale. The body exhales and forces the air out – you again inhale. Just watch your breathing: you pay more attention to inhalation; you go on inhaling. Exhalation is just left to the body. The body throws air out; you inhale again, because deep down you think that inhalation is life and exhalation is death. In a way it is true, because the first thing a child does after birth is to inhale.

Life starts functioning with inhalation. Hence, you identify life with inhalation. And the last thing a man who is going to die will do will be to exhale. You cannot die with inhalation, can you? You cannot die inhaling, you will have to die exhaling. So deep down the unconscious feels that exhalation is death and inhalation is life. You cling to inhalation. And if you cling to one pole you will become a mind. Exhale, inhale – remain in the middle and don't choose. Don't choose. Don't choose between the opposites – remain in the middle, because if you choose between opposites you become unbalanced. Imbalance is neurosis.

Then you become addicted to one pole, and life is a rhythm – it needs the other. It is neither sound nor silence, it is both. Silence is one pole and sound is the other pole, and life is just the rhythm between these two polarities. Don't choose! If you choose sound you will become addicted to sound, to noise, to the outside. You will become an extrovert, because sound is outside. Inside is silence. If you choose silence you will become an introvert. Then you will close yourself completely towards the existence that exists without. You will move in and in, and that movement will not be a rhythm because you have denied the other pole. Rather, this movement will be a dead stagnancy. You will be stuck with it, you cannot be ecstatic.

With silence and sound both, you simply move between these polarities because you are neither. You are just in the middle – you are the rhythm. My left hand and my right hand are both me; sound and silence are both me; life and death are both me. Don't cling. Exhalation, inhalation – both are me.

If you cling to one then your life will be a neurosis, because what will you do with the other? It is there. And whether you choose to or not, you have to move to the other. How can you stop exhalation? And if you stop exhaling, how will you be able to inhale? Look at the beauty: you exhale – the moment you exhale you have created a situation for a deep inhalation. When you inhale you have created a situation for a deep exhalation. The opposite is really not the opposite. How can it be the opposite? Inhalation depends upon exhalation, exhalation depends on inhalation. How can they be enemies? How can there be any antagonism? They are friends, they are not foes. They are playing a game in which they appear to be opposites, but deep down they are one earth.

Don't choose love against hate, because then you will be in trouble; then where will you put hate? Hate is there, as much part of you as love. Remain in the middle. Let hate have its own way, let love have its own way. You simply watch from the middle, don't move to the extreme. If you move to one extreme, what will you do with the other? You will then become afraid of the other. And the other is going to come, because that which you have chosen cannot remain alone, it depends on the other.

You fall in love with a man or a woman, then you become afraid of hate, anger and conflict. But what will you do? – they are bound to come. Your so-called love depends on them; it cannot exist alone, it is a rhythm. The opposite is needed. Have you ever seen a river with one bank? Life is a river, and mind tries to flow with one bank – that is the neurosis. There are peaks and there are valleys. There are high moments and there are low moments. Don't get obsessed with any high peak, otherwise what will happen to the valley? Have you seen a peak without a valley?

Go to the Himalayas: the higher the peak is, the deeper the valley will be. The deepest valley exists near Everest – it can only exist there. Only such a high peak can allow such a deep valley. And there is a balance: the valley has to be deep to the same extent as the peak has gone high. They balance each other. Watch a tall tree reaching to the sky: the roots are hidden, but the roots go deep down to the same extent...if the tree has grown one hundred feet, the roots have to grow one hundred feet deep down. Otherwise, what will support the tree? What will support this one-hundred-foot tree? And if the tree chooses just the height and tries to deny the roots it will die. And this is what you have been doing. This is what the whole of humanity has been doing. That's why the whole of humanity has shrunk, caved in. Everything has gone wrong, because you want only high moments.

People come to me and they say, "Yesterday I was ecstatic and now I am low." You have to be. What will support the ecstasy? What will support the peak? The peak could not exist alone; this valley was bound to follow.

Watch the waves in the ocean: the higher the wave goes, the deeper is the wake that follows it. One moment you are the wave, another moment you are the hollow wake that follows. Enjoy both, don't get addicted to one. Don't say, "I would always like to be on the peak." It is not possible. Simply see the fact: it is not possible. It has never happened and it will never happen. It is simply impossible – not in the nature of things. Then what to do? Enjoy the peak while it lasts and then enjoy the valley when it comes. What is wrong with the valley? What is wrong with being low? It is a relaxation.

A peak is an excitement, and nobody can exist continuously in an excitement. You will go completely mad. That's why when you love a person you have to hate the same person. But don't be afraid of hate, just accept it. If you love deeply you will hate deeply. If you don't love much you will not hate. The moment husbands and wives stop fighting, love disappears. If you see a couple absolutely okay it is a dead couple; the love has disappeared long before. They are no longer fighting – then they are no longer in love. Now there are no more peaks, no more valleys

Lovers fight. Only lovers can fight; they depend on fighting. And they know that nothing is wrong, because when they fight they create a situation to move deeper into love. It is a rhythm. If you have been a lover, which is a rare thing, you know that just before making love, if you have been fighting and angry and trying to kill each other and then you make love, then the orgasm has a high peak such as can never be attained ordinarily. Because when energies move farther away – hate means energy is moving farther away – there comes a point when you have moved as far from each other as you were before you fell in love. Just the same point has come again. You are two individuals, completely independent, all communication has dropped. You are again strangers, not knowing who the other is. This was the situation when you fell in love. If you don't escape you will fall in love again – the whole romance, a new honeymoon. And if you cannot get the honeymoon again and again, love will become stale. It will be just a dead thing, you will have to carry it like a burden.

That's why marriage exists. Marriage has been invented by cunning and clever people, mathematicians. In marriage there is no peak, no valley; you simply move on plain ground. You never fall in love, there is no trouble. Marriage is security, not love. Marriage is an arithmetic, it is not romance. It has been invented by cunning people. They simply stop all possibility of any fight, anger, hate. They simply stop all possibilities of dangerous situations, insecurities. Marriage is always an 'okay' affair: never at the peak where you can dance, never at the valley where you will weep. But a person who has not known dance, who has not known weeping, is simply not alive.

One should laugh and one should weep also. Laughter and weeping are two banks. A balance is needed. If you really laugh you will also weep. And what is wrong with weeping? Tears are beautiful. If you have laughed, if you have laughed deeply, tears become very very beautiful. They carry something of the laughter, because deep down the banks are one, they are not two. On one pole laughter, on another pole tears; one pole smiles, another pole cries, but deep down they are joined together. If you have laughed totally you will weep totally, and both are beautiful. Totality is beautiful.

But if you cling, then you can never be total. When you weep you cling to the laughter; you try to smile, you try to force a smile because you don't want this weeping and crying: "This is bad, this is ugly" – and you try and force a smile. Tears are in the eyes and you force a smile. This smile is false – this is neurosis. When the body wants to weep and you are smiling, this is schizophrenia. This is how the split starts, how a person becomes two. Totality is lost. Then remember, when you laugh it can never be total.

If you cling to one pole you become afraid of totality. If you cannot weep totally, how can you laugh totally? That's why the belly laugh has simply disappeared from the world. You don't know what a belly laugh is, when not only you laugh but the belly laughs, the whole body vibrates. Not only you, but from head to toe everything laughs. That laughter is mad because you are totally in it.

Look at the absurdity of the world: only a madman can be total. You are afraid because you know well that you have suppressed tears, so if you laugh deeply tears may come. And it happens: you may have noticed many times, if you start laughing deeply, immediately you feel tears are coming. You feel confused – why are tears coming? Tears are coming because you have been suppressing them, and you have never allowed a totality. And now you laugh totally: the suppressed needs expression, the suppressed flows, the suppressed seeks a moment. The door is open – it flows.

When you open the door, remember, the enemy will also enter with the friend. If you want that only the friend should enter, it is impossible. Then you will have to close the door so that the enemy may not enter. But then the friend cannot enter either; it is closed – because it is the same door. And if you see deeply, it is the same person who is the friend and the foe. So if you deny the foe entry, the friend is also denied. If you say, "I am not going to weep," you are saying, "I am not going to laugh." If you say, "I am not going to hate," you are saying, "I am not going to love." If you say, "I am not going to become low, depressed and sad," you are saying, "I am not going to be blissful." Both are one, so you cannot choose. You can simply be aware and remain in the middle. When you are in the middle you can see that both are your wings.

Think of this situation: if a bird flies with one wing, what will happen to it? If I can move wholly, totally to my right side, I will be paralyzed; the left will simply be paralyzed. And if the left is paralyzed, do you think that the right can be alive? How can the right be alive if the left is paralyzed? They live in a mutual dependence – not even dependence, they live in oneness. Can you say where your right side ends and your left side begins? Where exactly is the demarcation? No boundaries are there. It is a circle: left goes into right, right goes into left. It is a circle.

That's why in China they have made the yin-yang symbol. It is a circle, and this circle, moving, exists in every dimension. A man is not just a man, he is also a woman. A woman is not only a woman, she is also a man. There are moments when a woman is man, there are moments when a man is woman. And you become afraid: "I should not be a woman. I am not effeminate, I am male, and I should never betray any feminine qualities." This has been taught for centuries all over the world. Even to small boys you say, "Don't be a sissy." What nonsense! You even start poisoning a small boy: "You are a man. Behave like a man – don't be girlish." The right side is male and the left is female in the boy; the same is true in a girl. If the girl starts behaving like a tomboy, everybody is afraid. If she starts climbing a tree, then you say, "What are you doing? You are a girl! Behave like a girl. Girls never do this. They only play with toys and arrange marriage and make a house."

I was staying with a family. My friend and his wife had gone somewhere and three small children were playing. Two were playing in the room, and the smallest one was sitting just near the porch on the steps. So I asked him, "Why are you not playing?"

He said, "I am also playing."

But I had been watching and I said, "You have been just sitting here, outside on the porch."

He said, "Yes, because I am the baby who is going to be born. They are playing mommy and daddy, and I am waiting for the right moment."

Girls play 'house'; boys are not expected to do that. You create a division. You create the split from the very beginning. And then neither is man total nor is woman total, because man, always half-paralyzed, cannot be a woman. That's why a man is not allowed to weep. Only women weep. Man seems to be more clever than God. Then why are there tear glands in the eyes? If man is not to weep, then God seems to be a fool: he goes on giving man tear glands in the eyes. And you never weep, you never use your tear glands. Then you also cannot laugh, because the half is paralyzed – you cannot move. And a woman is not supposed to laugh loudly; that doesn't look feminine, that doesn't look lady-like. Then half is paralyzed there also.

Remember, you are both. And remember this always: wherever you see an opposite polarity you are both, and neither is to be chosen. You are both and you have to accept both and enjoy both. And nothing is wrong. If you are a man, nothing is wrong in moving to the other polarity sometimes and just being feminine. Just weep like a woman – it is so beautiful, so relaxing. It is such a benediction. Just weep like a woman, cry like a woman, and laugh like a man. It is such a great phenomenon, because the moment you move to the opposite you become total.

Psychoanalysis and psychiatry really can't help much, because basically they go on accepting the division. Even a Freud is as much a suppressed personality as anybody else, sometimes even more ...very uptight. Nobody seems to be relaxed. If you are relaxed there is no need to meditate, because meditation is medicinal – it is a medicine. If you are healthy there is no need for it. And I have not come across a single human being who is not in need of meditation. That means the whole of humanity is sick; the whole earth is a great hospital.

Try to look at it. And when I say try to look at it, look at it within yourself. Don't look to the right and to the left – I am talking to *you*. Just see the whole point. And if you can see the whole point of your split being, nothing is to be done. Simply drop helping this split. By and by, move from the extremes to the middle. Hence, Buddha called his path the middle way, *majjhim nikaya*. Hence, Lao Tzu says his path is 'the golden mean'.

It is said of Confucius that he was passing through a village and he asked a villager, "Have you got any wise men in this town?"

The villager said, "Yes, we have our own wise man."

Confucius said, "What is the reason that you call him wise? Can you say something?"

The man said, "Yes – he is a great thinker. Even coming out of his house he stops and thinks three times about whether to come out or not."

Confucius said, "Three times? Three times is too much. Once is not enough, three times is too much. Twice will do."

You see the point? He said, just the middle will do. Once is not enough, thrice is too much; you have moved to the other extreme. There are people who will not think once. These are the fools about whom it is said: Where angels fear to tread fools simply rush in. These are fools. But a person who thinks thrice has gone to the other extreme. Again the foolishness has entered, from the other extreme.

To be extreme is to be foolish. He is again stupid. People may call him wise because they are the first type of fools, and this man is just the opposite. But opposite to a fool, you will be a fool. Fighting a fool, how can you be a wise man? This extreme, that extreme, both are foolish. So Confucius said: Just in the middle... twice will do.

This has to be remembered because this is the whole point of this Zen story. Try to understand it.

Mokusen Hiki was living in a temple in the province of Tamba. One of his adherents complained of the stinginess of his wife.

Mokusen visited the adherent's wife and held a clenched fist before her face.

"What do you mean by that?" asked the surprised woman.

"Suppose my hand were always like that, what would you call it? – always clenched, always a fist, closed – *what would you call it?"* Mokusen asked.

"Deformed," replied the woman.

Then he opened his hand flat in her face and asked, "Suppose it were always like that – what then?"

"Another kind of deformity," said the wife.

"If you understand that much," finished Mokusen, "you are a good wife." Then he left.

After his visit this wife helped her husband to distribute as well as to save.

The first thing: Zen believes not in teaching but in situations. This Mokusen Hiki could have talked, could have given a long sermon, but he didn't do anything like that. He simply went to the woman and held a clenched fist before her face, he created a situation.

A situation is an existential phenomenon. Just talking, teaching, won't do, because talking and teaching go to the head. And even if the head is convinced, nothing happens out of it. You know this very well. You are convinced of many things, but you just go on doing the contrary. You are convinced that anger is poisonous, but does that make any difference to you? Whether you say anger is poisonous or not you go on being angry. You have been repenting continuously – again and again the same happens. It seems such an autonomous phenomenon, you feel completely helpless. The head knows anger is wrong, but nothing happens through it.

You know very well what is wrong, but that doesn't transform your life. You know very well what is right, but that doesn't come into your being. It remains something in the mind – a conviction, an argument, a rationalization. It remains knowledge but it never becomes understanding. Knowledge won't help. And this is the difference between knowledge and understanding. Understanding means that you have learned it through your whole being, you have learned it through an existential situation; it has not been given only through words. All the masters have been doing that – they create situations. In a situation you have to act. In a situation your totality is called in, challenged.

This woman must have been shocked. "What is this enlightened master doing? What a foolish thing!" He didn't say a single word, he simply came to arouse. He showed a clenched fist in her face – she must have been shocked. This was no way to behave when he had not said a single thing. He had not given a single opportunity for the head to come in. The whole woman was challenged – she must have been ready to fight. Something was going to happen. "This man seems to be mad!" And then he asked a question: "What would you call it if my hand continuously remained like this?" She said, "Of course, deformed."

This was a perception; something dawned on her. The whole situation showed that this is deformed: if you cannot open your hand, if it is always closed, this is a deformity.

And such a deformity has happened to you. You cannot exhale, you simply inhale: this is a deformity. You cannot give, you can only possess: this is a deformity. You cannot share, you can only go on hoarding. You go on hoarding everything, you cannot share it. You have completely lost the language of sharing – but this is a deformity. A miser is a deformed human being. He has completely lost something in him that can share. He hoards and hoards and hoards, and this hoarding just becomes a grave.

Why are you hoarding if you cannot share? Why are you alive if you cannot love? What are you seeking if you cannot be ecstatic? And ecstasy comes through a balance: if you simply possess a thing to share it, then possession is not ugly. Then you are simply waiting to share it.

It happened: Two monks were traveling. One monk believed in renunciation of everything, so he would not carry a single *paise*. He was against money, absolutely against – he would not touch it.

By the evening they came near a river, and they had to cross the river. The river was very vast: they had to ask the ferryboat man to take them. He asked for money. The other monk was a hoarder; whatsoever he could get he would hoard. He was a miser. And there had always been an argument, a continuous argument between them about what is right. One would say, "Money is useless.

It is dirt" – as all the ascetics have always said, which is nonsense. The other would say, "Money? – money is life. Without money you cannot even live. It is not dirt." And there was no end to their argument.

The ferryman asked for money. The money-hoarder, the miser, said, "Now, what will you do? I have money; I will go to the other shore, to the town, and you will have to stay here. This is a wild and dangerous area. Now what do you say?"

The other monk simply smiled and didn't say anything. Of course, the friend paid for him also. They both crossed the river.

When they had crossed, the man who had smiled, who was against money, said, "Now see what has happened. Because you gave the money to the ferryboat man, that's why we could pass. If you had been miserly about it we would have died on the other shore. You renounced that money, that's why we have come to this bank. Now we are safe. And I always say money has to be renounced. Now you see...!" The argument again came to the same point.

Who is right? Both are wrong. And remember this: in argument both sides are always wrong, because if there is not something wrong an argument cannot continue forever and ever. The worldly people are wrong, the other-worldly people are exactly as wrong as the worldly people; otherwise the argument cannot continue for centuries and centuries. Miserly people are wrong, and people who renounce are wrong. People who possess are wrong, and people who renounce are wrong. Somewhere there is a mid-point where you simply see that money is necessary and to renounce money is also necessary. To hoard money is necessary and to share it is just as necessary. If you can create a balance between hoarding and sharing, then you have come to the point from where understanding becomes possible.

So don't be for or against, just try to understand. Wherever there are opposites, always remember not to choose one opposite against the other. You will be wrong. It doesn't make any difference which one you choose; for me, to be at the extreme is to be wrong. Both the monks were wrong. But I was not there.... They must be arguing the same argument somewhere in other bodies, because this type of argument cannot be concluded.

That's why people who say there is God have not proved anything, and people who say there is no God also have not proved anything. Because God both is and is not – life and death, positive and negative, presence and absence – that's why they have not been able to prove anything. Both parties have been continuously arguing. Millions of ages have passed and not a single conclusion has been reached through philosophical argumentation. You can go on and on...if you have a clever mind you can go on and on. Mind never reaches any conclusion, it cannot reach. It chooses one part and the other is involved in it; you cannot deny it.

People who say God is not, if they really think that God is not then why bother? But they bother even more: they continuously argue, they write big books, they devote their whole lives to proving that God is not. What type of foolishness...? If God is not, why are you wasting your life proving it?

I know a man who has been writing against God continuously for thirty years. He came to see me and he said, "I would like to have a confrontation with you."

I told him, "There is no possibility, because whatsoever you say, I will say 'yes'."

He said, "Whatsoever I say? What do you mean? – for thirty years I have been trying to prove that God is not."

I told him, "Whether God is or is not, that is irrelevant, but why have you wasted your thirty years? Now who will give them back to you? There is no God, so you cannot even ask him for another life. But why bother? This is an obsession. You are neurotic. If God is not, simply drop the idea. You just live."

"No," he said, "I have to prove it to convince others."

But if God is not, let others believe. Why are *you* worried? He was worried, terribly worried: God was an obsession from the negative pole.

And then there are people who go on proving that God is. They too waste their time. If God is, live him! If God is not, then live his absence. Why be bothered?

But no, when mind chooses an extreme it always feels that something is wrong – the imbalance. You have to prove it. Why? – because you feel an imbalance. If God is then the imbalance becomes more apparent, so you try to prove it. You are not trying to convince others, you are trying to convince yourself that there cannot be any imbalance because there is no God. "I am right" – you are trying to prove this. And what is the need? If you are right, what is the need to prove it? You are right, you are happy, you live happily – finished. God will take care of himself.

But no, you cannot sleep because God is not. You are worried because God is not. There are people who worry that God must be; they go on making others believe – they try to convince. Who are they trying to convince? It is not a dialogue, it is a monologue. Whatsoever you try to prove is really of your inner imbalance. You would like it if the other didn't exist. Then, *then* you could feel a balance.

But the other is...the other is – it haunts you. Atheists, theists, for-against people – it haunts them. You have to balance yourself, then it simply drops. All problems drop when you are balanced. You cannot solve any problem, remember; problems simply disappear when you are balanced. Problems are just symbolic indications, they are not the real disease. The real disease is the imbalance.

There are people who live with a clenched fist; they hoard – they hoard everything. They don't know, because hoarding becomes their habit. They hoard everything, anything – rubbish. You may not be aware that they even become constipated because they hoard. You will always find a miser constipated. He cannot relax, he cannot give anything out of himself; he even hoards excreta. And then he seeks a remedy for constipation. There is no remedy for constipation. The remedy is to relax and share. When you share, the body relaxes totally because it is a total organic unity. A person who can love will never be constipated – impossible, because he shares all his energies. And if he can share his heart, why should he hoard excreta? No, the hoarding is a closing. You go on shrinking within yourself. You cannot give anything; you have lost the very dimension of giving.

Go to the misers' houses.... Just a few days ago there was news. Two brothers lived in New York. For thirty years they didn't allow anybody to enter their house. Nobody knew what they were doing within the house. They never married, because misers never want to fall in love; a woman can be dangerous. And when a woman enters, you never know what she will do with your money. She is bound to waste it. So they never married, they never fell in love, and they hoarded and hoarded things, every type of thing.

Just a few days ago, two or three months ago, they both died from an electric shock. Something went wrong and they died. Then the police opened the house. They found millions of dollars worth of every sort of thing; it was impossible to enter the house. There were fifty television sets, forty-nine never opened – just in their boxes; radios, refrigerators, many just unpacked – they had never used them.

They used to live on milk. One brother would go and bring the milk in the morning, that was all. He would bring the milk and a newspaper, they would read the news. And what were they doing inside? – arranging things. And they had made such a mess! It was a three-storey building, all three storeys filled with things; one had to creep because there was no space left.

It took many days for the police to bring the things out, to count how many things there were and how many dollars they had left behind. They had never put any money in the bank – because nobody knows, banks can go bankrupt. And they lived like poor beggars. They could have lived rich lives, but a miser always lives a poor beggar's life. A miser is really a beggar, the ultimate in beggary. You cannot find a greater beggar than a miser: he has it and he cannot use it.

Then there are other types of people: they are just the reverse image of a miser. They renounce everything, they escape. It was said of Vinoba Bhave that if you brought money to him he would simply close his eyes. He would not touch it; he would not look at the money. This seems to be another extreme. Why be so afraid of money – why this fear? Why close your eyes? What is wrong with money? Nothing is wrong with money, but you are afraid. This is the reverse image of the miser, because the man is afraid that if he looks at the money then the desire for it will arise.

Remember, if you are afraid of looking at money, at a beautiful woman, if you are afraid to look, what does it show? It shows that a fear is there that if you look at a beautiful woman, desire will arise. You are afraid of the desire and you have suppressed it: then you cannot even look. This is the most obscene type of mind. If you cannot look at a beautiful woman, what are you doing? – your whole sexuality has become cerebral. You cannot even use your eyes now. No, they are not eyes, they have become genital organs. You are afraid, because if you look then you don't know what will happen. You are afraid of yourself, that's why you cannot see. One can move from one extreme to another: one can hoard money or one can throw it to the dogs and escape from it to the Himalayas, but both types are the same.

Twice is enough, once is not enough, thrice is too much. Why can't you remain in the middle? – because in the middle, mind disappears. It is just like the pendulum: the pendulum goes on moving to the right and to the left. You know that if the pendulum is moving from right to left and from left to right the clock is functioning. If the pendulum is maintained in the middle, balanced, all movement gone, the clock stops. And when the pendulum goes to the left you only think it is going to the left, but it is gathering momentum to go to the right. So where is it going? When it goes to the left it is gathering momentum. This going to the left is nothing but a preparation to go to the right. It goes to the left, gathers the energy, the momentum, then it goes to the right. Left-right it moves – those two extremes keep it moving.

Mind is a movement between extremes; it is a travel, a continuous movement between two. In the middle mind simply disappears, because movement disappears. When there is no movement, you are a being for the first time, you are in a state of being. Everything stops – time, space – everything has disappeared. It doesn't mean that you stop functioning, it simply means that now your headquarters have changed: they are in the middle. Now you will function from the middle. You will go to the left, you will go to the right. You can go to the left without any fear, you can go to the right without any fear. You can go to the right and to the left, retaining yourself in the middle. That's why I call it the greatest art, to be in the middle.

If you are a miser, it is very easy to simply get fed up with your miserliness. And then you move to the other extreme – you throw everything. You renounce everything and you become an ascetic. If you are a playboy, it is very easy to become a monk and move to a Catholic monastery, or to become a Jaina, or to come to India and go to some ashram. If you are a playboy it is very easy, because you have touched one extreme. Now you are frustrated with that, finished. You think it is finished but it is now following you to the other extreme, it is pushing you to the other extreme. One bank is finished, but that bank is throwing you to the other bank.

Both banks are the same; neither is the river. You have to be in the middle so that you can flow with the river. This bank or that, what is the difference? You were stuck on this bank, now this bank is throwing you to the other bank and you will be stuck there. And what is the difference? The other bank is 'other' only because you are here; when you are there, this bank will become the other. And that's what happens to many people: they leave the world in search of the other world; then they are stuck with the other bank. This world looks at the other world and then the desire for it arises.

If you could open the heads of the monks, the ascetics, you would be surprised. If you could make a window in their heads and look into it, the whole world, this world, goes on and on. A man who has escaped from women will think continuously of women and nothing else.

Mulla Nasruddin was telling me one day about his new girlfriend, and he was bragging so much. He said, "She is the most beautiful woman in the world, a regular mirage."

I asked him, "You may be right, she may be the most beautiful woman in the world, but you are using a wrong word. Why a regular mirage? A mirage means you can see it, but you cannot touch it."

Mulla Nasruddin said, "Exactly. That's my girl. You can see her but you cannot touch her – a regular mirage."

Look at your monks: they live in a regular mirage. Girls are there: they can see but they cannot touch, that is the only difference. Your girls you can touch also. They cannot touch, they live in their dreams. If you escape from something, that something will become a dream in you, it will haunt you. Never try to escape from anything. Fear cannot help. Escape is simply foolish. Situations help, escapes never. Just try to find the middle in every situation. And what is the middle? How can it be maintained?

I talked about a peak and a valley. You can find a mid-point; that will not be the middle I am talking about. You can make a hut just in the middle, neither in the valley nor on the peak. You can just measure the whole thing, come to a point which is the middle, and make your hut and live there. But that is not the middle I am talking about. That's very easy, that too can be done. That too can be done; you can live just half-half: you hoard half and half you share. That is not the mid-point, because a mid-point is not a fixed point, it changes with every situation. It changes with every situation: it is not a static thing, it is a dynamic awareness. And one never knows....

Mulla Nasruddin once said to his wife, "I am going out. I have arranged a great feast for a friend. And that friend is not only a friend, he is a great businessman, and there is a possibility that we will come to some understanding and a new business can be started." And he was very very hopeful.

His wife was also happy. She said, "It's okay." So he went, and then he returned. The night had almost gone, it was two o'clock in the morning. His wife was waiting for him and she asked, "What happened? How was the deal?"

He said, "Fifty-fifty."

The wife asked, "What do you mean by fifty-fifty?"

He said, "Only I turned up there, my friend never came."

Your fifty-fifty can be a deception. It is not a fixed point, you cannot measure it. It is a constantly changing flow of awareness, and in every moment you have again to regain the balance. It is not something that once you have gained, forever.... It is just like a tightrope walker: it is not that once he has attained the balance, finished – then he goes on. With every single step the balance has to be attained again. Sometimes he feels that he is falling towards the left; immediately he leans towards the right to gain balance. Then when he feels that the opposite is happening, that he has leaned too much to the right, he leans immediately to the left. With every single step one has to attain balance. It is not something that you have attained and finished with. It is a process.

Be more aware. Be more aware when you exhale, be more aware when you inhale. And don't cling to either of them. Earn money, share, be aware. Don't think of the quantity. There are people, particularly Mohammedans, who share a fixed quantity: they have to share one-fifth of their income. So they have been sharing, but that makes no difference, because it is not a question of a fixed amount, it is a question of awareness. Sometimes you have to give all, that is the mid-point. Sometimes you have not to give anything, because that is the mid-point. One never knows but one moves. One is fully alert not to cling to any polarity.

And one cannot plan. Mind always wants to plan, because once you plan there is no need to be aware. You can become an automaton, and go on like a robot – you have a fixed discipline. That's why in all the monasteries they have a fixed discipline; no need to be aware. "Do this, this is right. Don't do that, that is wrong" – finished. You need not be aware, you simply become a robot. You know what is right, you know what is wrong.

I tell you, the right becomes wrong and the wrong becomes right when situations change. Sometimes something is right, because the situation is totally different; another time the same thing is wrong. And nobody can say beforehand what is right and what is wrong. So no moral code can be given. All moral codes kill you, they poison you. All commandments are poisonous because they give you a fixed thing: do this. But situations change, and in changing situations the same thing is immoral.

Morality and immorality are not commodities, things. They are not things, they are processes. And that is the subtlest point to be understood about life. People come to me, they say: We listen to you, but that is too difficult. You just give us a discipline – what to do, what not to do – so we will follow.

If you want moral codes, I cannot give you any because I know all codes are poisonous. And you ask for codes – that's your trick to escape from awareness, because without codes you will have to be constantly aware and constantly feel, "What is the situation? What is right now? What is wrong now? This moment will decide. Nobody else can decide." Then you have to be very very alert. To make you alert, I don't give you any code. I have no code. Awareness is the only discipline, the only commandment.

I have heard that this happened in a small class: The teacher asked, "Who is the greatest man in the world?" It happened in America, so one child said, "Abraham Lincoln." The teacher was not satisfied. She asked another child; the other child was a Negro. He said, "Martin Luther King."

Then a small child raised his hand. She asked, "Who is the greatest man in the world?"

He said, "Jesus. Of course, Jesus."

The teacher was surprised. She said, "Yes, your answer is right, but I am surprised because you are a Jew."

So the boy said, "Yes. I know, you know, everybody knows that Moses is the greatest man in the world, but business is business."

Life is always changing, nothing is static, and whatsoever you know will not be of much help. You have to look at the situation, the whole situation. And if your response to it is with a perfect awareness, it is right. Then you'll never repent for it. And then you grow through it, then you become more aware.

Awareness has no past, awareness has no future; awareness has only this here-now. And a man of awareness never thinks about the past again, it is finished. He did whatsoever could have been done. He never regrets, he has no grudge. He never thinks in terms of what should have been. A person who follows a dead code will always think, "I should have done this or that. This should have been the case, this should not have been the case." He is always regretting, repenting, because he acted out of a dead code. And a dead code never fits. It cannot fit, because every situation is new.

Be more aware, and don't create a code in the mind. Just live moment to moment and let life itself decide the code. Let awareness itself feel the code. And then there will be no past, because when you never think anything wrong has gone on in the past, there is no wound. You are completely clean of the past; it never clings to you like dirt, dust. You are completely fresh. And if you are aware you have found the mid-point.

Awareness is the mid-point. Then sometimes you open your hand, when it is needed; and sometimes you close your fist, when it is needed. You are addicted neither to the closed fist nor to the open hand. You have no addiction, you have no neurosis. You are neither a Christian, nor a Hindu, nor a Jaina, nor a Buddhist – because these are addictions, these are all neurotic attitudes. You are simply aware.

And when you are aware, sometimes you will act like a Christian, perfectly Christian, sometimes you will act like a perfect Buddhist, and sometimes you will act like a perfect Mohammedan. Nobody knows. Sometimes the Koran, sometimes the Gita, and sometimes the Bible; but you never decide beforehand, you are never prepared for it. Anybody who is prepared is wrong.

In life there are no rehearsals. You cannot rehearse a situation, you cannot be ready for it. You move unprepared. And when you realize this fact, that to move unprepared is to create the situation for being more aware, then the situation decides and you are not really the decider. The whole thing, you and the total, meet in that moment and the thing happens. You are not the decider, you are not a victim. You acted as the organic unity of existence decided at that moment. You are also not responsible: you have not done anything, you have just been a vehicle – this is the mid-point. To be a witness, to be aware, to be alert, to act consciously, with mindfulness, is the mid-point.

So remember, don't try to find a fixed mid-point. It is nowhere to be found. And nobody else can decide for you. Not even you can decide for the future. These are all tricks of the mind and they make you neurotic. Just move unprepared. This is the preparation: move unprepared. Move and let things happen. You just be aware and let things decide themselves. And I tell you, when you are aware, everything fits. Suddenly everything falls into a cosmos; it is not a chaos. Out of that unknown happens what is right. If *you* decide, out of you happens what is wrong.

He then opened his hand flat in her face and asked, "Suppose it were always like that – what then?"

"Another kind of deformity," said the wife.

The situation was such that the wife came to an understanding. The woman could understand, and the master said nothing else. He said, "You understand that much, that is enough. You have understanding. Nothing else am I to say to you. You are a good wife." Then he left, and it transformed the woman. She could understand, she could feel. Whatsoever he did in that moment became a light. The clingingness disappeared, but it was not replaced by the opposite. She became able to share.

But how can you share if you don't have anything? That's why in India you will find people who have renounced – they have nothing to share, *nothing*. They are simply unsharing, because they have moved from hoarding to the other extreme. Now they cannot even share, because they have nothing to share.

Don't move to the extreme; have something to share. And this is not only about things, this is about you. If you have yourself, only then can you share. If you have individuality, only then can you share. If you have love within you, only then can you share. If you *are,* only then is there a possibility of sharing.

And this is the mystery: you have to be there so that in some moments you disappear, you are not there. You have to attain to a presence, then you can also be absent. If you become too present and you cannot be absent, then you are hoarding. If you become absolutely absent, you have no presence, then you have renounced.

But remember, neither hoarding is sharing, nor renouncing is sharing. Sharing is just in the middle. You hoard a little, you share a little, and you always make a balance. You move in the middle. You sometimes go to this bank, you sometimes go to that bank. Sometimes you lean to the left and sometimes to the right; but you lean to the left just to be in the middle, you lean to the right just to be in the middle.

Become like a tightrope walker, for such is life – just a tightrope walk.

Enough for today.

五

Discourse 5

This Is Egoism

The prime minister, Kuo Tzu I, of the Tang Dynasty, was an outstanding statesman, a distinguished general, and the most admired national hero of his day. But fame, power, wealth and success could not distract him from his keen interest and devotion to Buddhism.

Regarding himself as a plain and humble devoted Buddhist, he often visited his favorite Zen master to study under him. He and the Zen master seemed to get along very well. The fact that he was the prime minister seemed to have no influence on their association.

There was no noticeable trace of politeness on the Zen master's part, or of vain loftiness on the part of the minister; the association seemed to be the purely religious one of a revered master and an obedient disciple.

One day, however, when he was paying his usual visit to the

Zen master, he asked the following question: "Your Reverence, how does Buddhism explain egoism?"

The Zen master's face suddenly turned blue, and in an extremely haughty and contemptuous manner he said to the premier, "What are you saying, you numbskull?"

This unreasonable and unexpected defiance so hurt the feelings of the prime minister that a slight sullen expression of anger began to show on his face.

The Zen master then smiled and said, "Your excellency, this is egoism."

Ego is the basic problem, the most basic. And unless you solve it, nothing is solved. Unless ego disappears, the ultimate cannot penetrate you.

The ego is like a closed door. The guest is standing outside; the guest has been knocking, but the door is closed. Not only is the door closed, but the ego goes on interpreting. It says: There is nobody outside, no guest has come, nobody has knocked, just a strong wind is knocking at the door. It goes on interpreting from the inside without looking at the fact. And the door remains closed. By interpretations, even the possibility of its opening becomes less and less. And a moment comes when you are completely closed in your own ego. Then all sensitivity is lost. Then you are not an opening, and you cannot have a meeting with existence. Then you are almost dead. The ego becomes your grave.

This is the most basic problem. If you solve it, everything is solved. There is no need to seek God. There is no need to seek truth. If the ego is not there, suddenly everything is found. If the ego is not there, you simply come to know that truth has always been around you, without and within. It was the ego which wouldn't allow you to see it. It was the ego that was closing your eyes and your being. So the first thing to be understood is what this ego is.

A child is born. A child is born without any knowledge, any consciousness of his own self. And when a child is born, the first thing he becomes aware of is not himself. The first thing he becomes aware of is the other. It is natural, because the eyes open outwards; the hands touch others, the ears listen to others, the tongue tastes food and the nose smells the outside. All these senses open outwards. That is what birth means. Birth means coming into this world, the world of the outside.

So when a child is born he is born into this world. He opens his eyes, sees others. 'Other' means the 'thou'. He becomes aware of the mother first. Then, by and by, he becomes aware of his own body. That too is the other, that too belongs to the world. He is hungry and he feels the body; his need is satisfied, he forgets the body. This is how a child grows. First he becomes aware of you, thou, the other, and then by and by, in contrast to you, thou, he becomes aware of himself. This awareness is a reflected awareness. He is not aware of who he is. He is simply aware of the mother and what she thinks about him. If she smiles, if she appreciates the child, if she says, "You are beautiful," if she hugs and kisses him, the child feels good about himself.

Now an ego is born. Through appreciation, love, care, he feels he is good, he feels he is valuable, he feels he has some significance. A center is born. But this center is a reflected center, it is not his real being. He does not know who he is, he simply knows what others think about him. And this is the ego: the reflection – what others think. If nobody thinks that he is of any use, nobody appreciates him, nobody smiles, then too an ego is born – an ill ego: sad, rejected, like a wound, feeling inferior, worthless. This too is the ego. This too is a reflection. First the mother – and mother means the world in the beginning – then others will join the mother, and the world goes on growing. And the more the world grows, the more complex the ego becomes, because many others' opinions are reflected.

The ego is an accumulated phenomenon, a by-product of living with others. If a child lives totally alone he will never come to grow an ego. But that is not going to help, he will remain like an animal. That doesn't mean that he will come to know the real self, no. The real can be known only through the false, so ego is a must. One has to pass through it. It is a discipline. The real can be known only through the illusion. You cannot know the truth directly: first you have to know that which is not true. First you have to encounter the untrue. Through that encounter you become capable of knowing the truth. If you know the false as the false, truth will dawn upon you.

Ego is a need; it is a social need, it is a social by-product. 'Society' means all that is around you – not you, but all that is around you. All, minus you, is the society, and everybody reflects. You will go to school and the teacher will reflect who you are. You will be in friendship with other children and they will reflect who you are. By and by, everybody is adding to your ego, and everybody is trying to modify it in such a way that you don't become a problem to the society.

They are not concerned with you, they are concerned with the society. Society is concerned with itself, and that's how it should be. They are not concerned that you should become a self-knower; they are concerned that you should become an efficient part in the mechanism of the society. You should fit into the pattern, so they are trying to give you an ego that fits with the society. They teach you morality: morality means giving you an ego which will fit with the society. If you are immoral you will always be a misfit somewhere or other.

That's why we put criminals in the prisons – not that they have done something wrong, not that by putting them in the prisons we are going to improve them, no. They simply don't fit. They are troublemakers. They have certain types of egos of which the society doesn't approve. If the society approves, everything is good.

One man kills somebody, he is a murderer, and the same man in wartime kills thousands – he becomes a great hero. The society is not bothered by a murder, but the murder should be committed for the society – then it is okay. The society doesn't bother about morality. Morality means only that you should fit with the society. If the society is at war, then the morality changes. If the society is at peace, then there is a different morality.

Morality is a social politics, it is diplomacy. And each child has to be brought up in such a way that he fits into the society, that's all, because society is interested in efficient members. Society is not interested that you should attain to self-knowledge. Society is always against religion. Hence, the crucifixion of Jesus, the murder of Socrates – because they also didn't fit.

Two types of people don't fit. One: someone who has developed an anti-social ego; he will never fit. But he can be put on trial, there is that possibility. You can torture that man, you can punish him and he may come to his senses. The torture may be too much and he may be converted. Then there is another type of man who is impossible for the society – a Jesus. He is not a criminal but he has no ego. How can you make a man who has no ego fit? He looks absolutely irresponsible but he is not: he has a greater commitment to God. He has no commitment to the society. One who is committed to God doesn't bother; he has a different depth of morality. It doesn't come from codes, it comes from his self-knowledge.

But then a problem arises, because societies have created their moral codes. Those moral codes are man-made. Whenever a Jesus or a Buddha happens, he doesn't bother about the man-made conventions. He has a greater commitment; he is involved with the whole. Each moment he decides his response through his awareness, not through conditioning; so nobody knows about him, about what he will do. He is unpredictable.

Societies can forgive criminals but they cannot forgive Jesus and Socrates – that's impossible. And these people are almost impossible. You cannot do anything about them because they are not wrong. And if you try to understand them, they will convert you – you cannot convert them. So it is better to kill them immediately. The moment the society becomes aware it kills them immediately, because if you listen to them there is danger – if you listen to them you will be converted. And there is no possibility of converting them, so it is better to be completely finished, to have no relationship with them. You cannot put them in prisons, because there also they will remain in relationship with the society. They will exist. Just their existence is too much – they have to be murdered. And then, when priests take over, then there is no problem. The pope of the Vatican is part of the society; Jesus never was.

That is the difference between a sect and a religion. Religion is never part of any society. It is universal, it is existential, and very very dangerous. You cannot find a more dangerous man than a religious man, a more rebellious man than a religious man, a more revolutionary man than a religious man, because his revolution is so absolute that there is no possibility for any compromise with him. And because he is so absolutely certain – he *knows* what he is doing – you cannot convert him. And he is infectious: if he is there he will spread like a disease, he will infect many people.

Jesus had to be killed. Christianity can be accepted, but not Christ. What is Christianity? Christianity is society's effort to replace Christ. Christ is dangerous, so society creates a Christianity around him. Christianity is okay because it is a social phenomenon, a social politics. The church is okay, the priest is okay – the prophet is dangerous. That's why three hundred religions exist on the earth. How can there be three hundred religions? Science is one. You cannot have a Catholic science and a Protestant science; you cannot have a Mohammedan science and a Hindu science. Science is one – how can religions be three hundred?

Truth cannot be sectarian. Truth is one and universal. Only one religion exists. Buddha belongs to that religion, Jesus belongs to that religion, Krishna, Mohammed, they all belong to that religion. And then there are three hundred religions – these are false religions, these are tricks the society has played with you, these are substitutes, imitations.

Look: Jesus is crucified on the cross, and what is the pope of the Vatican doing? He has a gold cross around his neck. Jesus is hung on the cross, and around the pope's neck the cross is hanging, and it is a gold cross. Jesus had to carry his own cross; that cross was not golden. How can crosses be golden? His was very very heavy. He fell while carrying it on the hillock of Golgotha. Under the weight he fell, he fainted. Have you seen any priest fainting under the weight of the golden cross? No, it is a false substitute. It is a trick. Now this is no longer religion, this is part of the social politics. Christianity is politics, Hinduism is politics, Buddhism is politics. Buddha, Jesus, Krishna, they are not social at all. They are not anti-social – they are beyond society.

So there are two dangers for society: anti-social people, criminals; you can tackle them. They may be dangerous but something can be done about them; they are not that dangerous. Then there is a group of people which is beyond society. They are impossible, you cannot change them. They will not be ready to make any compromise.

The society creates an ego because the ego can be controlled and manipulated. The self can never be controlled and manipulated. Nobody has ever heard of the society controlling a self – not possible. And the child needs a center; the child is completely unaware of his own center. The society gives him a center, and the child is by and by convinced that this is his center, the ego that society gives.

A child goes back to his home. If he has come first in his class, the whole family is happy. You hug and kiss him and you take the child on your shoulders and dance and you say, "What a beautiful child! You are a pride for us." You are giving him an ego, a subtle ego. And if the child goes home dejected, unsuccessful, a failure, he couldn't pass, or he has just been on the back bench, then nobody appreciates him and the child feels rejected. He will try hard next time, because the center feels shaken.

Ego is always shaken, always in search of food, that somebody should appreciate it. That's why you continuously ask for attention. That's why ego has always been a misery. If the husband comes into the room and doesn't look at his wife, there is trouble. If he is more interested in his newspaper there is trouble – how dare you be more interested in the newspaper when your wife is there? If a man is very very great, then his wife is always a problem. The contrary will also be so: if a wife is very very great, her husband will be a problem. Ask the wives of great men – because a great man has many deeper things to do. A Socrates...he was more interested in meditation than in his wife, and that was a wound. Socrates' wife was continuously nagging. He was more attentive to somewhere else – "something is more important than me?" – and this shakes the ego.

I have heard: Mulla Nasruddin and his wife were coming out from a cocktail party, and Mulla said, "Darling, has anybody ever said to you how fascinating, how beautiful, how wonderful you are?"

His wife felt very very good, was very happy. She said, "I wonder why nobody has ever told me this?"

Nasruddin said, "Then from where did you get the idea?"

You get the idea of who you are from others. It is not a direct experience, it is from others that you get the idea of who you are. They shape your center. This center is false. You carry your real center – that is nobody's business; nobody shapes it, you come with it, you are born with it.

So you have two centers. One center you come with, which is given by existence itself; that is the self. And the other center, which is created by the society, is the ego; it is a false thing. And it is a very great trick: through the ego the society is controlling you. You have to behave in a certain way, because only then does the society appreciate you. You have to walk in a certain way, you have to laugh in a certain way, you have to follow certain manners, a morality, a code. Only then will the society appreciate you, and if it doesn't, your ego will be shaken.

And when the ego is shaken you don't know where you are, who you are. The others have given you the idea. That idea is the ego.

Try to understand it as deeply as possible, because this has to be thrown. And unless you throw it you will never be able to attain to the self, because you are addicted to the center; you cannot move and you cannot look at the self.

And remember, there is going to be an interim period, an interval, when the ego will be shattered, when you will not know who you are, when you will not know where you are going, when all boundaries will melt. You will be simply confused, a chaos. Because of this chaos, you are afraid to lose the ego. But it has to be so. One has to pass through the chaos before one attains to the real center. And if you are daring, the period will be small. If you are afraid, and you again and again fall back to the ego and you again start arranging it, then it can be very very long; many lives can be wasted.

Enlightenment is always sudden. There is nothing like gradual enlightenment. The gradualness comes if you are not daring, it comes out of your fear. Then you take one step towards the center, the real center, and you become afraid – you come back. It is just like a small child standing at the door thinking to go, but there is darkness. He looks out, comes back, again gathers a little courage, again looks.

I have heard: One small child was visiting his grandparents. He was just four years old. In the night, when the grandmother was putting him to sleep, he suddenly started crying and weeping and said, "I want to go home. I am afraid of darkness."

But the grandmother said, "I know well that at home also you sleep in the dark. I have never seen a light on. So why are you afraid here?"

The boy said, "Yes, that's right – but that is *my* darkness. This darkness is completely unknown."

Even with darkness you feel, "This is mine. Outside, an unknown darkness." With the ego you feel, this is my darkness. It may be troublesome, maybe it creates many miseries, but still –

mine. Something to hold to, something to cling to, something underneath the feet; you are not in a vacuum, not in an emptiness. You may be miserable but at least you *are*. Even being miserable gives you a feeling of "I am." Moving from it, fear takes over; you start feeling afraid of the unknown darkness and chaos. Because society has managed to clear a small part of your being... It is just like going to a forest: you make a little clearing, you clear a little ground; you make fencing, you make a small hut; you make a small garden, a lawn, and you are okay. Beyond your fence, the forest, the wild.... Here everything is okay – you have planned everything.

This is how it has happened: society has made a little clearing in your consciousness. It has cleaned just a little part completely, fenced it; everything is okay there. That's what all your universities are doing. The whole culture and conditioning is just to clear a part so that you can feel at home there. And then you become afraid: beyond the fence there is danger.

Beyond the fence you are, as within the fence you are – and your conscious mind is just one part, one-tenth of your whole being; nine-tenths is waiting in the darkness. And in that nine-tenths somewhere your real center is hidden.

One has to be daring, courageous. One has to take a step into the unknown. For a while all boundaries will be lost. For a while you will feel dizzy. For a while you will feel very afraid and shaken, as if an earthquake has happened. But if you are courageous and you don't go backwards, if you don't fall back to the ego and you go on and on, there is a hidden center within you that you have been carrying for many lives. That is your soul, the *atman*, the self. Once you come near it everything changes, everything settles again. But now this settling is not done by the society. Now everything becomes a cosmos, not a chaos; a new order arises. But this is no longer the order of the society, it is the very order of existence itself.

It is what Buddha calls *dhamma*, Lao Tzu calls *tao*, Heraclitus calls *logos*. It is not man-made, it is the very order of existence itself. Then everything is suddenly beautiful again, and for the first time really beautiful, because man-made things cannot be beautiful.

At the most you can hide the ugliness of them, that's all. You can decorate them but they can never be beautiful.

The difference is just like the difference between a real flower and a plastic or a paper flower. The ego is a plastic flower, dead. It just looks like a flower; it is not a flower. You cannot really call it a flower. Even linguistically, to call it a flower is wrong, because a flower is something which flowers. And this plastic thing is just a thing, not a flowering. It is dead, there is no life in it.

You have a flowering center within. That's why Hindus call it a lotus – it is a flowering. They call it the one-thousand-petaled lotus. 'One thousand' means infinite petals. And it goes on flowering; it never stops, it never dies.

But you are satisfied with a plastic ego. There are some reasons why you are satisfied. With a dead thing there are many conveniences. One is that a dead thing never dies. It cannot, it was never alive. So you can have plastic flowers, they are good in a way: they are permanent; they are not eternal, but they are permanent. The real flower outside in the garden is eternal but not permanent.

And the eternal has its own way of being eternal. The way of the eternal is to be born again and again and to die. Through death it refreshes itself, rejuvenates itself. To us it appears that the real flower has died. It never dies; it simply changes bodies so it is ever fresh. It leaves the old body, it enters a new body. It flowers somewhere else, it goes on flowering, but we cannot see the continuity because the continuity is invisible. We see only one flower, another flower; we never see the continuity. It is the same flower which flowered yesterday. It is the same sun but in a different garb.

You need very penetrating eyes to see the invisible continuity. The invisible continuity is God. If you can see, this is the same flower in a different body. That's what Hindus call the theory of reincarnation. Christianity, Judaism, Mohammedanism, they all miss the beauty of it, so all three religions by and by became materialistic. They had to, because the invisible had been missed.

I am here. You are here. You have been here millions of times before. It is an eternal recurrence: in different bodies, different shapes, but the continuity is the same. And we call that continuity the soul. Not this body – forms change, the formless remains. And this is the way for it to be eternal; otherwise it cannot be eternal.

Death is a way to rejuvenate oneself again. You exhale, this is the way to inhale again. You die, this is the way to be reborn. Each moment you die, the body is doing the same.

You ask the physiologists – they say the body dies and renews itself every moment. Every cell will die. If you live seventy years, then at least ten times the body will have died completely. But gradually it changes: one cell dies, another is replaced...leaves fall down...it goes on.

Just a few days ago the almond tree outside became completely naked, all the leaves fell down. This is the way. Now it is young again. Now new leaves have come. The old have gone, the new leaves have come. But the leaves are not the tree: the tree is that source from which leaves come, and that source is hidden.

The old drops so that the new can come. The old body dies so that the new body can come. This is how existence exists eternally – always dying, always coming back. It is a wheel. The spokes go up, then they go down; this is how the wheel moves.

The ego is a plastic thing, but it looks permanent. Remember, eternity is not permanence. Eternity moves through movements. Eternity moves through change. Eternity is continuous change, and yet it remains the same: changing, yet remaining the same, moving, yet never moving.

The ego has a certain quality – it is dead. It is a plastic thing. And it is very easy to get it, because others give it. You need not seek it, there is no search involved. That's why, unless you become a seeker after the unknown, you have not yet become an individual. You are just a part of the crowd. You are just a mob. When you don't have a real center, how can you be an individual? The ego is not individual. Ego is a social phenomenon: it is society, it is not you. But it gives you a function in the society, a hierarchy in the society. And if you remain satisfied with it you will miss the whole opportunity of finding the self.

And that's why you are so miserable. With a plastic life, how can you be happy? With a false life, how can you be ecstatic and blissful? And then this ego creates many miseries, millions of them. You cannot see because it is "your own darkness"; you are attuned to it.

Have you ever noticed that all types of miseries enter through the ego? It cannot make you blissful, it can only make you miserable. Ego is hell. Whenever you suffer, just try to watch and analyze and you will find somewhere the ego is the cause of it. And the ego goes on finding causes to suffer.

I was staying at Mulla Nasruddin's house once. The wife was saying very nasty things about Mulla Nasruddin, very angry, rude, aggressive, just on the verge of exploding, very violent. And Mulla Nasruddin was just sitting silently and listening. Then suddenly she turned towards him and said, "So again you are arguing with me!"

Mulla said, "But I have not even said a single word."

The wife said, "That I know – but you are listening very aggressively."

You are an egoist, as everyone is. Some are very gross, just on the surface, and they are not so difficult. Some are very subtle, deep down, and they are the real problems. This ego comes continuously in conflict with others, because every ego is so unconfident about itself. It has to be – it is a false thing. When you don't have anything in your hand and you just think that something is there, then there will be a problem. If somebody says, "Nothing is there," immediately the fight will start, because you also feel that there is nothing. The other makes you aware of the fact.

Ego is false, it is nothing. That you also know. How can you miss knowing it? It is impossible! A conscious being, how can he miss knowing that this ego is just false? And then others say that there is nothing, and whenever the others say that there is nothing they hit a wound, they say a truth – and nothing hits like truth. You have to defend, because if you don't defend, if you don't become defensive, then where will you be? You will be lost. The identity will be broken. So you have to defend and fight – that is the clash.

A man who attains to the self is never in any clash. Others may come and clash with him, but he is never in a clash with anybody.

It happened that one Zen master was passing through a street. A man came running and hit him hard; the master fell down. Then he got up and started to walk in the same direction in which he was going before, not even looking back to see who this man was.

A disciple was with the master. He was simply shocked. He said, "What is this? If one lives in such a way, then anybody can come and kill you. And you have not even looked at that person, who he is, and why he did it."

The master said, "That is his problem, not mine."

You can clash with an enlightened man, but that is your problem, not his. And if you are hurt in that clash, that too is your own problem. He cannot hurt you. And it is like knocking against a wall: you will be hurt, but the wall has not hurt you.

The ego is always looking for some trouble. Why? Because if nobody pays attention to you, the ego feels hungry. It lives on attention. So even if somebody is fighting and angry with you, that too is good because at least the attention is paid. If somebody loves, it is okay. If somebody is not loving you, then even anger will be good. At least the attention will come to you. But if nobody is paying any attention to you, nobody thinks you are somebody important, significant, then how will you feed your ego? Others' attention is needed.

In millions of ways you attract the attention of others: you dress in a certain way, you try to look beautiful, you behave, you become very polite, you change. When you feel what type of situation it is, you immediately change so that people pay attention to you. This is a deep begging.

A real beggar is one who asks for and demands attention. And a real emperor is one who lives in himself: he has a center of his own, he doesn't depend on anybody else. Buddha sitting under his bodhi tree...if the whole world suddenly disappears, will it make any difference to Buddha? – none. It will not make any difference at all.

If the whole world disappears it will not make any difference because he has attained to the center.

But you...if the wife escapes, divorces you, goes to somebody else, you are completely shattered – because she had been paying attention to you, caring, loving, moving around you, helping you to feel that you were somebody. Your whole empire is lost, you are simply shattered. You start thinking about suicide. Why? Why, if a wife leaves you, should you commit suicide? Why, if a husband leaves you, should you commit suicide? Because you don't have any center of your own. The wife was giving you the center; the husband was giving you the center.

This is how people exist. This is how people become dependent on others. It is a deep slavery. Ego has to be a slave: it depends on others. And only a person who has no ego is for the first time a master, he is no longer a slave.

Try to understand this, and start looking for the ego, not in others – that is not your business – but in yourself. Whenever you feel miserable, immediately close your eyes and try to find out where the misery is coming from, and you will always find it is the false center which has clashed with someone. You expected something and it didn't happen. You expected something and just the contrary happened: your ego is shaken, you are in misery. Just look, whenever you are miserable, try to find out why.

Causes are not outside you. The basic cause is within you – but you always look outside, you always ask, "Who is making me miserable? Who is the cause of my anger? Who is the cause of my anguish?" And if you look outside you will miss. Just close the eyes and always look within. The source of all misery, anger, anguish, is hidden in you – your ego. And if you find the source, it will be easy to move beyond it. If you can see that it is your own ego that gives you trouble, you will like to drop it, because nobody can carry the source of misery if he understands it.

And remember, there is no need to *drop* the ego. You cannot drop it. If you try to drop it you will attain to a certain subtle ego again which says, "I have become humble." Don't try to be humble;

that's again ego – hiding, but it is not dead. Don't try to be humble. Nobody can try humility, and nobody can create humility through any effort of his own, no. When the ego is no more, a humbleness comes to you. It is not a creation, it is a shadow of the real center. And a really humble man is neither humble nor egoistic; he is simply simple. He's not even aware that he is humble. If you are aware that you are humble, the ego is there.

Look at humble persons; there are millions who think that they are very humble. They bow down very low. But watch them – they are the subtlest egoists; now humility is their source of food. They say, "I am humble," and then they look at you and they wait for you to appreciate them. "You are really humble," they would like you to say; "in fact, you are the most humble man in the world. Nobody is as humble as you are." Then see the smile that comes on their faces. What is ego? Ego is a hierarchy that says, "No one is like me." It can feed on humbleness – "Nobody is like me, I am the most humble man."

Once it happened: A monk came to me and he was talking about his humility, and I said, "You are nothing. I know a man who is more humble than you."

Suddenly anger, ego, and he said, "Who is that man? Show him to me."

"That is not the point," I told him; "that is not the point. I am not going to show him to you. But try to understand, because suddenly the ego comes in and says, 'How is somebody else daring to be more humble than me?'"

It happened once: A fakir, a beggar, was praying in a mosque early in the morning when it was still dark. It was a certain religious day for Mohammedans, and he was praying and he was saying, "I am nobody. I am the poorest of the poor, the greatest sinner of sinners."

Suddenly there was one more person who was praying. He was the emperor of that country, and he was not aware that there was somebody else there who was praying. It was dark, and the emperor was also saying, "I am nobody. I am nothing. I am just empty, a beggar at your door."

When he heard that somebody else was saying the same thing, he said, "Stop! Who is trying to overtake me? Who are you? How dare you say before the emperor that you are nobody when he is saying that he is nobody!"

This is how the ego goes. It is so subtle, its ways are so subtle and cunning; you have to be very very alert, only then will you see it. Don't try to be humble. Just try to see that all misery, all anguish comes through it. Just watch! No need to drop it. You cannot drop it – who will drop it? Then the dropper will become the ego. It always comes back. Whatsoever you do, it stands out of it and looks and watches. Whatsoever you do – humbleness, humility, simplicity – nothing will help. Only one thing is possible, and that is to just watch and see that it is the source of all misery. Don't say, don't repeat – watch; because if I say it is the source of all misery and you repeat it, then it is useless. You have to come to that understanding.

Whenever you are miserable, just close your eyes and don't try to find some cause outside. Try to see from where this misery is coming. It is your own ego. If you continuously feel and understand, and the understanding that the ego is the cause becomes so deep-rooted, one day you will suddenly see that it has disappeared.

Nobody drops it...nobody *can* drop it. You simply see; it has simply disappeared, because the very understanding that ego causes all misery becomes the dropping. The very understanding is the disappearance of the ego.

And you are so clever in seeing the ego in others; anybody can see someone else's ego. When it comes to your own, then the problem arises, because you don't know the territory, you have never traveled on it. The whole path towards the divine, the ultimate, has to pass through this territory of the ego. The false has to be understood as false. The source of misery has to be understood as the source of misery – then it simply drops. When you know it is poison, it drops.

When you know it is fire, it drops. When you know this is hell, it drops. And then you never say that 'I' have dropped the ego. Then you simply laugh at the whole thing, the joke that you were the creator of all misery.

I was just looking at a few cartoons on Charlie Brown. In one cartoon he is playing with blocks, making a house out of children's blocks. He is sitting in the middle of the blocks building the walls. Then a moment comes when he is enclosed, all around he has made a wall. Then he cries, "Help, help!" He has done the whole thing; now he is enclosed, imprisoned. This is childish, but this is all that you have been doing also. You have made a house all around you, and now you are crying, "Help, help!" And the misery becomes millionfold, because there are helpers who are also in the same boat.

It happened that one very beautiful woman went to see her psychiatrist for the first time. The psychiatrist said, "Come closer, please."

When she came closer, he simply jumped and hugged and kissed the woman. She was shocked. Then he said, "Now sit down. This takes care of my problem, now what is your problem?"

The problem becomes multifold, because there are helpers who are in the same boat. And they would like to help, because when you help somebody the ego feels very good, very very good – because you are a great helper, a great guru, a master; you are helping so many people. The greater the crowd of your followers, the better you feel. But you are in the same boat – you cannot help. Rather, you will harm.

People who still have their own problems cannot be of much help. Only someone who has no problems of his own can help you. Only then does he have the clarity to see, to see through you. A mind that has no problems of its own can see you, you become transparent. A mind that has no problems of its own can see through itself, that's why it becomes capable of seeing through others'.

In the West there are many schools of psychoanalysis, many

schools, and no help is reaching people but rather harm. Because the people who are helping others, or trying to help, or posing as helpers, are in the same boat.

I was reading Wilhelm Reich's wife's memoirs. He was one of the most significant psychoanalysts, one of the most revolutionary – but when the question comes to one's own problems, the difficulty arises. His wife has written in her memoirs that he was teaching others not to be jealous, that love is not possession, it is freedom. But about his own wife he was always jealous. If she would laugh with someone, there would be misery immediately. And he was making love to many women but he would not allow his own wife even to smile with someone; even just sitting and talking he wouldn't allow. Whenever he would go out – sometimes he had to go to see his patients – the first thing he would do when he came home was to inquire about where his wife had gone, who she had met, who had come to the house, and there would be a cross-examination. His wife says that she was simply surprised. This man was so wise with others, but with his own....

It is difficult to see one's own ego; it is very easy to see others' egos. But that is not the point. You cannot help them. Try to see your own ego. Just watch it. Don't be in a hurry to drop it, just watch it. The more you watch, the more capable you will become. Suddenly one day you simply see that it has dropped. And when it drops by itself, only then does it drop; there is no other way. Prematurely you cannot drop it. It drops just like a dead leaf: the tree is not doing anything, just a breeze, a situation, and the dead leaf simply drops. The tree is not even aware that the dead leaf has dropped. It makes no noise, it makes no claim, nothing. The dead leaf simply drops and settles on the ground, just like that.

When you are mature through understanding, awareness, and you have felt totally that ego is the cause of all your misery, one day you see the dead leaf simply dropping. It settles onto the ground, dies of its own accord. You have not done anything so you cannot claim that you have dropped it. You simply see that it has disappeared, and then the real center arises. And that real center is the soul, the self, God, the truth, or whatsoever you want to call it. It is nameless, so all names are good. You can give it any name of your own liking. Now listen to this beautiful story.

The prime minister, Kuo Tzu I, of the Tang Dynasty, was an outstanding statesman, a distinguished general, and the most admired national hero of his day.

Remember, when you are at the peak it is very easy to be humble. I will repeat it: when you are successful, when you have come to the peak, it is very easy to be humble. When you are nowhere, nowhere in the hierarchy, it is very difficult to be humble. A poor man finds it more difficult to be humble than a rich man. A politician who is defeated finds it more difficult to be humble than the politician who has won. Look at the top people in the world: they are always humble – they can afford to be. Now there is no danger to their egos. They have already attained; they don't bother about your attention. You don't mean anything to them, now they have attained. They can be humble, they can afford to be. That's why great leaders are always humble. But that humility is not the humility of a Buddha, not that of a Lao Tzu; that humility is false.

When you are no one, then to be humble is very difficult. When you are defeated, then to be humble is very difficult because the ego is so hurt – it needs food, it is hungry. When you have won, you are victorious, you are on the crest of a wave reaching higher and higher, you can bow down because everybody knows without anything being said who you are. There is no need for you to declare it; the whole world knows it already. Then you can bow down and be humble.

Kings are more humble than beggars. And then people think, "What beautiful persons these kings are, these leaders!" Nothing is beautiful. You can see their real face when they are defeated, never before. Then to be humble is very very difficult. When the whole of life is humiliating, then to be humble is difficult. When everybody appreciates and everybody cheers you, then you can bow down with a smiling face. There is no need for you to claim, it is already established.

This has been my experience with people: if somebody comes to me and he has already arrived somewhere in life, he is always humble. He bows down deeply, he sits on the floor. He is established... this humbleness is good for his ego. Whenever somebody comes who is frustrated, who has gambled and lost, who is nobody, then it is hard for him to sit on the floor.

One man wrote a letter to me saying, "I can come and see you only if I also have a chair, otherwise I will not come." I know this man is very very defeated, humiliated by life. He cannot bow, he cannot surrender, he cannot be humble. He is so humiliated that it has become a wound. Now humility looks like humiliation.

But both are in the same boat. One is defeated, one feels hurt; one feels that he has to stand, he has to claim, he has to fight for it. The other is established, there is no fight – he already knows.

It happened that Henry Ford once went to England. At the airport he inquired about the cheapest hotel in London. And the man recognized him, because just the other day there had been pictures in the newspapers about Henry Ford's coming. So he said, "If I haven't forgotten, if I remember well, you look to me like Henry Ford. But you are dressed so shabbily; your coat looks so old, rotten, and why are you inquiring about the cheapest hotel?"

Henry Ford said, "Whether I have a new coat or old I am Henry Ford, and everybody knows about it. It makes no difference – I am Henry Ford. Whether the coat is old or new makes no difference."

The man said, "And I know well that when your sons come they ask for the costliest hotel."

Henry Ford laughed and said, "They are still not established and they feel insecure. They are known as sons of Henry Ford; they are nothing by themselves. I am something by myself, so the cheapest hotel won't make any difference."

A rich man need not declare that he is rich. A poor man always declares. The richer you grow, the less declaration there is.

Have you observed it in life? It happens everywhere. An ugly woman will have more ornaments, a beautiful woman need not. The more a country becomes beautiful, the more women become beautiful, the more things drop, by and by. There is no need for ornaments and gold; by themselves they are enough. But an ugly woman cannot afford that, she has to carry many, many ornaments – diamonds, rubies – because only through those ornaments is she somebody, otherwise not. This happens in all the dimensions of life. But both are in the same boat.

This prime minister was a very humble man...

...But fame, power, wealth and success could not distract him from his keen interest and devotion to Buddhism. Regarding himself as a plain and humble devoted Buddhist, he often visited his favorite Zen master to study under him.

This too has to be understood: *But fame, power, wealth and success could not distract him from his keen interest...* They never distract anybody. It is difficult to be devoted to religion when you are poor, a failure. It is very very easy when you are a success to have a keen interest in religion, because those who have succeeded in this life, who have reached the top.... And this man is a prime minister, he has reached the top; there is nowhere else to go now. Now he will take a keen interest in meditation, religion, God – because a man like Kuo Tzu, a prime minister, a hero, has to possess God also. Such a successful man has to succeed in the other world also. That's why, whenever a country becomes rich, affluent, immediately a keen interest in religion arises.

Nowhere else in the world now is there such keen interest in religion as in America. It has to be so. If you ask poor Indians why so many Westerners come to India, they simply think them crazy – there is nothing here.

I am here in Poona; how many people do you see here from Poona? – not a single one that you can recognize. They are simply wondering why you madmen have come from the West to listen to me. You must have gone crazy, or I must have hypnotized you: something must be wrong. They need not bother even to come and listen and to see whether something is wrong or not, they are already convinced of it. Why? They are not rich, they are not successful, they are not established. When you fail in this world.... You struggle to succeed here in this materialist world first; when you succeed, then you would like to succeed in the other world also.

So this is my understanding: that only a rich country can be religious; poor countries can never be religious. Sometimes poor persons can be religious, because individuals can be exceptions, but the masses, never. Sometimes it happens that a poor person becomes religious and achieves to the ultimate – a Nanak, a Kabir, a Jesus – but ordinarily the masses cannot afford to be religious unless they are established.

Religion is the last luxury. And I am saying it not in any condemnatory tone, it is so: you have to be able to afford it. And when you have got everything and you feel you have nothing, then for the first time a keen interest arises to seek the unknown.

He and the Zen master seemed to get along very well. The fact that he was the prime minister seemed to have no influence on their association. There was no noticeable trace of politeness on the Zen master's part, or of vain loftiness on the part of the minister; the association seemed to be the purely religious one of a revered master and an obedient disciple.

But this is only on the surface. Deep down the prime minister is the prime minister; deep down he is somebody very very important. Deep down he has the same ego as everybody else. This situation, this appearance on the surface is just skin-deep. To find the reality you will have to go a little deeper. The prime minister may have been fooled, but the master is not fooled by it. Others may have been fooled; they may have thought, "What a great man this prime minister is! So humble, comes and sits at the feet of the master, so religious...rare to find such a man."

But the master is not fooled by the appearance. Appearance means nothing, the real thing is that which is deeper. And this prime minister is a polished man. He has succeeded with the world, now he is trying to succeed with this master also with his polished mannerisms. But you cannot deceive a master. If you can deceive a master, he is not a master at all.

One day, however, when he was paying his usual visit to the Zen master, he asked the following question: "Your Reverence, how does Buddhism explain egoism?"

Deep down, you cannot really fool yourself either. How can you? You know what you are doing. While you are deceiving, then too you know that you are deceiving. You can deceive the whole world, but how can you deceive yourself? It is impossible. You may not be alert, but the moment you become alert you know what you have been doing.

This too is a deception: he doesn't ask a direct question. He doesn't say, "I am an egoist, so Master, tell me what to do about it." These cunning people always ask indirect questions. I know many of them.

One man came to me and he said, "One of my friends is impotent. What to do?" And I could see that this man was impotent, but he was talking about his friend. So I asked him, "Why didn't you send the friend? He could have told me that one of his friends is impotent – what about it? What to do? Why did you trouble to come? Your friend could have come and told me the same." Then he became disturbed.

People talk indirectly and problems are personal. And they talk philosophy; they ask questions like: How in Buddhism is egoism explained? What nonsense! What has it to do with Buddhism? Egoism is *your* problem. Why make it indirect? If you make it indirect you will miss. You will not be able to understand because from the very beginning you are deceiving. And you may be thinking that you are asking about Buddhism and egoism; then a theory can be given to you, a hypothesis, a philosophy, a system, but that won't help – because each individual has his own problem, and each individual has his own problem in a unique way.

If you say, "I am an egoist, what to do about it?" my answer will be different. If you ask what Buddhism says, the answer will again be different. Buddhism – then it becomes a generalized thing, and no individual is a general thing. Every individual is so individual, so authentically individual, unique, that you cannot help an individual by a general theory. No, it will not suit. Every individual needs a direct approach. Never ask a philosophical question: it is useless. Just ask a personal question, just ask directly.

And that's what the master had to do with this prime minister. He had to bring him down from the peaks of Buddhism to the reality of his own being, because those peaks didn't belong to him. That was not his problem, really.

People come to me; they ask whether God exists or not. What are you going to do with God? Leave him to himself. What are you going to do? If he exists, what will you do? If he doesn't exist, what will you do? It looks like your mind is not facing real problems and is avoiding them through imaginary problems.

God is an imaginary problem for you. Anger, ego, sex, passion, hate – they are real problems. You don't ask about them, you ask about God. How are you concerned with God? There is no relationship. I see people who believe in God and people who don't believe in God; I don't see any difference. Can you detect whether a man is an atheist just by looking at his behavior? No. How can you know whether this man believes in God and that man doesn't believe in God? They both behave the same way. If you insult them, they will both get angry. What is the difference? If you hurt their egos they will both get mad, so where does God come in? This is a trick – you want to avoid real problems. The words 'god', 'moksha', 'truth', are like blankets: you cover all the problems with them and hide them. They are not problems, they are blankets. And those who answer them help you to avoid the reality.

"Your Reverence, how does Buddhism explain egoism?"

The Zen master's face suddenly turned blue, and in an extremely haughty and contemptuous manner he said to the premier, "What are you saying, you numbskull?"

Now everything has changed immediately. The master has beautifully brought the prime minister to the reality, to the earth, just with a single word: numbskull! A single word can make that miracle happen – because you are not aware, that's why. Otherwise, the premier would have laughed and he would have said, "Yes, you are right. Now what about Buddhism and how it explains egoism?" But just a single word....

How much you are addicted to words! A single word, and the whole situation changes? And what is a word? – just a sound with no meaning really. Meaning is just a contract of the society, between people: we will mean this by this. It is just a social contract. What does 'numbskull' mean? – nothing, just a sound. If you don't understand English, what does it mean? – nothing, just a sound. If you understand English, then there is trouble. Somebody calling you 'numbskull'? – immediately philosophy disappears and reality comes up. All mannerism was skin deep. "Your Reverence" – all skin deep. He was bowing down and saying "Your Reverence." What type of reverence is this which a single word can destroy? Skillful are the Zen masters....

"What are you saying, you numbskull?" This unreasonable and unexpected defiance so hurt the feelings of the prime minister that a slight and sullen expression of anger began to show on his face.

Yes, it was unreasonable, and unexpected. Masters *are* unreasonable and unexpected; you cannot predict them. They are like the wind, or like the clouds moving in the sky. Where they are going nobody can say, because they don't follow any map. They simply go wherever the wind moves. They have no goal, they have no direction; they simply live in the moment. You cannot say what a master is going to do, never. A master is unpredictable because he has not planned for the future. He is not prepared in any way. He moves in the moment, looks at the situation, and responds. A master never reacts, he responds. A man who is aware never reacts, he responds. You react. Try to understand the difference.

Reaction is a deep-rooted habit. Response is not a habit, it is an alive sensitivity to the moment. Response is real, reaction is always unreal. Somebody insults you and you react. Reaction means: between the insult and what you do, between these two, there is not a single moment of awareness. You react through habit as you have reacted in the past – but the situation is totally different. Somebody insults you on the street and then a master insults you; the situations are totally different. Somebody insulting you on the street is just like you. It is a totally different situation. And then a master, a buddha insults you – he insults in a totally different way. He is creating a situation. He is giving you a chance not to react, not to follow the old pattern of habits, not to move and behave like a robot but to become alert and aware.

If this man had been a little alert, a little aware, a little mindful, he would have laughed, he would have bowed down and touched the feet of the master, because a master insults you only when there is deep love and compassion. Otherwise, what is the use? A master insults you to show you something. A master can get angry in some moments – but he is not angry, it is part of his compassion.

Just the other day, one sannyasin told me that he had been in contact with a Gurdjieff group, and he said there seems to be no compassion in that system. He is right. Gurdjieff was deeply compassionate, but he never showed it. He was very ferocious – even Zen masters could not beat him. But if you could tolerate him a little, if you could be with him in spite of him, then by and by you would feel what deep compassion he had. And it was only because of deep compassion that he was so hard, because he knew that with you compassion wouldn't help. Your hearts have gone so dead, they have become stony. Much hard work is needed.

If one is simply kind to you, he will not be able to change you. He has to be very hard. But if you can be a little aware and live with a man like Gurdjieff, be around him, be in his presence for a few days, by and by you will see the inner core. One of the most deep people – deep in compassion, love, but he has become hard through experience. If he shows compassion from the beginning, you think you are allowed to have your weaknesses, you think you are allowed to remain as you are; you think there is no need for any transformation. His compassion becomes a food for your weaknesses. No, that won't do.

When a master insults or becomes angry, don't judge by ordinary standards, don't judge by your ordinary experience. Wait a little and don't react. The prime minister reacted immediately.

This unreasonable and unexpected defiance so hurt the feelings of the prime minister that a slight and sullen expression of anger began to show on his face.

He must have really been a polished man. Even anger was coming, but very slightly, it was not exploding. He must have suppressed himself very deeply. He was a cultured man, really cultured, but even to that cultured man just a small word, 'numbskull', and a sullen expression and a slight anger started to show on his face.

Now the situation is real. A master is there, without any ego; and the prime minister is there – now the ego is showing up, now the real has surfaced.

The Zen master then smiled and said, "Your excellency, this is egoism."

...And it has nothing to do with Buddhism, it has something to do with you. The master was really skillful: he created such a situation by just using a single word.

Once it happened that a press reporter went to see Gurdjieff – and you cannot find greater numbskulls than press reporters. They are the most surface people; they have to be, because newspapers exist on the surface.

Gurdjieff looked at the man, then looked at one woman who was sitting just by his side, a disciple, and he asked the woman, "What day is it today?"

She said, "Saturday."

Gurdjieff became suddenly angry and said, "How is it possible? Yesterday was Friday, so how can today be Saturday, you fool?"

The woman was shocked. Had he suddenly gone mad? And the reporter simply left. Then Gurdjieff laughed. What a way to get rid of numbskulls! And he said, "If this person cannot see the point of my being unreasonable and mad, he will not be able to understand what I am doing here. It will be impossible, because it is without reason. It is unreasonable, it is irrational; you cannot sort it out through the head. If he cannot wait, if he judges so immediately, then he will not be able to judge what I am doing here. So it is better to get rid of him in the very beginning."

You live through reason, and whenever you see something irrational you immediately make a judgment. Immediately! That is a reaction. Otherwise there are millions of possibilities. This press reporter could have thought, "It may be just a joke, no need to judge." This press reporter could have thought, "This man seems mysterious. Let's see...wait. And the whole thing is so absurd, this Gurdjieff asserting that this can't be Saturday when just yesterday it was Friday. The whole thing is so absurd. There must be some deep hidden meaning in it. Wait, don't judge." But this needs awareness. And what are you going to lose if you wait?

Gurdjieff created many situations, and millions of misunderstandings are still rumored about him around the world. Nobody knows what type of man he was. Nobody can know, because you try to reach through reason, and the work that a master is doing is beyond reason – it is supra-rational. But to you it will look irrational because you don't know what supra-rational is. To you it will look irrational; that is because of your standpoint, the place where you are standing, from where you are looking, your attitude, your prejudice, your over-addiction to reason. It will look irrational.

If you follow a master, by and by you start feeling that it is not irrational, it is supra-rational. It is not rational, that is right, but it is not irrational either. It may not look rational to you, but when your quality of being changes, then a new vision, a new clarity, a new perceptiveness happens to you. And then things settle in a different way. Then it starts seeming to be supra-rational; not irrational, but superior to reason, greater than reason, vaster than reason. But then one has to wait. And masters always try to create situations, because through situations reality surfaces. What a beautiful thing the master said.

Then the master smiled. You cannot smile immediately after anger, no – because you are not a master. Even if you try to smile you will feel so much tension in your lips that you will not be able to relax them. After anger you cannot smile immediately; you will need time so the anger subsides.

It is said of Gurdjieff that sometimes he would create two impressions on two people in a single situation. If somebody was sitting to his right and somebody to his left, he would look to the left with such anger, and then he would look to the right with such a beautiful smiling face – then both friends would carry different interpretations. One man would say, "This man is dangerous, looks like a murderer!" The other would say, "I have never seen such a gentle, smiling, buddha-like face." To some he would look like a Rasputin, a Genghis Khan, a Tamerlane; to some he would look like a Buddha, a Jesus, a Socrates – and he could create this immediately just by turning left and right.

This is possible. This is not possible for you, because you react. When you react you are a victim, you are possessed by the emotion; you are not a master. When you don't react you simply create a situation.

The master looked angry, condemning, when he insulted the prime minister. And when the insult had done its work and the real prime minister had surfaced, he smiled and said, *"Your Excellency, this is egoism."*

Enough for today.

Discourse 6

THE TWO CONCUBINES

When Yang Chu was passing through Sung he spent the night at an inn.
The innkeeper had two concubines – one beautiful and the other ugly. The ugly one he valued and the beautiful one he neglected. When Yang Chu asked the reason, the fellow answered, "The beautiful one thinks herself beautiful and I do not notice her beauty; the ugly one thinks herself ugly and I do not notice her ugliness."
Yang Chu said to his disciples, "Remember this: if you act nobly and banish from your mind the thought that you are noble, where can you go and not be loved?"

The ego exists through self-consciousness; it cannot exist otherwise. But remember, self-consciousness is not the consciousness of the self: self-consciousness is not self-remembering. Self-consciousness is in fact not consciousness at all. It is an unconscious state. You are not alert when you are self-conscious, you are not aware; you don't know that you are self-conscious. If you become aware, self-consciousness disappears. If you become a witness, then it is not found there.

Remember one criterion: whatsoever disappears through awareness is illusory, and whatsoever remains through awareness – not only remains but becomes more crystallized – is real. Make it a criterion. Consciousness is the touchstone.

In a dream, if you become aware that you are dreaming then the dream disappears immediately. Not even a split second it can remain there. The moment you become aware that it is a dream it is no longer there, because the very nature of a dream is illusory. It exists because you are not. When you are, it disappears. It exists only when you are unconscious. If you take this touchstone and touch all that happens to you on it, there will be so much happening within you, such a great transformation is possible through it, that you cannot imagine it beforehand.

Anger is there; if you become aware, it disappears. Love is there; if you become aware, it becomes more crystallized. Then love is part of existence, and anger is part of dreaming. If you are unaware, then you exist; if you become aware you simply dissolve, you are no longer there – then God exists. And you both cannot exist together – either you or God. There is no choice and there is no compromise. You cannot say, "Fifty-fifty, a little 'I' and a little God." No, that's not possible. You are simply not found, and God is.

So self-consciousness is not a right word, because consciousness is used in it, and it is a very unconscious state. It will be better, if you will allow me, to call self-consciousness self-unconsciousness. Whenever you feel you are, something is ill.

Chuang Tzu says: If the shoe doesn't fit, then you are conscious of the feet. If the shoe fits, the feet are forgotten. It is because of a headache that you become aware of the head. If the headache disappears, where is the head? Along with the headache, the head also disappears. When something is wrong it becomes like a wound. When you are ill, then this so-called self-consciousness exists. When everything fits, is a harmony, and there is no discord – the shoe is not pinching, everything is absolutely okay – you are not self-conscious. Then you are. In fact, for the first time you are – but you are not self-conscious.

For example, whenever you are ill you become body-conscious. You are weak, you have a fever, something is wrong in the body; you become body-conscious. It hurts – you become body-conscious. When the body is absolutely okay, healthy, in a state of well-being, you are not conscious of it; not that you don't know that you are healthy, but no self-consciousness is needed. You are simply healthy. A state of well-being surrounds you.

But in this state there is no division between the state and the knower. You are one with it. It is not that you feel well-being: you *are* well-being, so who will be conscious of it? There is no division, so who will know about it? Only in disease does the division come in. You are totally one with the body when the body is healthy. When the body is ill a rift happens; you are broken asunder, you are not together. The body exists somewhere, you exist somewhere else.

In meditation you are one with your consciousness, so it doesn't function and exist as a mind. You are one, there is no division. When there is no division and unity comes in, all self-consciousness disappears. Let me repeat, because you can misunderstand it. It is not that the Self disappears, just the self-consciousness disappears.

And remember, you will not be in a state of unconsciousness; you will be perfectly aware but not self-conscious. You will be perfectly aware, fully aware, but there will be only awareness, no division – who is aware of whom; no subject, no object, simply a complete, a total state, a circle of awareness. That awareness in which self-consciousness is not, is egoless. And that awareness has a grace, a beauty, a beauty that doesn't belong to this world. Even an ugly person will become beautiful in that state – ugly as far as the criteria of this world go, but suffused, illuminated with something from the beyond. The body, the shape may not be beautiful, but it is filled with some unknown grace. And then you forget the body; the grace is so much that you simply cannot attend to the body – you feel the grace.

All saints are beautiful. Not that their bodies are always beautiful, no, but they are filled with some unknown bliss which touches you, a grace which fills the milieu around them. They carry their own climate and, wherever they are, suddenly you feel the climate has changed. And that is such a tremendous force that you cannot look at their bodies; their bodies simply disappear, their bodilessness is so much.

Your body is seen because the bodilessness is not there. You are just the body; nothing is illuminating it from within. You are an unlit lamp, so only the lamp is seen. When the light comes you forget the lamp; when the light comes out of it then who bothers about the lamp? And if the light is so much, you cannot even see the lamp.

All saints are beautiful. All children are beautiful. Observe the fact: every child is born beautiful; you cannot find an ugly child. Difficult, very very difficult to find an ugly child. All children are born beautiful. Then what goes wrong? – because later on all people are not beautiful. All children are born with grace but then something goes wrong; somewhere the growth stops and everything becomes ugly. Later on you cannot find so many beautiful persons in the world. And as you grow old you become more and more ugly.

It should be just the opposite, if life moves in the right direction. If you know the art of how to live beautifully, how to live with grace, how to live through the divine, not through the ego, then just the opposite will be the case. Every child will grow more and more beautiful, and old age must be the culmination of beauty. It has to be. If the life has been lived according to nature, Tao, Dhamma, if it has followed an inner discipline, not forced; if you have loved, if you have been aware, if you have been meditative, then every day you become more and more beautiful. And an old man who has passed through all the turmoils, all the ups and downs of life, who has known maturity, who is now seasoned, will have a beauty which nobody else can have.

In the East it has happened. That's why the East worships the old, not the young, because the young is still incomplete. The young has to pass through many things yet, and there is a possibility that something may go wrong. When an old man is beautiful, now there is no possibility of his falling down; he has known all, he has passed through all the experiences, all the anguish of existence, all the miseries, all the blessings. He has seen nights and days, he has moved to the peaks and to the valleys, and he has attained an inner integrity through all these experiences. Now he is balanced; now there is no right or left, now there are no extremes. Now he neither longs for peaks nor avoids the valleys; he simply accepts. Life has prepared him for this acceptance. Life has prepared him not to fight but to let go. And when you can let go you have attained.

A young man tries not to let go and he fights. A young man tries to conquer. A young man is foolish; he does not know that the victory comes through let-go. He cannot know, it is difficult to know. He will have to pass through many frustrations; only then will he become aware that frustrations are the other aspect of expectations. He will have to pass through many defeats; only then will he come to know that victory belongs to those who don't fight, who give way, who don't fight against the current, who don't try to go upstream, who simply leave themselves wherever nature puts them.

Only those who have come to an inner harmony with nature are victorious. Now there is no fight, because how can the part fight the whole? And how can the part be victorious against the whole? It is absurd, but a young man has to try.

An old man reaches total acceptance; in this total acceptance he is the most beautiful. And he is not self-conscious – he cannot be, because ego is created, self-consciousness is created because you fight. So the first thing to understand is not to be self-conscious. Be aware. Be conscious but not self-conscious – consciousness without the self, just being alert. And what is the difference? When you are conscious you are conscious of yourself; when you are self-conscious you are conscious of yourself in relation to others – what others are thinking about you, what others are feeling about you, whether they think you beautiful or not. You come in the room, others are sitting there; you become self-conscious. You were a different person just a few minutes before outside the room. You were alone. In your bathroom you are totally different – singing, humming, even making faces before the mirror. You are totally a child, enjoying; you are not worried about anything else – you are not self-conscious. But suddenly you become aware that somebody is peeping through the keyhole. Immediately everything changes. You are no longer the same; you have become self-conscious.

Self-consciousness is related to others – and that is what ego is. Ego means continuously thinking what others are thinking about you, whether they appreciate you or not, whether they pay attention to you or not. And when you become so much aware of others you will be ill at ease; you cannot be at home because you cannot control others. Others change like the weather. Sometimes they appreciate you – in fact, they are not appreciating you: by accident you have come to them at a time when they are in a good mood! They appreciate you because they are feeling generous, in a good mood. Come to them when they are in a bad mood; then they cannot appreciate you, then you look ugly to them. Their appreciation doesn't depend on you; their appreciation or condemnation depends on their own moods. And how can you control the moods of others? They are millions, there is no way. You cannot control your own mood; how can you expect to control others' moods? If you depend on others you will always be in a continuous trembling and shaking.

A mature man, a man who understands, simply drops the whole idea. It is absurd, it is meaningless. He simply lives his whole life unself-consciously. And then beauty arises, then grace happens; then something from the beyond starts pouring into him. And here is the paradox: when this happens, many will become aware of you. Many will feel the beauty, the benediction that you carry with you, the grace that happens just in your presence. Many will feel it when you are not self-conscious. When you are self-conscious you become ugly. When you are self-conscious, the very effort to impress makes you ugly.

And this you can watch in life. It may be difficult for you to catch it in yourself, because it is very difficult to watch oneself. Watch others. Why does a prostitute look ugly? She may have a beautiful body, but why does she look ugly? Because she is too self-conscious. She depends on the attention of others. She is a commodity, she is on sale; she is always in the window for others to appreciate and look at, because that is her whole life, her business. A prostitute cannot live without self-consciousness. How can she live without attracting others? The body may be beautiful, but you cannot find beauty in a prostitute – it is impossible.

And sometimes a homely woman suddenly appears to be beautiful, just a homely woman doing her housewife's work: preparing food because the husband may be coming, waiting for children, just waiting for the lover, sitting near the steps looking far away in the distance, suddenly you feel a beauty around her. She is homely; in no way can you call her beautiful, but you feel the beauty. Why? What is happening there? Waiting for the lover she is unself-conscious. She is not worried about you, she is not asking for anybody's attention; she is totally absorbed. She is not self-conscious, she loves somebody.

If you love somebody then you need not be self-conscious; and if you are self-conscious you cannot love, because the ego will become the barrier. If you are not self-conscious, only then is love possible. That's why the more egoistic a person is, the less possibility is there of love. And when there is no love you are in a vicious circle: you think people don't love you because you don't appear beautiful, so you try to be more beautiful; you become more and more self-conscious. The more self-conscious you become the less possibility is there, and if you become absolutely self-conscious it is almost impossible – nobody can love you. You will simply put off anybody who comes near. You are a closed person; nobody can enter you.

An unself-conscious person is simply open. He doesn't expect much but much happens. If you expect too much then nothing happens. This story is beautiful. Try to understand it.

When Yang Chu was passing through Sung he spent the night at an inn.

The innkeeper had two concubines – one beautiful and the other ugly. The ugly one he valued and the beautiful one he neglected.

This is a parable so don't take it literally. In fact, everyone has two concubines. You may have one wife, but that is only on the surface. Everybody has two wives, one beautiful, one ugly, because every person has two aspects, one beautiful, one ugly. Even a beautiful person in certain moments is ugly, and just the reverse is also true; an ugly person is in certain moments beautiful, because ugliness and beauty are not parts of the form – they belong to the within.

Have you observed a beautiful person in certain moments when he or she becomes totally ugly? Have you seen a beautiful woman with lust in her eyes? – suddenly everything goes ugly, because lust is ugly. Have you seen an ugly woman with love in her eyes? – suddenly everything becomes beautiful. Love beautifies; lust makes you ugly, anger makes you ugly – compassion beautifies.

The more you think inside your mind, the more ugly and tense your face becomes. If you don't think, if you live without much thinking, more meditatively, everything becomes beautiful. The faces of buddhas always become feminine. That's why Hindus never depict their enlightened persons with beards and mustaches, no. Have you seen any pictures of Buddha or Mahavira or Krishna or Rama with a beard or a mustache? Not that beards never came to them, because that would have been a deformity; that would have meant that something was biologically wrong, physiologically wrong, some hormone was missing. No, they had beards and mustaches, but the Hindus have completely dropped them. They don't depict them because they are depicting something of the inner.

They are showing through the statues of buddhas that these men became completely feminine. Why feminine? – because grace is feminine, beauty is feminine.

The body loses all violent concerns; it becomes more round. Muscles are not needed for a buddha; muscles belong to wild animal-hood. The body becomes more and more round, shapely, more and more feminine. When aggression disappears, muscles also disappear, because they exist for a particular purpose: for aggression, for violence.

Look at the pictures or at the bodies of Mr. Universes: they are wild animals, they are no longer human beings. And their bodies are also not healthy. They have been forcing their bodies into unnatural shapes. They may look like lions but they are not even human beings. They are appreciated because we are still animalistic.

If you become more beautiful and graceful, less aggressive and violent, then you will choose a man like Buddha to be Mr. Universe; not the animals that you choose but a body which has lost violence and aggression, which is completely at ease, relaxed, ready to love, not to fight.

Everybody has two aspects. Just watch people. I say watch people so that finally, eventually, you can watch yourself. It is very difficult to watch yourself because you are so near to yourself. There is no distance, so observation becomes difficult.

Once, Mulla Nasruddin was put in a mental hospital – he had to be. But after just a few minutes he pushed the call bell. The nurse rushed in and she asked, "What is the matter?"

Nasruddin said, "You people, why have you put me in this room with this nut?" – there was another person there. "Why have you put me here with this nut?"

The nurse said, "The hospital is crowded and it is difficult to find a single bedroom for you. And we know that he is a nut, but is he annoying you in any way?"

Nasruddin said, "Yes, it is impossible for me to be here with him. He is annoying me. He goes on looking all around and saying,

'There are no lions here, no scorpions, no snakes, no tigers, no crocodiles; no, nothing is here.' He goes on saying this and it annoys me. As you can plainly see, the room is full of them."

It is very easy to see what is wrong in somebody else; it is very very difficult to observe oneself. That's why I say, first start watching people. They are you – through them you will understand yourself. Just start watching people; they are you. Watching them you will come to a point where you can understand yourself better. Look at people on the street, at how self-conscious they are, how continuously ego-oriented. Look at your leaders, politicians, your so-called saints, how self-conscious they are: continuously on show, in the market, in the show-window – but never at home. They are like commodities for sale. And it doesn't matter whether you are a very costly commodity or a cheap commodity; a person is not a commodity.

Mulla Nasruddin once met a woman in the train, and he said, "Would you like to sleep with me? I will give you one thousand rupees."

The woman hesitated a little and said, "No, what do you think I am?"

Mulla Nasruddin said, "Then I can give you ten thousand rupees." Now it was difficult to say no to the offer, because to everybody there comes a limit, when the price reaches a certain amount.

The woman said, "Okay."

Nasruddin said, "How about one hundred rupees?"

The woman said, "What are you saying? What do you think I am?"

Nasruddin said, "That we have decided. Now, a little haggling about the price. What you are – that we have decided."

Ten thousand or ten rupees, that is not the point. Are you a commodity? Why are you so worried about what people think about you? Are you for sale? Then why so much self-consciousness? And everything goes wrong.

You notice people talking beautifully with each other – everybody talks. But just put the man or the woman on a platform and tell him to talk to you; something goes wrong. He was never at a loss for words before, now he cannot find them; he starts stuttering, trembling. What happens? And he's a good talker; with friends he talks perfectly well. Now he has become self-conscious. Standing on the platform he has become a commodity: "Now what will people say, will they appreciate me or not?" Now he is troubled. Now it is an ego-trip. When he is talking with friends it is not an ego-trip; he is a charming talker. But on the platform almost everybody becomes boring.

Mulla Nasruddin once became mayor of his town. He was a good talker, you could talk with him for hours together; a good story-teller, a beautiful man. But he became the mayor and it was very difficult. He started boring the people of the town. He would talk too long, and then he would be at a loss when to stop. So he told his secretary not to write such long speeches, because people were getting bored.

The next day he delivered a talk; there was some celebration, the year was ending, but people still got bored. He was very angry. He told the secretary, "What is the matter? I told you to write a short speech and you again did the same, and people got bored."

The secretary said, "I had written a short one, but you read all three copies."

When you are self-conscious you are completely unconscious. You don't know what you are doing. You are so afraid that you don't know what is happening. Self-consciousness is a disease.

Animals are beautiful, all animals. Have you seen an ugly animal? Have you ever seen an ugly bird, an ugly deer? Can you find an ugly tree? Then what has happened to man? When everything is so beautiful in the world, what has happened to man? There is nothing like an ugly tree or an ugly bird or an ugly animal. They are all beautiful, they are all graceful; they are so perfectly alike. If you go into the forest and see one thousand deer moving, you will not find a single deer too fat, too thin, ugly or beautiful. You will not be able to make any distinction – they all look alike.

What is the matter with man then? Why do so many people become so ugly and so fat; either thin or fat, but never in balance? They don't exist in a relaxed way. They are tense, self-conscious. When you are tense you will start eating more. When you are relaxed you eat only as much as is needed. The body decides, not you. If you are tense you will eat more. Tense people tend to eat more because eating becomes an occupation; through eating they can forget themselves. Tense people become ugly because the tension is not only in the mind, it affects the body.

Body and mind are not two, there is no division. Mind is just the other pole of the body and the body is the other pole of the mind. Visible mind is body, invisible body is mind. Subtle body is the mind, gross mind is the body. You have a psychosomatic structure – it is one.

When the mind is tense, then your face starts showing the worries, then your skin starts showing the tension. And if it has become a deep-rooted thing, then the body takes the shape; the mind becomes the mold and the body takes the shape. Just by watching the face of a man you can see what is happening in the mind. Hence, face-reading exists as a science. It is a science, because your face shows what is happening in your mind. You see that whatsoever you do – eating, sleeping, moving, walking, relating with people, sitting alone, whatsoever you do – the body and mind are always together.

If you eat more, that shows that your mind needs love, and you are in such a deep need of love that food has become a substitute. People who are in need of love will eat more, and the more they eat the less exists the possibility of anybody falling in love with them. Then it becomes a vicious circle – they eat more. And a deep association exists between love and food, because every child receives love and food together, from the same mother – they become deeply associated. In fact, the child gets food first, milk, and then by and by he becomes aware of the love that is flowing from the mother. So whenever you cannot find love you will fall back on food, you will start eating more; it will become a substitute.

You walk – everything shows around you. If you are tense you walk in a tense way, as if you are carrying a burden, a mountain on your head; something is hanging around your neck. Even if you shake hands, if you are worried and tense the hand will be dead, there will be no warmth in it, it will be cold. It is like a dead branch of a tree: no more life moves in it. When you are tense the whole energy is absorbed in the head. When you are relaxed the energy moves all over; then the energy has a flow. When you are tense it becomes blocked. Tense, you are like a river in hot summer: only in some spots little pools are left, but the bed is dry. Somewhere you can find a little dirty pool, but there is no flow; then again sand, then again a little pool.

This is how a tense man is: there is no flow of energy – many blocks, many dry beds, and somewhere a little pool exists, and that pool is bound to become dirty. When energy is flowing you are fresh. When energy is moving without any blocks you are river-like, and the ocean is not far away. When you are a summer river – when everything is dried and only pools of energy exist, and there is no interlink between your energy pools – then you can never reach to the ocean; then God is the farthest thing possible. Flowing, he is near; non-flowing, he is very very far away. Flow is needed, and when you flow you are beautiful. Look at a child, watch a child: he is a flow, a river-like flow. He moves like wind and he never tires. If you walk like a child....

They have been doing some experiments at Harvard. One very very healthy person was told to follow a child for twenty-four hours. Whatsoever the child did, he had to do – whatsoever. If the child jumped he had to jump, if the child went out he had to go out, the child lay down, he had to lie down. Within eight hours he was completely exhausted; he couldn't follow for twenty-four hours. And the child was never tired.

What was happening? – the river was flowing. When a river is flowing, a constant source of energy is available. The man simply said, "I cannot follow anymore. This boy is driving me crazy and I am tired, exhausted. I feel that my mind will crack any moment because he is doing such absurd things, without any rhyme or reason, and I have to follow him." And the boy enjoyed tremendously that somebody was following him and he had become the leader.

Just watch a small boy. What is happening? Nothing, just a simple thing: he is not a dry river in the summer, he is a flood. He is a river in the rainy season: millions of streams are falling into him. And you can be the same. But the more you become self-conscious, the more a deep tension goes into you. Self-conscious, you start shrinking; unself-conscious you open and spread.

And everybody has two concubines. Everybody is himself the two concubines.

When Yang Chu was passing through Sung he spent the night at an inn.

The innkeeper had two concubines – one beautiful and the other ugly. The ugly one he valued and the beautiful one he neglected.

This looks irrational, but it has a deep reason.

When Yang Chu asked the reason, the fellow answered, "The beautiful one thinks herself beautiful and I do not notice her beauty; the ugly one thinks herself ugly and I do not notice her ugliness."

Try to understand this arithmetic of existence, paradoxical but real. And if you can understand it many things will change in you immediately.

If you demand something it will not be given to you. If you don't demand, you will suddenly find millions of streams falling into you – every door is open. Demand and you will be denied; don't demand and the whole existence belongs to you. Possess and you will lose; don't possess and nobody can take it from you. Be self-conscious and you will not be a self; be unself-conscious and you attain to the inner crystallization, the integrity which is the self.

The fellow said, "The one thinks herself beautiful...." When somebody thinks himself or herself beautiful, there is a constant demand: "Look at me, I am beautiful, appreciate me." And beauty is a delicate phenomenon – you cannot demand. If you demand, in the very demand you have become ugly. If you demand, I repeat, in the very demand you have become ugly, because demand is ugly. If you demand and you are asking for it too much, nobody is going to give it to you. Your demand becomes aggression; it is violent, and how can violence be beautiful? How can aggression be beautiful?

Somebody who thinks himself or herself beautiful is constantly aggressive. You cannot live with such a person happily – almost impossible, because the demand is too much. And when somebody demands you will feel a sudden feeling not to give, because one wants to share, one wants to give, but one wants to remain one's own master. If you have to fulfill a demand you become a slave. Nobody wants to be a slave.

And this is not only so for beauty, it is so for every dimension of life. If somebody says, "I am a realized man," and demands recognition continually, it is difficult. In the very demand the man proves his ignorance.

Hence the Upanishads say that the man who thinks he knows does not know. Hence Socrates says that, "When I became a knower, I realized that I am the most ignorant one."

A man who knows becomes ignorant, and all those who are ignorant know much. They demand: "I am a knower...." It is the demand of an ignorant mind. Those who know, they never demand, because the moment you become knowing, you know. What do you know? – you know nothing. Existence is so vast, so mysterious, how can you know it? All claims to knowledge are egoistic, and only one who is not egoistic, who becomes completely unself-conscious, who does not know who he is, enters into the mysteries.

It happened: Bodhidharma reached China. He took the lotus flower of silence, the light of Buddha, the awakening, the secret, the key. The emperor came to visit him. He asked many questions. He said, "I have done many many things, good deeds. What will the outcome be?"

Bodhidharma said, "Nothing. You will fall into the deepest hell. One who has done a good deed should not be self-conscious about it, because a good deed becomes a bad deed if you are self-conscious about it – that is the only sin."

The emperor was a little shocked. He asked other questions and he received only shocks. He asked, "Tell me something about the holy, sacred Buddha."

Bodhidharma said, "There is nothing holy and nothing sacred" – because if you think something is holy then self-consciousness takes it over. If you think, "I am holy," then you are bound to look at others as sinners. So Bodhidharma said, "There is nothing holy, nothing sacred."

Angry, the emperor asked, "Who are you to be talking like this before me?"

Bodhidharma said, "I don't know." This is the perfect knowledge. Bodhidharma said, "I don't know who I am talking here before you." Look at the beauty of it: he says, "I don't know who I am." In this no-claim, he claimed all.

When you claim you miss. Saying "I don't know," he effaced himself completely, utterly. This man is absolutely unself-conscious; he has attained to the self.

"The beautiful one thinks herself beautiful and I do not notice her beauty..."

She would like it to be noticed. Whatsoever you want that people should notice, nobody will notice. You will be a constant drainage of their energy; you will drain them of their energy, you will be a burden, a bore. And everybody will escape from you; nobody will like being near you.

A self-conscious person is like a heavy burden: you come near him and suddenly you feel a fever because he is demanding something.

"The ugly one thinks herself ugly and I do not notice her ugliness."

And the ugly thinks herself ugly.... She is humble, she doesn't claim anything, she doesn't ask, she doesn't demand any notice. She doesn't say that she is this or that, she simply knows that she is ugly. So if you love her she feels grateful. If somebody notices her she feels thankful. And when you feel thankful and grateful you become beautiful. Whatsoever somebody says to her, she feels it is too much: "I was not in any way worthy of it. I am ugly." She is not expecting anything, so whatsoever happens is a bliss, a happiness. If you expect you will be frustrated; if you don't expect you will be fulfilled.

Said the fellow: "*The ugly one thinks herself ugly and I do not notice her ugliness*. She has become so humble, so simple, so egoless, so unself-conscious that I cannot notice any ugliness in her."

Yang Chu said to his disciples, "Remember this: if you act nobly and banish from your mind the thought that you are noble, where can you go and not be loved?"

You are destroying yourself by claiming things. You claim that you are wise and then life proves you to be a fool; you claim yourself to be very attractive and life doesn't take any notice of you. You try to prove that you are very beautiful and everything proves that you are ugly, because there is nothing more ugly than the ego, and all claims are egoistic.

Drop claims and simply remain with the fact. Don't claim anything, don't ask anything, don't demand. Don't think that you are very very worthy and then much will happen to you. The whole existence will accept you. When you accept existence, existence accepts you. When you claim, in every claim you are complaining:

"I was more worthy."

Just a few days ago a man came to see me – he insisted. Ordinarily, I don't want to see persons who have never meditated, who have never listened to me, because it is going to be futile. But he insisted, so I said okay. He had been writing letters to me for many years in which he said there is a deep problem that he would like to discuss with me, and he is in much misery. He talked continuously for half an hour saying that he is a graduate of Oxford, that he is in the secretariat on a very high post of the ministry of education in New Delhi, and he has done this and that. I tried again and again to bring him to the point: "What is the problem?" But he would not come to the point. He went round and round. I said, "But your time is nearly finished, so come to the point. These are not problems. You are a graduate of Oxford, okay, it is not a problem. What is the problem?"

Then he said, "The problem is that too much injustice has been done to me. I am a very capable man with many degrees and achievements, and nobody takes any notice of me, so how can I tolerate this injustice?" He would have liked to be the prime minister or the president or something, but then too it would not be just because nothing can be just if you have expectations.

I told him, "There is no problem. The problem is not how to tolerate injustice, the problem is how to drop the claim of being worthy."

If you think too much of yourself, if you think of yourself as somebody very significant, then every day, every moment you will find that injustice is being done to you. Nobody is being unjust. Who bothers about you? Who has time to do injustice to you? Who cares? But you feel that the whole world is being unjust to you. Nobody is being unjust to you; it is your claim.

Lao Tzu says: If you want to be the first in the world, you will find yourself to be the last. And if you are able to stand at the back, just to be the last, you may find yourself to be the first.

Effface yourself completely; a clean slate, not claiming anything, nothing written on it. Become clean, don't be self-conscious, and suddenly you feel that all the doors that were closed have opened. They were never closed – it was you.

A rare phenomenon happened. You must have heard about Houdini, the great magician. Only once in his life did he fail, otherwise he could open any type of lock within seconds without keys. How he did the whole thing has yet remained a mystery. He would be tied with chains, locked into a trunk and thrown into the sea and he would escape within seconds. He was thrown into all the great prisons of the world and within seconds he was out. England has one of the best police forces, one of the best detective departments, Scotland Yard, but they could not do anything. Whatsoever they did, within a few seconds he was always out. Only once did he fail; it was in France. He was thrown into a cell in a prison, and he couldn't get out for three hours. Nobody could believe what had happened: Is he dead? And then he came out, perspiring, completely tired. A joke had been played on him and he missed: the door was not locked and he was trying to open it.

How can you unlock a door which is not locked? If it is locked there is a way, something can be done. He never expected the door not to be locked. He tried and tried in every way, but the door was not locked, there was no lock on it, and he couldn't see it for three hours. Then how did he come out? – just from tiredness he fell down and the door opened.

Existence is not denying you anything. There is no injustice, there has never been, there cannot be. How can the mother be unjust to the child? Existence is your mother: you come out of it, you go back into it. How can existence be unjust to you? It is your claims, your egoistic claims, that create the problem.

Yang Chu said to his disciples, "Remember this: if you act nobly and banish from your mind the thought that you are noble, where can you go and not be loved?"

If you efface yourself, love rushes towards you from every side. Everybody falls in love with you. If you efface yourself, if you are nobody, everybody falls in love with you – everybody, even a stranger suddenly feels love for you. This I say to you from my own experience, that if you efface yourself everybody is in love with you. If you try to be somebody it is impossible: nobody can love you.

Without ego you are accepted everywhere: you are a guest, you are accepted everywhere. Without ego, whatsoever happens you will feel a benediction; with ego, whatsoever happens you will be miserable. Because it is not what happens that matters, it is the you to whom it happens.

The ego is a deep discontent; it cannot be satisfied, it is a bottomless pit. Whatsoever you throw into it disappears, it always remains hungry; that is the nature of it. Nothing can be done about it. You can simply drop it, otherwise you will always remain dissatisfied.

Egolessness is contentment. Egoless, you don't expect anything, and just a small child smiles at you...but it is so beautiful. What else could you need? Suddenly you see a flower and the flower sends its perfume to you. What else could you need? What more could you want? The whole sky goes on filling with stars, the whole life becomes a celebration, because now everything is beautiful. Without expectations, everything fulfills. Just to breathe is enough, just to breathe is such a bliss. Otherwise, with the ego....

I have heard: Mulla Nasruddin went to his bank. The bank was celebrating the hundredth year of its existence, so they made it a point that whosoever came first was to be given many presents: a car, a television set, this and that, and a cheque for ten thousand rupees. By coincidence, Mulla Nasruddin entered. He was garlanded, photographed, interviewed, and many gifts were piled on him: notes, a TV set, and a car which was standing outside.

When everything was finished he said, "Now, is everything finished so that I can continue to my destination?"

They asked, "Where were you going?"

He said, "To the complaint department." He had come to complain about the bank, and even all that had happened would not do. He couldn't forget the complaint.

The ego is always going to the complaint department. Whatsoever happens is meaningless, because even if God comes to you, you will say, "Wait, let me first reach the complaint book." The ego is headed towards the complaint book, nothing can satisfy the ego.

The whole effort is useless; drop it. Simply efface yourself, abide in non-ego, abide in egolessness; drop self-consciousness and become more conscious, and then suddenly everything fits, suddenly everything falls into a harmony. Nothing is wrong, there is no injustice going on. You feel at home everywhere, and only in this moment of at-homeness does the existence take a new color; it becomes divine, it becomes spiritual – never before it.

So the search for God is not a search for some person outside of you. The search for God is a search for this moment of total fulfillment. Suddenly the door is open – it was never closed. It appeared closed to the ego. With no ego in between, the door is open. It has always been open.

Existence is open, you are closed; existence is simple, you are complex; existence is healthy, you are ill. Nothing is to be done to existence, something is to be done to you. And nobody else can do it for you, you have to do it.

Watch your self-consciousness, feel the misery that follows it like a shadow. If you want to get rid of the shadow you have to get rid of the ego. You have been trying to get rid of the shadow, but how can you get rid of the shadow? – it follows ego. You have to drop the ego, then the shadow disappears.

Enough for today.

Discourse 7

Snowflakes As Beautiful As These

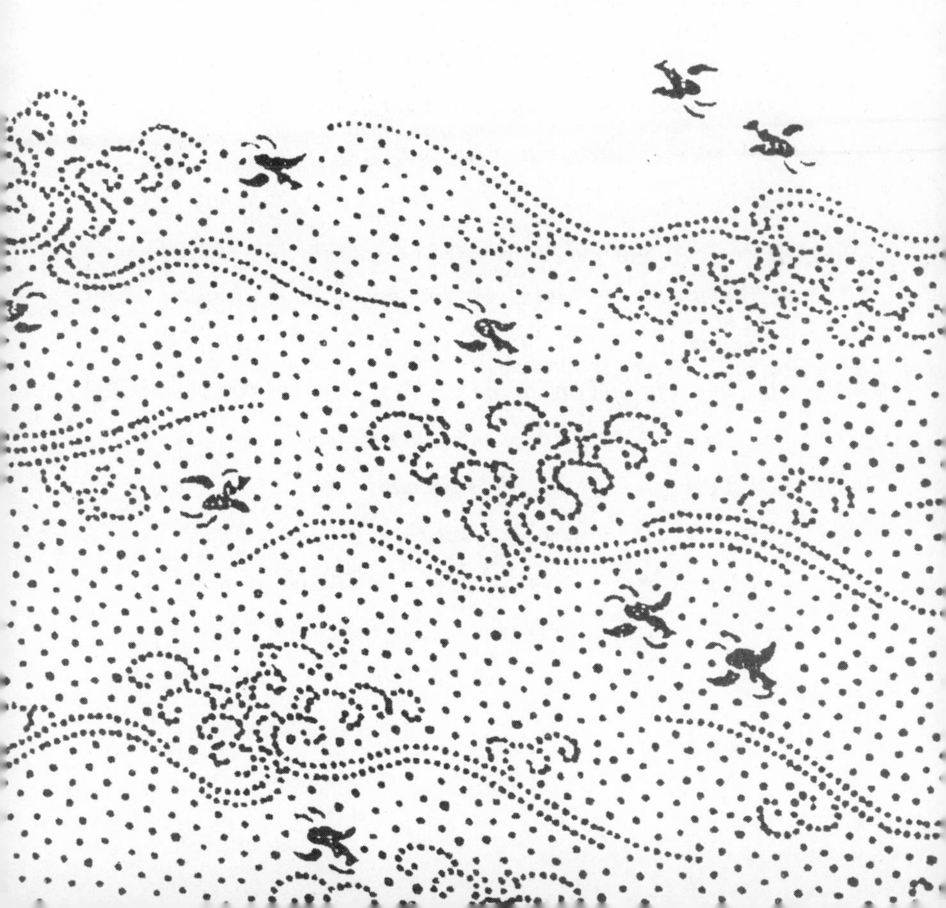

For nearly twenty years, Houn, a layman devoted to the study of Zen, lived at Yakusan Temple, and undertook discipline under Master Igen.

The day came when he decided to return to his family. The master asked ten of his disciples to see him off at the gate.

It was snowing, and Houn, looking up, said, "Lovely. Snowflakes as beautiful as these don't fall elsewhere."

"Elsewhere?" said one of the ten, "where is this elsewhere?"

At this Houn slapped his face.

"Why did you do that, dear layman?" asked the disciple, rubbing his cheek.

"How can you pose as a Zen man?" Houn said angrily. "You're doomed to hell."

"And you?" the disciple cried. "What about yourself?"

Houn slapped him again. "You've eyes, but you won't see," he said over his shoulder as he moved off, "and you have a mouth, but you're dumb."

A few things before we enter this beautiful anecdote. First, time should be forgotten completely. If you want to enter meditation time should not be of concern to you. If you are in a hurry then nothing is possible, and this has become a most deeply rooted problem for the modern man. The West has made people too time-conscious, not knowing where they are going, but speeding to get there because time is short.

I have heard: Once a pilot communicated on the intercom to his passengers: "It seems everything has gone wrong. The radar is not functioning, the radio is out of order, even the compass has ceased to function. But don't be worried, we are keeping the same speed."

But this is what is happening to the modern mind: everything is out of order except speed. Where are you going? For what are you going? Of course you are going fast, but you are going so fast that you have no time to look at where you are going and why you are going.

People come to me and they say, "I can stay here only one day. Is meditation possible?" They ask, "Can you give me something so that I can know the divine?" They are childish, juvenile; they have not grown up at all. They don't know what they are saying.

Is God something one can give to you as a gift? Is God a certain technique so that the formula can be given to you and you can work it out later on? Is it something like a material key that can be given to you and you can unlock the door? This search needs tremendous patience, infinite patience. This is the first requirement: you should simply forget about time.

What is time? It is a very anxious state of mind. You are too much worried about tomorrow, too much worried about the future, too much worried about the past. You are pulled in these two opposite directions, the past and the future, and you are worried because you have not gained anything in the past. You are worried: who knows, the same may also happen in the future as has happened in the past – nothing. You have achieved in the past, and it may be that you may not achieve anything in the future, so you are in a hurry. But just hurry won't help, because it disturbs you.

The modern man is farther away from God not because he is more materialistic, no. Man has always been materialistic, has to be so because a man is ninety-nine percent body. Man has always been materialistic – this is nothing new. Is it because of too much scientific training and education? No. Science is not against God. It may not be for God, but it is not at all against God. It simply says: God is not my concern at all. It is not; they exist on different planes. Science cannot say yes or no to God; they are not moving in the same dimension, the dimensions differ. So science has not made man atheistic.

Then what is making people atheistic, farther away from God? No, not even communism. Communism may have created new gods but it has not destroyed the old one – it cannot. Communism itself is a religion. Then what? To me, it is time-consciousness – which is a new factor in the world, a new factor in human consciousness – that is creating the trouble. And it has become deep-rooted, particularly in Christianity and Judaism; it has become very very deep-rooted. And the cause of it is that Christianity, Judaism and Islam are all three from the same source – Judaism. All three are Jewish.

In the world there are in fact only two religions: one is Hindu, the other is Jewish. Mohammedanism and Christianity come out of Jewish sources – just offshoots. Buddhism, Jainism and Sikhism come out of Hinduism – they are just offshoots.

There is a deep-rooted problem in Jewish thinking, and that is that they deny rebirth; they deny the theory of a circle of births. They believe in only one life, and that dominates the West. If there is only one life then you will be in a hurry, because time is short and too many things have to be done; you cannot move at ease. That's why so much speed: everything is moving fast, everybody is worried that life is slipping out of their hands, and you have only one life.

In the East it is believed that you have millions of lives: there is no hurry, time is not short, no need to be worried about it; enough to waste and even enough always there in reserve – it is eternal. You will be born again and again, again and again. It is a circle. You move...you go, you come again, you go, you come again, so there is no need to be worried about time. That's why in the eyes of the West the East looks lethargic, lazy, not doing anything. Nobody is worried, people can relax under the trees – no hurry. But this 'no hurry' helps religion. The mind which is too time-conscious may create many materialistic miracles but it will miss the inner dimension, because the inner dimension is approached only when you are absolutely patient.. You will miss many things if you are patient, that is right, but you will never miss yourself.

If you want to create an empire of things, possessions, then be in a hurry; then think that time is money and very precious, and use it to create more and more things. But you will be lost. When you die you will have piled up a great empire of things, but dying you will come to realize that you have not achieved anything. The whole effort has been a failure, because unless you achieve yourself, nothing is achieved. Unless you come to yourself, you have not come to any point. Life may have been a journey, but you have not reached the goal.

So about this you have to decide: you have to drop time-consciousness. Simply forget about time; time is always available. It is not like money, it is like the sky – it is always available, you cannot exhaust it. So don't run. You can sit at ease, you can relax, you can sit like a buddha. Look at the statue of Buddha, sitting as if there is no time. He doesn't seem to be in a hurry.

It is said in one of the old Zen stories: Once two monks were crossing a stream in a ferryboat; one was very old, the other was very very young. When they got off the ferryboat they asked the man who had brought them to this shore, "Will it be possible for us to reach the town where we are headed before the sun sets?" – because it was a hilly track and the sun was just going down; at the most they had one hour. They had to arrive before sunset because once the doors of the town were closed, then the whole night they would have to remain in the forest outside the town. And it was dangerous, wild animals were there. The ferryboat man said, "Yes, you can reach if you go slowly."

The old man could understand because a certain wisdom happens in old age. Youth is always in a hurry. This is paradoxical. An old man should be in a hurry because time is short, but it is always the opposite. The young man is always in a hurry even though there is enough time, because this hurry comes from an inner energy – ignorance. An old man can understand.

The old man said, "Yes, I understand."

But the young man said, "You are fools, you both. How can one reach if one goes slowly? I am not going to listen to this stupid nonsense!" He started running.

It was a hilly track, and he was in such a hurry that that which was to happen, happened. He fell down. He was hurt, wounded, all his things scattered. Then the old man caught up...because he was coming slowly. He looked at the young man – he was crippled, blood was flowing – and he said, "Now how will you be able to reach? You tried to reach quickly and now you cannot reach at all."

It is said that the young man was devoured by wild beasts, but the old man reached by the time the sun was setting. He reached the door just in the nick of time and he entered the city.

This is a parable. In fact, the track is hilly. When you are moving towards the divine, the track is hilly. There are valleys and peaks and you can fall at any moment. The territory is dangerous and millions of wild animals are all around. You have to reach the gate before the gate closes. But if you run fast you will not be able to reach, because when you run fast you cannot be conscious.

Have you ever tried running fast? If you run very fast, the very speed gives you an intoxication. That's why there is so much addiction to speed. If you drive a car, the mind wants to go more and more and more and more fast. It makes you intoxicated. Speed releases certain chemicals in the body and in the blood; that's why you would like to go on pressing the accelerator. More people die every year in car accidents than in a world war. The second world war was nothing, more people die every year in car accidents. People go on getting more and more speedy; then they become intoxicated. A moment comes when they are not in their minds and the speed has taken over.

Start running one day and just watch what happens – a moment comes when the speed takes over: that is the acceleration of speed. And just the opposite happens if you slow down. What is Buddha doing under the tree? – slowing down the speed, nothing else. What am I continuously teaching you? – slow down the speed. Come to a point where there is no speed within you, nobody running. In that moment awareness happens – you become enlightened.

And there are two poles: one is speed – then you are intoxicated, you become unconscious; the other is no speed – slowed down completely, totally, an absolute stop. Suddenly you become enlightened.

This is the first thing to be understood: slow down your speed. Eat slowly, walk slowly, talk slowly, move very very slowly, and by and by you will come to know the beauty of inactivity, the beauty of passivity. Then you are not intoxicated, you are completely aware and conscious.

The second thing: you cannot pose as an enlightened man. Many people try it and they can also deceive many others, because fools are everywhere. But you cannot pose before a man who knows, you cannot deceive one who knows himself. There is no possibility, because he can look into you; you become transparent. Never try to pose. But the mind is so cunning – even if you come to a master you try to pose before him. You would like to show your knowledge, you would like to show that you have attained something. And the very effort to show shows that nothing has been attained, because when one attains the exhibitionist disappears; then you don't pose. Then you are simply there; wherever you are you are there. And remember continuously, because even a single moment of unawareness and the mind starts posing. It has become a routine habit.

Once Mulla Nasruddin's doctor told him, "Now you are behaving absolutely madly. You are going to kill yourself, and I warn you for the last time that you are behaving in a suicidal way. I have told you: now stop all irregular habits. Live a regular life, otherwise you will die soon."

Nasruddin said, "But I have always lived a regular life."

The doctor said, "Who are you trying to deceive? Just the other night I saw you coming out of a prostitute's house in the middle of the night, and the way you were walking I could see you were completely drunk. So who are you trying to deceive?"

Nasruddin laughed loudly and he said, "But that is my regular habit. I have always lived a regular life."

Deceiving others is your regular habit. It has gone into the very roots. You do it without knowing you are doing it, that is the problem. You go on posing. If it is a regular habit, how can you suddenly drop it when you come to a master? There also the regular habit will persist.

Mahakashyapa, Sariputta, Moggalayan, all great disciples of Buddha, had to wait for two years before Buddha would start teaching. Sariputta asked, "Why do we have to wait for two years?"

Buddha said, "Just to provide a gap so that your old habits slow down, because if they persist you will not listen to me; if they persist it will not allow you to see me; if they persist, whatsoever you do will be a confusion. Just two years – let things slow down. Two years, don't do anything. Just remain silent, watchful, so that you can become aware of things which you have been doing continuously without knowing that you were doing them."

Posing, showing, being that which you are not, is dangerous. And with a master it is absolutely dangerous because it is not going to help anybody and you are missing an opportunity. Never pose. If you pose then the authentic cannot surface; then the posture remains all around you. If you have many faces, then when and how will the original face surface? Allow the original face to come; drop all postures, drop all faces. For a few days you will feel dizzy without a face. You will feel very uncomfortable without your old pattern and habits. For a few days you will feel that you have lost your identity. That's okay, that's how it should be.

One has to lose one's identity in order to regain the real identity. One has to lose all faces to gain the real face – that which you had before you were born, and that which you will have after you have died. When you are no more, the original will be with you. Never pose. Now try to enter this story.

For nearly twenty years, Houn, a layman devoted to the study of Zen, lived at Yakusan Temple, and undertook discipline under Master Igen.

Twenty years! One-third of life, and he waited as if there was no hurry. Twenty years! Just think! Two days seem to be too long, two months, two years – twenty years seem just a whole lifetime. He must have come when he was nearabout twenty, a young man, and when he came out of the temple he was already old. Your whole youth, your whole energy has to be devoted to the search. Remember, time-consciousness will be a barrier.

There is a Zen story: One old man was dying. He called his son and told him, "I would like you to attain to meditation before I die, because in my whole life I have come to realize that nothing is more important. So I am not giving you riches, I am not giving you any prestige or power of this world; this is going to be my only gift. So you go to a master and learn meditation."

The boy was afraid to leave because the father was old and any day he could die; he was just on his deathbed. But when the father said, "You have to go," he had to go.

He reached a Zen master and told him the whole thing. "My father is very very old, almost dying, and he wants me to learn meditation before he dies. He would like to see my meditative face and I would like to make him happy, so just tell me how long it will take for me to become meditative."

The Zen master said, "Three years."

The young man said, "I will make as much effort as possible, I will put my total energy into it; then how much time will it take, how long?"

The Zen master said, "Thirty years."

He said, "What are you saying? I am saying that I will put my total energy into it – and before that you said three years."

The master said, "I thought that you would put your total energy into it, that's why I said three years. But when you say, 'Now I will put my total energy' – thirty years. And if you ask about time again, it will be impossible – ninety years."

The boy said, "But my father is dying."

The master said, "What can I do? Everybody has to die, that is not my concern. Meditation doesn't bother about who is dying or who is not dying. Never ask about time again, or else leave me."

The boy watched the master: he was the right man, the fragrance was there, the quality that exists around a master – he could feel it, he could touch it exactly. It was there all around him like a light, an aura.

He said, "Okay." He touched the master's feet and said, "I will never ask about time, and you start the teaching."

The master said, "Good. You clean the house and whenever the time is right, I will start."

Three years passed and he had not even started, but by this time the young man had also become perceptive. He could understand that he had been foolish to ask about time. These three years slowed him down. He was just cleaning the house the whole day, and cleaning the house is not a mental thing. You have to do it with the body, so by and by the mind stops. He became perceptive and he could see that he had been foolish – the question was non-sense. And now there was no point in asking.

The master knows whenever the right moment comes and he will start. One day he thought inside that he knew, and the time was right. On that very day the master started – and what was the start? He came from behind and attacked the boy. The boy was sweeping and he attacked him with a wooden sword. The boy screamed and jumped. The master said, "This is my first teaching – now be aware. At any moment I will attack, so don't just simply clean and wash and sweep. Be alert, I am a dangerous man." And then the attacks started.

Within three months the boy was so alert – he had to be, because at any moment from anywhere the master would come like the wind and attack. He started dodging, he learned the trick, he became more and more alert and more and more happy.

By the third month the master said, "This won't do. Now in sleep also remain alert. I will come at any moment and jump on you." The master brought his mattress into the boy's room and said, "I will sleep here."

Now even sleep was not to be left alone. The boy learned by and by – because the master would jump at least twelve times each night. He would attack at any moment. The moment the boy would be falling into sleep, he would attack. He became so alert that again by the third month the body slept, but he remained alert; he started dodging in his sleep. The moment the master would jump, he would already be out of his bed. Even in his sleep, with closed eyes, he became so perceptive – he had to.

Then the master said, "It is not enough. Now tomorrow I am going to purchase a real sword. This wooden sword won't do. Remain alert because now I will be attacking you with a real sword. You miss once, and finished!"

But by this time the awareness was penetrating very very deeply. The boy laughed because he knew that now he could not miss a single moment. Now he became so perceptive that the master had no need to attack, because the moment the master would think to attack, the boy would say, "Wait! No need. You are an old man. Why...?" Just by thinking – the master would think inside and the boy would say, "Wait, you may kill yourself."

Three months passed, nine months, and the master said one day, "Now you are ready, you can go to your father."

The boy thought, "This old man has been torturing me in every possible way; I'm grateful because I have become aware and meditative, but would it not be good before I leave to attack this old man and see what happens?"

The old man started laughing. He said, "Remember, I am an old man."

Time should not be a concern, because time is against meditation. Time is mind and in meditation there is no time. Meditation is beyond time; there is no space, no time.

When you are deeply in meditation you don't know what time it is, you cannot know, you cannot feel time; and you don't know where you are, you cannot feel space. And if you go a little deeper, you don't know who you are. Everything disappears – time, space, and all the configurations of time and space: the ego, everything disappears. You simply are. This is the being, this is the truth. Twenty years?

...Houn, a layman devoted to the study of Zen, lived at Yakusan Temple, and undertook discipline under Master Igen.

Zen doesn't believe in renouncing the world. If you renounce, it is okay; if you don't renounce, it is also okay. It is up to you, both are good. The basic thing is not the world or renouncing the world; the basic thing is to be alert and aware wherever you are. Even a layman, a householder, can attain to the perfect enlightenment. In this, Zen is very very liquid. It gives you total freedom. Your style of life in this world doesn't matter.

Hindus have insisted that you have to renounce the world. Jainas have insisted that you have to renounce the world. Even Buddha insisted. Buddha in fact had no householders as his disciples. The whole Indian tradition is for renouncing the world. But Lao Tzu, Chuang Tzu, they lived in the world; they lived fully aware.

Chuang Tzu's wife died and the corpse was lying there. People were gathering, the neighbors, waiting to take the body, and he was sitting under a tree beating a drum and singing. The king himself had come to pay his respects. He also respected Chuang Tzu very much, and Chuang Tzu's wife was dead so he had come. But when he saw Chuang Tzu beating a drum he couldn't contain himself.

He said, "Not weeping I can understand, but this is going too far. Not to be sad I can understand, but singing and beating a drum! – it is going too far. What are you doing?"

Chuang Tzu said, "She lived with me, she was a beautiful woman, she served me, she loved me, she gave me many beautiful moments, she was really lovely – can't I even give her a good goodbye? She is leaving, it may not be possible for us to meet again. Can't I even sing and beat a little drum while she is leaving? She lived so long with me and she has done so much for me. Can't I do even this much?" This is a perfectly alert man. He has not renounced his wife, he has lived in the world like an ordinary man. But he is not ordinary, he is extraordinary.

Buddhism and Tao met, and Zen was born. So Zen says both are good: if you live in the world, it is okay, but live with alertness. If you renounce, if you feel like renouncing, that too is good, but renounce with alertness. So the basic thing is not the form but the spirit.

This Houn was a layman. He was not a *bhikkhu,* he was not a sannyasin; he had not renounced life. But what a man! For twenty years he had not gone to his family. What more of a renunciation can you ask? For twenty years he had not remembered the family, for twenty years he had not talked about it; what more of a renunciation can you ask? And when he became enlightened and the master said, "Now you can go"...now he is going back to his family. He is totally transformed but he is going back. The wife may be waiting, the children may be there, the old parents may be there; maybe they are dead. He is going back.

There is a saying in Zen that before you are enlightened, rivers are rivers and mountains are mountains. When you start meditating, rivers are no longer rivers and mountains are no longer mountains; everything is topsy-turvy. Then you attain and again everything falls into line – rivers are rivers again, mountains are mountains again. Just in the middle everything is disturbed, then everything settles again. Of course, it settles on a totally different plane.

Now this man is returning to his wife but he is no longer a husband; this man is returning to his children but he is no longer a father; this man is returning to his old parents but he is no longer a son; this man is returning to his shop but he is no longer a shopkeeper.

Zen says it is up to you. And there are different types of people; Zen gives freedom to all. There are people who would like to remain in the mountains – good. There are people who would like to remain in the markets – very good. Zen says that it is up to you; the style of your life is up to you. That is not the thing to be worried about. The basic thing is to be alert. This Houn attained alertness: he became aware and conscious.

The day came when he decided to return to his family. The master asked ten of his disciples to see him off at the gate.

He was ready, he was going back, and the master asked ten of his disciples to see him off at the gate. This 'ten' is symbolic. Ten are the senses: five senses – touch, smell, sight, hearing and taste – are outward; and five are the inward senses. As you can see outwardly, so can you see inwardly. When you see outwardly, your outer eyes function. When you see inwardly, the inner eye functions. Five are the senses for moving out, five are the senses for moving in. And these five senses each have two vehicles: two eyes, two ears, two hands – there is a duality. The five senses through which you enter inwards each have one vehicle, one eye – that is called the third eye; one ear – you can call it the third ear; one nose – you can call it the third nose. Five pairs going outwards, five units going inwards. In all they are ten. So the master tells his ten disciples to go and give him a good goodbye at the gate.

This is symbolic, this happens. When someone attains enlightenment, the senses come up to the gate from where they leave you, from beyond where they cannot go, from where enters the beyond. The senses come to a certain point from where they leave you. And they have lived with you so long, it is good that they should come and see you off at the gate.

It was snowing, and Houn, looking up, said, "Lovely. Snowflakes as beautiful as these don't fall elsewhere."

A buddha also has to use your language, an enlightened person also has to use your words, but the significance changes. He cannot use it in the same sense that you do because the sense comes from the user, not from the words. His meaning is different. For example, no buddha – one who has attained – can make any comparisons or use comparative words. If he says, "This is good," he doesn't mean that something is bad also.

But for us duality exists. If somebody says, "You are beautiful," immediately you compare it with ugliness. But when a buddha says, "You are beautiful," he is simply saying it to you, not in any comparative sense; he is not thinking of anything which is ugly and comparing it to you. His words don't carry any comparison. He says, "You are beautiful," and he will also say the same to somebody else, and somebody else: "You are beautiful." He can even say, "You are the most beautiful person in the world"; but don't think that he is comparing the whole world to you. Wait a little – he will say the same thing to somebody else, because to him everything is 'the most beautiful'. He is not saying anything about you. In fact, he is saying something about his own quality: whosoever comes near him he feels to be 'the most beautiful'.

It is his feeling that he is showing through it, it is nothing about you. Don't be deceived by his words, because you will think in comparisons.

One day Mulla Nasruddin came to me and I said to him, "Nasruddin, many people say that you are effeminate."

He said, "They are right; in comparison to my wife, I am."

We think in terms of comparison. If somebody says to everybody, "You are beautiful," to us the meaning of that word 'beautiful' is lost. Because if you don't tell anybody that they are ugly, what do you mean by your word 'beautiful'? If somebody says, "Everything is good, nothing is bad," then what is the meaning of his word 'good'? To us the word 'good' carries meaning only in comparison to 'bad'.

An enlightened person has to use your words with the different quality of his consciousness. He doesn't compare.

This man Houn is enlightened. He says, *"Lovely. Snowflakes as beautiful as these don't fall elsewhere."* How many comparisons he is using! *"Lovely"* – to us it simply appears that this man must be saying that something else is not lovely; otherwise what is the meaning of 'lovely'? *"Snowflakes as beautiful as these"*...immediately to our minds it seems that he is making comparisons with other snowflakes... *"as these don't fall elsewhere."* Immediately we think that he is comparing this moment, this here and now with something else, somewhere else.

But he is not; he is simply expressing how he feels at this moment. He is not comparing. At another place he will again look up and say, "Lovely, such snowflakes, such beautiful snowflakes fall nowhere else." He will say the same thing everywhere.

Buddha is reported to have said: You taste the sea anywhere and you will find it salty. You have to watch a man who has attained, a man of understanding – you have to watch and you have to drop your old habits of comparison.

Once it happened: A man came to Buddha, and Buddha said,

"Beautiful. You are a beautiful person. I have never come across a person like you."

One of the chief disciples, Ananda, was sitting nearby. Ananda was always present. He became uneasy. When the man left he said, "But you told me the same thing, and you have been saying the same thing to others, to many people, and I have been hearing this. What do you mean?"

Buddha laughed and said, "Everyone is beautiful, so beautiful that everyone is more beautiful than everybody else." Nonsense! How can everyone be more beautiful than everybody else? Everybody else is included in everyone.

He is not saying anything about the person, he is saying something about his consciousness. When you attain, the whole world simply becomes a blessing. When you attain, suddenly everything is beautiful, illuminated, luminous; nothing is dark, nothing is sin, nothing is evil. When you are fulfilled you look around and everything is so fulfilled, so complete, so perfect: that perfection is total because you have attained it. A man who has attained cannot condemn.

Just a few days ago the roof fell down at the back of this house. And the first thing that came to me was: What a beautiful ruin! It was so perfect, you could not make a better ruin than that. It was simply perfect. Everything fell so beautifully, in such a pattern, as if someone had done it. It was not just an accident; it was as if someone had created it.

If you can see things with perfect awareness, everything is good. You feel blessed by everything and you can bless everything. This is what was happening.

He said, looking up, "Lovely. Snowflakes as beautiful as these don't fall elsewhere."

"Elsewhere?" said one of the ten, "where is this elsewhere?"

And he is right, because a man who has attained is expected not to compare. Comparison belongs to the ignorant mind. Comparison is part of the ignorant mind, so how can a man who has attained talk in terms of comparison? An enlightened man is always here and now. How can he talk about elsewhere? There is no elsewhere for an enlightened man.

This disciple must have heard all these things; he must have accumulated them in his memory and reason, he must have been a head-oriented person. He immediately raised a question: "Elsewhere? What do you mean? Where is this elsewhere? You are bringing in comparisons, and we have heard that a man who has attained never compares – he lives without comparison, he does not know comparison at all."

If you live only this moment, how can you compare? How can you say, "This moment is beautiful." You are bringing other moments in and you are comparing. Then other moments were not so beautiful. What type of attainment is this? Where is this elsewhere?

At this Houn slapped his face.

Why did he slap his face? – to bring him to his senses. You need to be slapped many times, because sometimes just an answer won't help, it will create more questions. And when there is a head-oriented person you cannot answer him, because the answer will create many more new questions. The more you answer, the more questions arise. Slapping is needed.

Have you ever observed, if somebody suddenly slaps you, the mind immediately stops for a moment? And when it is unexpected, absolutely unexpected...who would expect such an irrational act? And they had come to see this man off. They were not thinking that he would be rude. He slapped – he tried to bring the disciple back down.

Remember, neither has your consciousness any mind, nor your body. Mind exists just in between; it is a ghost phenomenon. If you are totally in the body, mind disappears. If you become totally conscious, then too mind disappears. If you cannot become totally conscious, then a master will slap you to at least bring you back to the body, because at that moment also there is no mind. That's the beauty and the appeal of sex: it slaps you so deeply that you come back to the body – for a single moment thinking is lost. And that is why in a war people feel very exhilarated, euphoric, because when you are facing death, suddenly you are in the body; the mind has disappeared.

Many things appeal to you only because they give you a shock. A gambler – what is the appeal in gambling? He puts all that he has at stake; now nobody knows what is going to happen. The unexpected is waiting just around the corner. He is thrilled but he cannot think; thinking leaves for a moment. When the dice fall on the table there is no thinking, there is simply waiting. In that waiting there is no mind. The man has come totally to his body.

Mind disappears, and that is the best moment, the most relaxed. But with the body it cannot disappear forever, only for a moment. It is just like when you take a dive into the water. How long can you remain there? You can force yourself to remain a little bit and then you will be out again. You can take a dive into the body – sex is a dive into the body, gambling is a dive into the body, alcohol is a dive into the body. You can take a little dive and then you are back again, more frustrated.

But Zen masters have used slapping because it can make you a little more awake, and in that awakening it is possible to see the man who has slapped you. And he is the answer; no answer can be given. Whenever you ask, the person is the answer. He is bringing you to the body so that mind disappears. And you can look at this person, but you can also miss. If you become too concerned about the slapping and why you were slapped, you are also making a question out of the slapping. Then you miss.

This man is saying, "Please come closer. Stop asking, stop thinking, just look at me." In the shock you can look.

At this Houn slapped his face.

"Why did you do that, dear layman?" asked the disciple, rubbing his cheek.

He is too concerned with the slap. The point is missed, he has made a question out of it; and that was the point – not to make a question out of it but to look at the man who has slapped.

And this Houn was really beautiful at that moment, at his peak; twenty years' effort had come to its culmination. He was moving back into the world; he was returning to the point where mountains and rivers again become mountains and rivers. He had touched the source and was moving to the circumference, to the world, to test whether it is real or not.

It is easy to attain something in an isolated monastery. It is easy to feel that something has been attained there, but the real test lies in the market, in the world, there where the situations are, where the challenges are. Will he be able to stand it?

This man was coming from the source, carrying the freshness, the fragrance of the source. At this moment he was most beautiful; just as fresh as a dewdrop in the morning, as fresh as a new lotus just opening its petals. That is the most beautiful state of consciousness.

He slapped this man in a deep compassion to bring him to feel: Don't bother about questions. I am here. Look at me.

"Why did you do that, dear layman?" asked the disciple, rubbing his cheek.

"How can you pose as a Zen man?" Houn said angrily. "You're doomed to hell."

"How can you pose as a Zen man? You are asking a question as if you know."

Remember, there are two types of questions: one question comes out of ignorance – it is beautiful; and one question comes out of your knowledge – it is ugly. A question that comes out of ignorance can be answered. And a master will help you to find the answer. A question that comes out of your knowledge – you cannot be helped.

That's why Houn said, *"How can you pose as a Zen man? – you are doomed to hell"* – because all those who know without knowing, they are doomed to hell. All scholars, if they don't become alert, aware, and see that they are hiding their ignorance through theories, creating a screen of knowledge around themselves, trying to hide the fact that they don't know but posing as if they do know, are doomed to hell.

A sinner can reach heaven, but it's unheard of for a scholar ever to reach. Because if you think you already know, all doors are closed for knowledge to enter. That's why he said angrily, "You are doomed to hell. How can you pose as a Zen man?"

"And you?" the disciple cried. "What about yourself?"
Houn slapped him again.

Houn is present there, he can be felt. You can drink and eat him in that moment; he can become part of you, he is available.

And this disciple asks, *"And you?" the disciple cried. "What about yourself?"* His ego is hurt: He – and doomed to hell? His ego comes in. The slapping has not awakened him; he has gone deeper into sleep. Now he is in a fighting mood, his anger is arising. And he says, "What about you? Where are you going? I am going to hell, but where are you going?"

Houn slapped him again. "You've eyes, but you won't see," he said over his shoulder as he moved off, "and you have a mouth, but you're dumb."

A man at the peak of his glory..."I am here," he said; "I am here and...*you have eyes, but you won't see, and you have a mouth, but you're dumb."*

A mouth is dumb if it is used by the mind. Then it is just chattering mechanically. A mouth is not dumb when it is not used by mind but by silence. So remember, there are dumb people chattering continuously and there are silent people who really have a mouth, who are not dumb, but they don't chatter. They only say that which they have known, they only say that which can be helpful, they only say that which is needed by you. Talking is not their need; they talk just to help you.

You talk – it is a mad need within you, because you cannot be silent. You go on talking just to avoid silence. Your talk is a monologue. You are not talking to the other, the other is just an excuse; and he also is not talking to you. He is not listening to you, neither are you listening to him. He is posing as if he is listening; he is just waiting for the right moment when he can start talking. He is just waiting for the right link from where he can go on, from where he can take over.

I have heard: A leader had come to a town. Many people gathered to listen to him, but by and by they all left. By the time the leader had finished his talk, only Mulla Nasruddin was left. The leader was very thankful and he said, "I'm very very grateful. I never thought that you were such a lover and such a follower of mine."

Nasruddin said, "I'm not, that is not it. I am the next speaker here, so if you are finished, I should start."

When somebody is listening to you, remember, he is the next speaker; he is just waiting for you to finish. And if you go on and on, he will tell people that you are a bore, but what he really means is that you never gave him a chance to bore. Those people who never give you any chance to start are called bores. They go on and on and on. They never give you a small space so that you can take over.

A master speaks – his words come from his silence, from his inner silence. You speak – your words come from your inner madness. That's why Houn says, "You have eyes, but you won't see." Why can't you see? – because your eyes are filled with many thoughts. Just as if the sky is covered completely by clouds in the rains, you cannot see where the sky is; when thoughts are too many, floating in your eyes, you cannot see. When thoughts are floating too much in your mind, you are dumb.

Be silent. First attain to silence, then your word carries a tremendous force and energy; then whatsoever you say or don't say has a significance, every gesture of yours is a poem. Even if you sit silently you release a tremendous energy around you – it is a communion.

Silence is the source of all energy, but you talk through your madness. You have an obsession with talk. That's why if you are put into isolation for a few days you will start talking to yourself. After the third week you cannot wait anymore for somebody to listen; you start talking to yourself. You cannot wait anymore. Now there is so much talk that it has to be thrown out.

Your talking is a catharsis, it is a cleansing. But why cleanse yourself on others? Why throw your dirt on others? If you want to clean yourself, clean yourself alone. Close your doors and talk to yourself as much as you like. Ask questions and give answers and make it a game. It will be good, because that's all that you are doing anyway. But when you do it with others, you are never aware of what nonsense you are doing. Alone, you will become aware. Do it alone and soon you will realize what you have been doing your whole life.

Then by and by, the more you become aware, the more words disappear, clouds disappear. And when the inner sky is without clouds, when your eyes are without words and thoughts and your mouth is filled with silence, then...then you have eyes, then you have ears, then your senses are completely vacant. They are vehicles, mediums. Then communion is possible.

Enough for today.

Discourse 8

The First Principle

There are some beautiful letters carved over the gate of the Oaku Temple in Kyoto which say: The First Principle. People come from far and near to admire them. The original calligraphy was done on paper by the Master Kosen. When Kosen was drawing the characters there was a pupil standing by who had mixed the ink. "Not so good," said the pupil at Kosen's first try. "That's worse than the first one," said the pupil to the second try. And so it went on. After the sixty-fourth try, the ink was running low, so the pupil went out to mix some more. "Just a quick one with the last of the ink," thought Kosen, "while that pupil is out of the way."

When the pupil returned, he took a good look as this latest effort, and said, "A masterpiece!"

A few things before we enter this beautiful story. First, if you are divided, then a conflict arises not only in the mind but in your bio-energy. Then you are two. And if you are two, the energy is wasted in the conflict; the energy is dissipated. Unless you are one, nothing can be done. As far as the inner journey is concerned, your oneness will be needed more and more. On the surface it is okay; you can go on doing the day-to-day work even if you are divided.

Just imagine a circle with a center: if you draw two lines from the periphery towards the center, on the periphery they are divided; the more you come towards the center, the gap becomes less and less and less. Just near the center the gap is almost not; at the center the gap disappears. At the center everything becomes one; at the periphery everything is divided, is two.

When you are self-conscious you are two, because then you exist at the periphery. When you are not self-conscious you are one, because then you don't exist at the periphery, you exist at the center.

If you are an egoist you are dissipating your energy, because the ego exists at the periphery. The ego exists for others; it has to be on the periphery. When you are totally alone in your innermost being the ego doesn't exist. You are but the ego is not, and when you are without the ego your energy is tremendous. When you are without the ego you are a god. Then you are undivided and the source of energy is infinite.

At the periphery everything is divided, and not only divided but in conflict. It is as if both my hands are fighting – right fights the left, left fights the right. What will happen? Is there any possibility of either hand being victorious? – no possibility, because both hands are mine. The right cannot win because it is mine; the left cannot be defeated – it is mine. Behind both hands I am one, so there is no possibility of any victory. And all victories will be just dreams, pretensions. I can fool myself, I can put my right hand on top of my left and say, "Now the right has won." I can change the situation in a single moment; I can put the left on top of the right and say, "The left has won." This is what you have been doing continuously.

If you fight with yourself there is no victory. Nobody is going to be defeated, nobody is going to win; the whole game is stupid. But one thing is certain: if you go on fighting with yourself you are dissipating energy. The right cannot win, the left cannot win – you will be defeated in the end. It is suicidal, you are destroying yourself.

When you are one you become a creator, when you are two you become suicidal – you destroy yourself. And how do you become two? Whenever self-consciousness arises, you become two. Whenever you look at others and feel, "What do they think about me?" you become two. That's why all that is beautiful cannot happen when you are two. A creator has to forget everything, he has to forget the whole world; only then something from beyond descends.

It is said about one of the greatest poets of India, Rabindranath Tagore, that whenever he was writing or painting a picture he would become so self-unconscious that he would forget to eat, he would forget to drink, he would forget to sleep. Even his wife would come and he would not be able to recognize who was standing in front of him. So whenever he was in a creative mood nobody would disturb him, nobody would come near him, nobody would pass by his house, because he was in such a different state of being that to disturb him could be fatal. For three days, four days, even for a week, he would not eat, he would not 'do' anything. He had become just a vehicle. He was one.

One great English poet, Coleridge, has left only seven poems completed, and he was one of the greatest masters. He left thousands of poems incomplete; forty thousand in all have been calculated, only seven completed. Just before his death somebody asked, "What is the matter with you? The whole house is filled with incomplete poems, and a few poems need just a touch, the last line. Or three lines are there, one line is missing. Why can't you complete them?"

Coleridge is reported to have said, "Who can complete them? I have never written a single word. When I am not, then something descends. Only three lines came; I was waiting for the fourth but it never came. And I cannot complete it because that won't be right.

I cannot complete it because it will come from a different plane of being. I was not when these three lines came, and I would be there too much when the fourth is added. I could add it, but that would be just false. It would be something imposed – it won't have a flow, it won't be authentic, it won't be true. So what can I do? I can simply wait." He waited for certain poems for twenty years, and then the line, the missing line would descend, and he would add it.

It happened: Rabindranath's book Gitanjali, for which he was awarded the Nobel prize, became world famous. He translated it himself – because he wrote in Bengali; the original was Bengali, then he translated it himself. But he was not so confident: it is easy to translate prose, it is very very difficult to translate poetry, even if it is your own, because poetry exists somewhere beyond grammar. It is more music, less language; it is more a feeling, less a thought. It eludes, and that is the beauty of it. You cannot fix it; it is like a river, moving, it is not like a pond. Prose is like a pond, poetry is like a river.

Rabindranath tried. He worked for many days on single pieces. Then he translated it completely. But, not confident, he asked C. F. Andrews for help. C. F. Andrews was one of the colleagues of Mahatma Gandhi; he worked for India's independence very deeply. C. F. Andrews looked through it and he said, "It is wonderful, beautiful! Only at four places would I like to change it, because at four places it is not grammatical." So he changed it at four places, just four words, and Rabindranath was very happy. Andrews said, "It is okay now."

So Rabindranath took it to London. Before it was to be published he called a small gathering of poets at the house of Yeats, one of the great poets of England. Almost twenty poets, all known, had gathered. They listened, then Rabindranath asked, "Do you feel that something is missing?"

Yeats stood and he said, "At four places something is wrong." Rabindranath was surprised. He couldn't believe it because nobody else knew that C. F. Andrews had changed the book at four places. He asked, "What are those four places?" – and they were exactly the same places. Yeats said, "At these four places the flow has stopped. Someone else has put in those four words, not you."

Yeats was a very perceptive poet; he could feel that the river had somewhere become a pond, that someone else from a different plane of being had entered, that something had become like a block; the river was not flowing as easily afterwards as it had been flowing before. There was a stone, a rock somewhere. Grammar is like a rock – it is dead.

Rabindranath then said, "Yes, C. F. Andrews suggested these words, and he is an Englishman, so he knows better. English is not my mother tongue." He added, "These were the four words I had used before Andrews corrected it."

Yeats said, "They are ungrammatical but they are poetic, they have the flow, so forget the grammar and retain the flow."

At the very center, the flow is the thing. Grammar is irrelevant, grammar exists on the surface; at the center, only a flow of energy. A different plane of being is needed. When something from the beyond descends into you, you are needed to be one.

These are the two planes of humanity: duality, the plane of duality, what Hindus call *dwaita,* the plane of two; and non-duality, the plane of one, the plane of the non-dual. When you are divided you are in this world; when you are undivided you have transcended – you are no longer here, you have penetrated into the beyond. Then boundaries meet and the boundaries meet in you. So the whole effort is how to become undivided, how to become one.

Just the other night a girl came to me and she said, "I am already a sannyasin inside." Why divide the outside from the inside? Is there really a division between inside and outside? Where is the demarcation line? Can you draw a line and say, "Beyond this is inside"? Where? – at the body can you draw a line? If the body dies, you die. If the body is not there, where are you? At the mind then? – if the mind becomes unconscious you become unconscious. Who are you without the mind? Where do you divide? – everything is linked.

At the periphery it is outside, at the center it is inside, but the periphery belongs to the center. Can you have a center without a periphery? – then what type of center would that be? The center belongs to the periphery. Can you have a periphery without a center? – they belong to each other. They are just like two banks of a river: the river flows in between and you cannot divide.

You are hungry – you don't say, "Hunger is inside so how can I eat the food which is outside?" You eat the food and the food becomes your blood, and the blood becomes your bio-energy, and your bio-energy becomes your thinking, and your thinking becomes your heart, your feeling, and your feeling becomes your witness, and your witness becomes the divine, the ultimate. There is a subtle digestion on every plane. You take the food, it is outside. The moment you have taken it in, you digest it, the non-essential is thrown out again; the essential moves towards the center. You have digested it; it has become blood, bones, flesh – the body. Then again a digestion takes place; the most subtle of it is again absorbed. It becomes your bio-energy, what scientists call bio-plasma. It becomes electricity in you. But then again a digestion happens; the essential in it is again absorbed inwards – it becomes your thoughts. Thought is subtle electricity. Then again you move inwards. Thinking is digested into feeling – it becomes your heart.

So love is still a more subtle bio-energy than thinking, but that too is not the end. Again, in love, that which is more subtle is absorbed and digested – it becomes your witness, your meditation. It becomes your awareness. But that too is not the end, because the witness is still there, and when the witness is there the division is there. The division has become narrow; you are coming almost to the center but the division is still there. You are a witness – the subject and the object. Of what are you a witness? The division is still there.

Then at the last jump energy has become totally centered; the object and subject disappear. Then there is no witness, then you have gone to the beyond, then you are as if you are not. You are and you are not; you have become the whole. This is the state, the final state, where in one way you are totally, utterly annihilated, and in another way you have become the whole. The son disappears, now you have become the father. Now there is no Christ, just the supreme-most father exists – the son is absorbed. Where will you draw the line between that which is outside and that which is inside?

Many people come to me and they say, "Inside we are already sannyasins, but outside...?" But is there really a division? And if you divide you become two; if you become two, then the conflict arises, the whole game of inner war. An inner politics arises – who is to dominate whom? Either the outside is to dominate the inside, or the inside is to dominate the outside. If the outside dominates the inside you become a materialist. If the inside dominates the outside you become a spiritualist. In either case you are half, you are not whole.

When the outside and inside disappear, nobody dominates anybody, because a domination is not a good state of affairs. The one who dominates will be thrown sooner or later; the oppressors will become the oppressed, and the oppressed will become the oppressors. It is just a fight between your left hand and right hand, and the whole game is a pretense. Remember this paradox: the more you go inwards, the less of the outer there is. When you really reach to the innermost, inner and outer both disappear. Then you are nothing, and everything.

In a school a teacher was asking tricky questions, and then she said, "Charlie Brown, how will you define nothingness?"

Without a single moment's hesitation Charlie Brown said, "Nothingness is a balloon with its skin off."

That is you at the last moment – the skin off...nothingness. But then you have become the whole because the skin was dividing you from the whole.

And where is your skin? Self-consciousness is your skin, the ego is your skin. When the ego is off you become nothing and the whole simultaneously, because they both mean the same thing.

The second thing to be understood: you may have observed in yourself and in others also, that there is a very deep urge to become unconscious; hence the appeal of all types of alcohol, drugs, chemical intoxicants. Puritans cannot understand it, moralists cannot understand it. Why? Preachers go on preaching against it but it has not changed a single person; not a single man has been changed through it. Humanity goes on moving on its path: puritans go on condemning, but nobody listens to them.

It cannot be an ordinary thing, something extraordinary is involved. That's why it is so difficult to try to change an alcoholic – very very difficult, almost impossible. Why is there so much appeal in becoming unconscious? – because self-consciousness is such a disease, it is such a burden. And there are only two ways to go beyond it: one is to fall into unconsciousness, the other is to become superbly conscious. Either move to superconsciousness or move to unconsciousness. Self-consciousness is such a tension, such an anguish and anxiety, so move either to alcohol or move to God.

God and the devil are not opposites really; God and alcohol... If God is supreme consciousness, then unconsciousness is the opposite pole.

I have heard: Once it happened that a social worker who was trying to convert people towards religion and against sin, against alcohol, came to see Mulla Nasruddin. She said, "Last time I came to see you, you were sober, and it made me tremendously happy. But now you are again intoxicated and it makes me very very unhappy."

"True," said Mulla Nasruddin beaming with happiness. He said, "This time it is my turn to be happy."

Alcohol, unconsciousness, may not give you happiness but at least it helps you to forget unhappiness. You forget your anxieties, and through the chemical help you drop the division, the division into two, the self-consciousness.

Self-consciousness is the greatest tension in the mind. That's why sometimes you would like to be alone; you would like to go to the Himalayas and forget the whole society. Society is not the problem, but when the other is present, it is very difficult to be self-unconscious or to be unself-conscious – both are the same. It is difficult when the other is present to forget yourself; the thou creates the I within you, they are two polarities. When nobody is there and you are alone, you feel a certain relaxation. That's why people go to the forests. But then too they become bored, because when you are alone tension is not there, but boredom enters because excitement disappears.

Excitement is a sort of anxiety, anxiety is a sort of excitement. If you are after excitement you cannot be meditative, you cannot move to a solitary place, you cannot move inwards, because there you will be alone and there is no excitement. Excitement needs the other. Alone, how can you be excited? – nothing is happening, how can you be excited? For anything to happen the other is needed. So if you are alone you become bored. If you move with society, live in relationship, then you become much too tense.

So going into loneliness won't help. But if you can drop your self-consciousness while living in society, with others, in relationship, if you can drop your self-consciousness, suddenly there is no tension and no boredom, and life is a constant celebration without any excitement. It is a very silent celebration. It is a joy, but without any excitement. It is a very very cool happiness; it is a deep fulfillment, but without any excitement.

A buddha is so fulfilled, but there is no excitement about it. He's simply fulfilled. He has not achieved anything, nothing new has happened; he has simply become so content with himself. It is a very very cool state of enjoyment – it is a cool state of bliss.

Remember, that is the difference between bliss and happiness: happiness is excitement; bliss is happiness without excitement. If there is excitement, sooner or later you will get bored, because only when the excitement is new is it excitement. But how can you be excited about the same thing again and again? You are excited about a woman or a man, but when the honeymoon is over, then the excitement is also over. Almost always, by the end of the honeymoon a marriage ends. Then there is just a hang-over, because you are looking for excitement and excitement cannot be a continuous phenomenon. Unless your love is cool – not cold remember, but cool; cold is dead, cool is alive, but without any excitement – it is bound to end in boredom.

In the world everything ends in boredom, it has to. When you attain to the innermost core of your being you are happy without any cause, you are happy without any reason, you are happy without any excitement. There will be no boredom. And this is what happens in love also. You need love, because only in love do you become self-unconscious; only in love does the other disappear. There is no need to be 'I'. With someone you love you can be alone. Even if the lover or the beloved is present you can be alone. The deepest possibility in love is that it helps you to drop self-consciousness.

But if you have to continuously carry the other's presence, if you have to behave accordingly, if you have to follow rules, if you have to plan even in love what to say and what not to say, then this love is sooner or later going to turn sour, bitter, because self-consciousness is there.

Wherever you find self-consciousness disappearing – in alcohol, in love, in meditation – you feel good. But alcohol cannot give you a permanent state; love can give that to you, but that possibility is very very difficult. Remember, love is more difficult than meditation because love means living with the other and without the self. Meditation means living with oneself, forgetting the other completely – it is a less difficult dimension than love. That's why those who can love don't need meditation; they will reach through love.

Jesus says: Love is God. But to love is very difficult. It is difficult because the other enters with all his problems. The other is ill, you are ill; and when two ill persons meet illness is not only doubled, it is multiplied. It is very difficult to love, but if you can love then there is no need for any meditation. Love will become your meditation and you will reach through it. If you cannot love, if you feel it difficult, then meditation is the only door. Only one in a million reaches through love; others reach through meditation. Once you become meditative love also becomes easy; then you can love. If you love, then meditation comes as a shadow of it.

You have to decide how to drop your self-consciousness. There are two methods: one is through love, relationship, living with the other and growing. It is a difficult path, very very arduous – there is nothing more difficult than that. And the other is living in meditation. You have to choose.

If you grow in love, meditation will happen like a shadow. Love and meditation are two aspects of the same coin; if you have gained control of the one aspect, the other follows. If you meditate, love will follow; if you love, meditation will follow. This you have to choose. Meditation is easier, love is difficult. Unless you want to move into the difficult unnecessarily – that is for you to decide; otherwise with meditation love comes automatically. This is my feeling: that ninety-nine persons in one hundred have to go through meditation, then love will happen. Only one percent can go through love and meditation happens. This is the state of affairs, this is how things are. But one thing is certain, that in either case self-consciousness is to be dropped.

Now try to understand this story.

There are some beautiful letters carved over the gate of the Oaku Temple in Kyoto which say: The First Principle. People come from far and near to admire them. The original calligraphy was done on paper by the Master Kosen.

Zen uses all types of skills to grow into meditation; calligraphy is one of them. If you have seen Japanese or Chinese calligraphy, you will become aware of a certain quality – there is flow. No other language can do that, because every other language has an alphabet. These far eastern languages – Chinese, Japanese – don't have an alphabet. They are pictorial languages: not the pen, but the brush is used, and the flow is the quality.

So a calligraphy is not only that which is written, it also carries something of the master who has done it – the flow. Change is not allowed, you cannot correct it; you have simply to do it in one stroke. A very skilled master, a very mindful state is needed. You cannot change it, you cannot correct it. If you correct it, the whole point is lost, because then the ego enters. You simply have to flow with it.

These are pictures, and the basic thing is not that which is written, the basic thing is that which is hidden. You will be surprised: on the gate of a temple only these words are written – The First Principle. What type of message is that? – The First Principle. It says nothing. If you go and read these words, 'the first principle', what does it say? There is no message in it.

The first principle is 'flow'; it is not written, these words are just an indirect way. If you look at the calligraphy, there is the first principle, the flow. If you can flow, if your energy can flow without any blocks, you will achieve. But the moment you become self-conscious a block enters, immediately. It is just like falling into sleep: if you become self-conscious you cannot fall into sleep. Now the West is suffering from insomnia, and sooner or later the whole world will suffer, because sleep needs self-unconsciousness.

And yet the whole civilization teaches you how to be more self-conscious. Walk, do, move in life – the whole training is how to be a subtle egoist. Western psychology says that a mature ego is needed; the whole Eastern effort is that a mature egolessness is needed. In fact, when you become egoless, only then are you mature, never before.

Ego is a juvenile phenomenon. It is childish, it is foolish, it is idiotic, because through ego you simply cut yourself off from the universal flow; then you are no longer a part of it. It is as if a wave in the ocean says, "I am total, I do not belong to the ocean – I have nothing to do with the ocean. I am separate." Ego is separation, and whenever a wave says, "I am separate," the wave is foolish. The wave is one with the ocean; the ocean 'waves' in it.

Real maturity is to attain an egolessness, a balloon with the skin off; then you are fully mature, a buddha, one who is now awakened. Western psychology teaches that you should become a mature ego. It is good – if you are attaining it just to throw it, then it is good, because you can throw a thing only when you have it. So it is good: attain an ego, but don't get caught in it. It is something to be attained and thrown. It is something you have to get, because if you don't have an ego, how will you achieve surrender?

This has been a constant problem for me. Eastern people come to me: Indians, Japanese, they can surrender very easily. They are almost ready to surrender, but they have nothing to surrender. Western people come to me: they are very very antagonistic to surrender, and they have something to surrender. If they surrender they will grow. And Eastern people, before they surrender something they have to attain a mature ego.

Remember, only that which you have can be surrendered. If you don't have an ego, what are you going to surrender? Western psychology takes the first step and Eastern religion takes the last. They are complementary. Unless Western psychology and Eastern religion meet, man is going to remain in trouble.

What is in these words, 'the first principle'? They say nothing. But 'the first principle' is not the point, the words are not the point. The point is, the point was, for the master to make them with such a flow that not even a touch of self-consciousness is in them. Whosoever loves to read between lines will be able to read at this temple gate.

And why at the gate? – because that is the gate of the temple. If you are self-conscious you cannot enter a temple; that is the first principle. If you have self-consciousness, an egoist mind, you cannot enter the temple. If you drop your self-consciousness, only then you can enter.

And what is a temple? – it is an emptiness. It is nothing surrounded by walls, it is an emptiness. You drop the ego outside. This was the problem for the master: to write these three words in such a flow that while he was writing them, not even a single touch of the self entered into them. Difficult, because you will not be able to judge this unless you know how self-consciousness can destroy the flow. The first principle is to be in such a flow that 'I' is no block; you simply live in a let-go.

Nothing is like Japanese or Chinese calligraphy; no language can do that, only they can do it – pictorial, flowing, doing it with a brush. Years of training are needed. First a man has to be taught the skill of calligraphy, and that alone won't do because just skill is not the point. A very egoist person can become very skillful but that is not the point.

So first one has to learn calligraphy for years, and then the master says, "Now drop it. For a few years forget about it." For three or four years the disciple has to forget about it. He will do other things: gardening, cleaning, many millions of things, but not calligraphy. He has to completely forget it so that the skill doesn't remain in the ego, on the surface, but the skill settles and settles, and settles at the center, reaches to the very bottom of the river.

Then the master says, "Now – now you can do calligraphy. But do it without any self-consciousness, do it as if you are not the doer, as if someone else is doing it through you; you become just instrumental and just move with the energy." That was the point, and it was going to be on the gate.

The original calligraphy was done on paper by the Master Kosen. When Kosen was drawing the characters there was a pupil standing by who had mixed the ink.

...standing by who had mixed the ink. The ink has to be mixed fresh constantly; ready-made ink is not used. These are all symbolic things – everything should be fresh, moving in the moment. A pupil stands by who goes on preparing the ink, and the master goes on doing the calligraphy.

But when the pupil saw the first calligraphy complete, he said, "Not so good." At Kosen's first try this became the problem: immediately the master became aware of the disciple, that he was standing there judging, looking. And when somebody is judging it is very difficult to remain self-unconscious. He became self-conscious – a slight tremor in the hand, a slight fear, a slight effort, because somebody was going to judge – he became afraid, a slight nervousness entered him.

Mulla Nasruddin was invited to speak in a ladies' club. A woman entered the room and asked Nasruddin, "Are you feeling nervous?" – because he was just about to speak in a few minutes.

Nasruddin said, "No, I have never felt nervous, never in my life!" – but he was trembling as he spoke.

The woman said, "Then what are you doing here in the ladies room?" Nervous, he had not noticed that he was in a ladies' room. He was not conscious, he was walking up and down.

When you are nervous you are not yourself. When you are self-conscious, you are not your true self; you are afraid, there is a slight trembling inside because others are going to judge whether they appreciate you or not – a fear has entered.

I have heard about one Zen master, Bokuju, that he would talk to his disciples even though sometimes the disciples would not come at the right time. He would start talking and there was no one to listen. Sometimes he would talk for so long that the disciples would simply disappear, but he would continue.

I have known a man in my own life. I had a teacher, a rare teacher. I was the only student in his subject, so he told me, "Remember one thing, because I don't follow rules; when I am speaking I cannot remember time, so if you feel uneasy or you would like to go to the bathroom, simply go and don't disturb me. And then return silently, sit and I will continue. While you are gone I cannot disrupt my flow, so it is for you to go and come, but don't disturb me. And don't wait, because nobody knows when I will stop. I may start when the bell rings, but I cannot stop, because how can the bell control me? Starting by it is okay, but stopping? If something is incomplete, how can I stop? – I will have to complete it. So if you are fed-up or bored, simply go."

I tried many times – I would be outside up to half an hour, and when I returned he would be speaking and there was nobody there.

This type of man cannot be nervous because he is not bothered about whether somebody is listening or not; he was not bothered about whether somebody was judging him or not. But Kosen was bothered; he was not yet a perfect master. This shows that he was more interested in the judgment of others than in doing his own thing. He was not yet centered. He was almost at the center, approximately he had reached, but something was missing.

"Not so good," said the pupil at Kosen's first try. "That is worse than the first one," said the pupil to the second try. And so it went on.

He must have become more and more worried

After the sixty-fourth try, the ink was running low, so the pupil went out to mix some more. "Just a quick one with the last of the ink," thought Kosen, "while that pupil is out of the way."

The pupil was outside, so while he was out of the way Kosen wanted to give it a last try. Because when the pupil was out Kosen was not self-conscious; nobody was there to judge.

"Just a quick one with the last of the ink while that pupil is out of the way."

When the pupil is out of the way, the ego is also out of the way. While the pupil is out Kosen is also out. Because of the pupil, Kosen could not not be; because of the pupil he had to be there. When the pupil was out of the way, Kosen was also out of the way – the passage was clear, there was nobody. The pupil and Kosen had both disappeared.

When the pupil returned, he took a good look at this latest effort, and said, "A masterpiece!"

How had it happened? Sixty-four times he failed and the sixty-fifth time he attained. How did it happen? – sixty-four times he was there to do it; the last time he was not there to do it – it had been done by the beyond. When you are not, the beyond functions; when you are, the beyond cannot function because you are in the way.

Not only did this calligraphy become a masterpiece, but through this calligraphy Kosen became a perfect master. Never again could anybody bother him, never again was he nervous, never again was he self-conscious – never again! This became a revelation, a realization. He could see through and through what the problem was: it was not the pupil, it was he himself; it was not his eye and judgment, it was his own ego.

Remember this, because a moment will come in your meditation when only you will be in your way, nobody else. A moment is bound to come in your own growth also when everything is clear and only you are in the way. So never think about what others are thinking about your meditation. Never think about others – why they are judging you, how they are judging you. Their judgment is their affair; it is their business, it has nothing to do with you. You do your thing and do it totally. Efface yourself utterly, then everything starts happening.

The moment the doer leaves, everything starts happening. The doer is the problem if meditation is not happening; you are still doing it. Let it happen. You are still a doer, you are still watching how and what others are thinking, whether they will judge you mad. If their judgment is in your mind you cannot be total, you are divided.

Only the ego thinks about others, because it depends on others. It is nothing but a collection of others' opinions, what others say about you. You are continuously on display, an exhibitionist: "What are others thinking, what are others saying?" Because of these others your ego remains, becomes more and more solid, crystallized.

Have you ever observed that whenever you are not thinking of others and not thinking of what they think about you, suddenly you have a different flow of energy within you, an unblocked flow? – there is no block and the river flows to the ocean. And then whatsoever you do becomes a masterpiece – whatsoever! Your quality is now totally different. Now you exist on a different plane altogether, and whatsoever you do, even a very small thing, becomes totally different. It becomes The First Principle.

If you are total, even just if you remove your shoes before you enter this house, you remove them in a different way. It becomes The First Principle. If a calligraphy, just three words, 'the first principle', can become a great message, why not shoes? The way you walk becomes the first principle. You walk unself-consciously – you walk like an animal, like a bird, or you sit under a tree and you sit like a tree, unself-conscious. And then suddenly many millions of things start flowering within you. The only problem is that you are, and the only solution is that you should not be there.

Just give way; don't stand there, just give way, just put yourself aside. Difficult – that's why it is the first principle. But once you can do it the temple is opened, you have entered. There is nobody blocking the way except you.

Look at how you do things and you will always find the ego. People saying prayers always look around; go to a mosque and watch, go to a temple and watch. If many people are there, then people say their prayer with a fervor. If there is nobody to look at them they simply do it in haste, as if the prayer is not addressed to God but to the bystanders, to the onlookers.

This is happening continuously whatsoever you do. You are not enjoying the act, you are enjoying others' opinions. And what value does it carry, what is the meaning in it? Why are you here? – just to be judged by others that you are a very good man, a religious man, a meditator, a seeker after truth? Truth doesn't seem to be so important as others saying that you are a great seeker after truth.

People come to me every day. I watch. Something is happening to someone's back, maybe just a backache. He comes to me, and if I say, "It is nothing but a backache, go to the doctor," he doesn't feel very good. If I say, "It is your kundalini rising," and look at his face, he feels very happy, tremendously happy. And in a hundred cases, ninety-nine cases are backache. He says, "Something is happening in the third eye." But it is nothing, just a headache. But if I say, "Go and take aspirin" or something, he simply feels badly. I see it in his face. He had come for something else, for recognition that he is growing, that he is reaching somewhere. Through headaches no one has ever reached. Not only does headache have to be left behind but the head itself.

Watch yourself, be alert to what you are doing. Don't be a fool, and don't befool yourself. It is so easy to, but the ultimate can happen only when this foolishness disappears. Nothing will help...unless you want to go on accumulating more junk around your ego. Watch whatsoever you do and remain alert. Don't go on moving like a somnambulist and don't try to seek any recognition from others. Just be alert and watch and wait, and the ultimate will happen to you. Because through watching you will disappear. Through forgetting about others you will forget your own ego.

Even with God people have the same relationship – they pray loudly just to get some recognition from the ultimate. Because no recognition can come from that source, they have created mid-agencies: priests, popes. They can give you recognition. God never recognizes you; God recognizes you only when you are not, and that's the trouble. That's why priests exist: they can give you recognition. They can tell you, "Yes, you are growing." If you are growing, there is no need to ask anybody; the growth will speak for itself, and even if the whole world denies it, it doesn't matter. If you are growing, the growth itself will say; you will feel it, you will be fulfilled through it. You will not go asking. God gives no recognition to you. That's why in this century we have said that God is dead. If he doesn't give us recognition, how can he be alive? If he does not come and give us a certificate, how can he be alive? He should recognize us – only then....

We would like to carry our egos to the very end, because he is not there to affirm. But unless you also become a nobody like him, there is no possibility of meeting him. We have created priests, great churches; they give you certificates.

I know a man: he is the head priest of a small Mohammedan community in India. He gives a letter – exactly, literally a letter – he writes a letter referring a man's name who is going to die to God, saying that he has donated this much and he has done that much, and this and that, so "Take care of him." The letter has to be put into the grave with the man. And people feel very, very happy; they donate, they give money, they fast, they pray, just to get a big certificate. You are lying in your grave and the letter will remain there.

I was speaking to this community once. I told them, you just go and dig up your old graves and you will find those letters there. But they were afraid to dig, because if they were to find the letters there, then the whole edifice would fall. Then what to do? Then who would give them recognition?

Don't ask for recognition, because all recognition is the effort of the ego. Don't look at others, just watch yourself. When you grow, you know. When you flower, you know. When you are blessed you will know. If you grow there is no possibility not to know; it is absolutely certain that you will know. But because in our lives we continuously live with others, always looking in their eyes, at how they feel, at how they think about us, we go on and on. Then the habit becomes a fixed pattern. When you move into the other world you carry the same habit.

Just a few days ago one man came to me and he said, "I have become enlightened."

I said, "It is very good, now everything is finished. Why have you come to me?"

He answered, "Just to check." What type of enlightenment is this that you are not certain of it?

There was a case against Mulla Nasruddin, because he was drunk, he had insulted somebody, so he was taken to court. The magistrate said, "Nasruddin, are you here again? Are you guilty or not?"

Nasruddin said, "Guilty, your honor, but I would like to be tried to make certain." Nobody is certain even about himself, and everybody is looking at the other.

Once it happened that Mulla Nasruddin's four-year-old child asked him, "Daddy, why did you marry Mummy?"

Mulla Nasruddin stared at the child for a few seconds and said, "So you also are not certain why? You also are asking why? I am also not certain." He added, "If you can find out someday why I married your Mummy, please tell me."

You live in an uncertainty; your only certainty is others' recognition. When you start moving to the beyond this is not needed. And that is the temple, and the first principle is at the door: drop yourself, drop yourself utterly. You cannot be allowed to enter. When you are not, then you are allowed. Then you flow into the temple; then there is no blockage of energy.

Try it. Be watchful and move in the world as if you are alone – there is nobody. Move in the world as if it is a total loneliness – there is nobody. If nobody is there your self-consciousness will drop by and by. Then the pupil will be out, and with the pupil you also will have gone out.

"Just a quick one with the last of the ink," thought Kosen, "while that pupil is out of the way."

When the pupil returned he took a good look at this latest effort, and said, "A masterpiece!"

If you can put yourself out of the way, your whole being will say, "A masterpiece!" You become the masterpiece. There are two types of creators in the world: one type of creator works with objects – a poet, a painter, they work with objects, they create things; the other type of creator, the mystic, creates himself. He doesn't work with objects, he works with the subject; he works on himself, his own being. And he is the real creator, the real poet, because he makes himself into a masterpiece.

You are carrying a masterpiece hidden within you, but you are standing in the way. Just move aside, then the masterpiece will be revealed.

Everyone is a masterpiece, because God never gives birth to anything less than that. Everyone carries that masterpiece hidden for many lives, not knowing who they are, and just trying on the surface to become someone. Drop the idea of becoming someone because you already are a masterpiece. It cannot be improved. You have only to come to it, to know it, to realize it. God himself has created it; it cannot be improved.

Here, I'm not teaching you to improve your life – no, not me. I am simply teaching you to know the life that is already there, that has always been there, that is already the case. Just put yourself aside so your eyes are not filled with the ego, your being is not cloudy, and the sky becomes open. Suddenly, not only you but the whole existence says, "A masterpiece!" This is The First Principle.

Enough for today.

九

Discourse 9

The Practical Joke

An old man who was born in Yen but grew up in Chu'u decided to return to his native country. While he was passing through the state of Chin his companions decided to play a joke on him. Pointing to a city they said to him, "This is the capital of Yen." The old man composed himself and looked solemn. Inside the city they pointed out a shrine: "This is the shrine of your quarter." He breathed a deep sigh. They pointed out a hut: "This was your father's cottage." Tears welled up. They pointed out a mound: "This is your father's tomb." He could not help weeping aloud. His companions roared with laughter: "We are teasing you – you are still only in Chin." The old man was very embarrassed.

When he reached Yen and really saw the capital and the shrine of his quarter and his father's cottage and tomb, he did not feel it so deeply.

Your whole world is in your mind. Or rather, your whole world *is* your mind; nothing else exists. Whatsoever you see is a projection. Whatsoever you feel is also a projection. That's why Hindus have always been saying that the world is illusory. It is a mirage; it appears but it is not there. And how can this illusion be transcended?

If you can understand it as an illusion you are already on the way to transcending it. If a dream is realized as a dream you are already moving away from it, you are awakening.

The world that you see is not the reality, because the reality can be seen only when there is no mind. With a mind in between, the reality cannot be seen, it is colored. You project your mind on it – it becomes a screen.

You see a woman as very very beautiful; others don't see that beauty at all. Does the beauty belong to the woman or to your mind? If it belongs to the woman, then everybody would see her as beautiful. But you can find people who will look at her and will be simply disgusted, you can find people who will not become in any way aware that she is beautiful. And you think that the woman is beautiful – so where is beauty? Is it in the woman or in your mind? Is it objective or just a subjective phenomenon?

It happened once: I was sitting near the Ganges in Allahabad with a friend. We were talking of God, of meditation, when suddenly the friend lost contact with whatsoever we were saying. I also felt that something had happened, so I asked, "What has happened? – because you are no longer here."

He said, "I cannot be. Look!" Just near the bank a woman was taking a bath, but we couldn't see her face. Her back was towards us, a very slender, proportionate body with long hair. And the friend was too much excited – he *was* excitement. He said, "Wait, I cannot talk about God and meditation right now, it is impossible. I will have to go and look at this woman. The body seems to be so beautiful and proportionate."

So I said, "You go and be finished." You can imagine the romance that was in his step. He walked filled with an illusion, a projection. He walked very softly and delicately, but when he reached her he suddenly became sad. He came back, and I asked, "What happened?"

He said, "She is not a woman at all. He is a sannyasin with long hair." But for a moment he was in a dream....

But he could have been a homosexual; then just the opposite would have been the case. If she had been a woman, useless. Then the sannyasin, a beautiful male body, would have become the poetry within him.

A homosexual exists in a different world, his projection is different. A heterosexual exists again in a totally different world, his projection is also different. Then there are auto-erotic people who do not bother about homosexuality or heterosexuality; they are so confined to their own bodies – they exist in a totally different world. And there are people who have transcended sex; they exist in a totally different world. So the world is not out there, it is somewhere within you.

Then there is a point when there is no mind: this world that you have known up to now simply disappears. Not that nothing remains, not that everything dissolves into nothingness – no. But all that you have known simply disappears, and the unknown is faced for the first time. The world is a projection, existence is not. When the world disappears, existence is there in its absolute glory – magnificent! But now it is not a projection because there is no projector inside. Mind is a projector – watch it, because this is one of the roots of all your misery...and all your happiness also.

A man who understands is neither happy nor unhappy, he is neither in anguish nor in bliss – and that is the bliss. He simply exists without any projection. Nothing can make him more happy, nothing can make him more unhappy. He is simply in a deep contentment for the first time – nothing disturbs – and he can see what existence is.

Those who have seen in such a way, without the mind, say that the world is not, God is. The world is a projection; God is not a projection, God is the reality. And you have been missing it. You have been missing through the projections; you see something else, what you would like to see.

A woman doesn't exist, a man doesn't exist. Woman exists because you are sexual. If within you sex disappears, woman disappears. But there will be somebody – your wife will not simply disappear into thin air. She will be there but she will no longer be a wife, and she will not be a woman. Suddenly all projections disappear, and there is God. Your wife becomes a god, your child becomes a god, the tree becomes a god, the rock becomes a god. Existence is God. Existence is divine – but that you cannot see, because that is the screen on which your projections are being imposed.

That's why buddhas have always said that if you have any desires you cannot know the truth – because your desire will color it. If you want to achieve something you will not be able to know reality. The very effort to achieve something – a desire – will color it. When you are desireless, when you are not in any way ambitious, when you are not moving to achieve something, when you are simply a being, totally still and quiet, then suddenly the reality appears to you.

So this is the mechanism: you and the reality, and in between these two, the mind. This is the mechanism of the unreal, the illusory, *maya*. You and the reality and no more mind in between – suddenly, all that is there is revealed, all mysteries open. But when the mind drops the bridge drops, you and reality become one because now there is no dividing line. Right now, you are there, the mind is there and the world is there: the trinity that all the religions have talked about – the father, the son, the holy ghost. Hindus call it *trimurti*. You must have seen the three images of Brahma, Vishnu, Mahesh – three faces together. These three faces disappear, because these three faces are illusory. Hidden just behind these three faces is one. With that one there is no object, no subject; you simply see whatsoever is. That which is, is revealed. But to come to this understanding you will have to understand your illusions, and you have known many. But you never learn anything.

Somebody asked a very old Sufi mystic, Bayazid, when he was

dying on his bed, "Would you like to say something about man so he can be profited by it?"

He said, "One thing: man never learns."

You have passed through many experiences, and what have you learned? You remain the same, you go on playing the same game. Have you watched this, that you remain the same? Situations may differ, but the game remains the same.

You fall in love with one woman. The moment you fall in love, you cannot believe that a moment will come when this love will disappear – you cannot believe it! It is simply impossible to think that your love can disappear. Then it disappears, then you are fed-up with the woman. The same woman was your dream, your desire; if you had not possessed her you would have cried and wept your whole life. You possessed her, you achieved, and sooner or later the boredom sets in. You are fed-up, you would like to escape. In that moment you never think back. You never move backwards and see that this is the same woman that you were mad for. One day you were mad to get her, now you are mad to get away from her. One day you were thinking that this was the most beautiful person in the world, and now this same person is the most disgusting. How often do husbands think of killing their wives? How often do wives think of killing their husbands? How often do children, small children, think of killing their parents?

A small boy came back home from school and he was very sad. The mother asked, "What is the matter? Why are you so sad?"

He said, "There was a psychoanalyst in our school. He came to test all the boys, and I am the only abnormal one, so I am sad."

The mother said, "What is your abnormality? What has he said?"

The boy said, "He asked a question, that the children should write whether they would like to kill their parents or not, and I am the only one who wrote no. Everybody else wrote yes, so the psychoanalyst said, 'You are the only abnormal child. Every child wants to kill his parents.'"

A moment comes when the lover would like to kill the beloved; and she was the goal of all his desires, of all his dreams, of all his poetry. How happily he was thinking of being with her, but it was only in the dreams. Reality is difficult – it destroys, shatters all dreams. Now he wants to get rid of her, and he will never learn anything. Sooner or later he will fall in love again with another woman, and the same thing will be repeated again. The same, with no difference. Again he will think that this is the most beautiful person. Again he will think that now there is no need to seek anybody else, now he is fulfilled, he has got the right person. And he will not be able to see that this is the same pattern. Within a few days again he is finished; again the search starts – somebody else.

Do you ever learn anything? Have you ever learned anything? And if you don't learn, how can you become mature? And if you don't learn and you repeat the vicious circle again and again, it becomes more and more solid within you, reaches to your very foundations. This is the state of ignorance.

If you start learning, then the circle breaks from somewhere. Then you start seeing the whole pattern of your mind, how it functions – first in love, then fed up, then again in love, then fed up: the circle revolves. And if you understand it, suddenly one day the very understanding of its nonsense brings you out of it. Nothing is to be done; you have just to understand, you have just to learn through life.

Move. Have as many experiences as possible, because experience is the only school. Move and don't be afraid; but learn – just moving won't do. You have been moving and traveling; that won't help. If you just go on moving in an unconscious way things become more and more engraved. You become almost a robot, you become predictable; everything can be said about you. That is why astrology exists, not because anybody knows what stars say, not because anybody knows what is written in your hand, no. Astrology exists because you are predictable, you move in a vicious circle.

One young girl was showing her hand to a gypsy woman. The

woman looked at her hand and said, "You have fallen in love" ...the girl was surprised because she had been hiding the fact from everybody..."and the man you have fallen in love with is six feet three inches in height." She was even more surprised: exactly! "...And he has black hair, long flowing black hair." Now it was unbelievable! Then the gypsy girl said, "On his right thigh he has the small mark of some wound."

It was too much, so she said, "How can you know these things through the hand?"

The gypsy said, "Who is knowing it through the hand? It is because of your wedding ring! That wedding ring was mine three years ago."

You are predictable because you move in a certain pattern, and everybody moves in a certain pattern. If you say just anything to anybody, there is a fifty percent chance of its being right, and fifty percent is too much. Astrologers are just clever, nothing else, just cunning. They go on talking and just watching you, how you are feeling. They feel the right track just by your face, because you are nodding. You also have a very subtle nod when you say yes inside.

A doctor comes to check me, a very good man. But I need not ask him anything because he goes on nodding or saying no inside. If he checks my chest he nods. Then I say to myself, okay, no need to ask him – a very subtle nod. He will take my blood-pressure and he will nod but he is not aware.

You also are not aware that when you show your hand to somebody you are making indications: Yes, this fits. When a line fits then you are caught, because now you will move robot-like on that line. You become predictable. Only for a few minutes in the beginning is the palmist in a puzzle, just a few seconds. Once he catches the scent, once he finds the line on which you have been moving, once you nod, you are caught. Now he can go on saying things and they will fit. You are a robot. Only when you become enlightened do you become unpredictable. Then no astrologer can say anything about you.

One astrologer came to see me in Bombay, a very famous man. We were discussing and he was saying, "No, this is a science."

I said, "You do one thing: you predict one year for me and I will contradict it completely. If you say that I will not die I will die; if you say that I will die I will not die. You predict one year and then decide."

He said, "Okay, I will come back." He never came again. I inquired many times, because before that he often came.

But things can be said about you because you move like a mechanism. You cannot change, you are in a grip. If you have fallen in love, you will say the same things that you have said to other girls.

Mulla Nasruddin fell in love with a woman. He said, "You are the most lovely person in the world."

The girl felt great, of course. She became very happy, flattered. Looking at her face, Nasruddin said, "Wait!...because I have been telling other women this also."

You are the same – just watch. When you fall in love you repeat yourself exactly, *exactly!* Not a single thing changes.

Mulla Nasruddin divorced his wife, and after twelve years they met at a function. By accident they were sitting side by side when Nasruddin became very drunk. He had been drunk the day he proposed to this woman, and again he was drunk. He said, "What about one more try? – can we get married again?"

The woman said, "Over my dead body!"

Nasruddin laughed and he said, "You have not changed a little bit."

She had said exactly the same thing thirty years before when they got married, and exactly the same situation was repeated on that day also: they met at a function, accidentally sitting by each other's side, and Mulla Nasruddin became very drunk, so he proposed. No man can propose if he is not drunk. How can he propose? And that day also the woman had said, "Over my dead body!"

Just go back, just see, watch. You may have missed the moment of watching but you can do one thing – you can relive it. It is also easier. Reliving is a very beautiful process, a great and deep meditation. If you can live with full awareness in the moment, then there is no need. But you cannot; right now it is not possible. So do one thing – relive. Just close your eyes every night before you go to sleep and go back. Don't remember, relive! When you remember you stand aloof; that won't help. Just relive the whole moment.

You are proposing to a woman; what are you saying? What did you say exactly? Say it again, move into the situation again, become the young man you were. And the woman – look at her, as beautiful as she was that day. Move slowly...and you will see many women, and the same.

That's why Hindus say the world is a wheel. The word *samsar* which Hindus use for 'the world' means a wheel. The symbol on the Indian national flag is a wheel. That symbol is taken from Buddha, because Buddha said that the world is like a wheel. And you are clinging to the wheel, and you go on moving with the wheel.

Become aware that you are repeating. Repetition is unconscious. Become aware that you have been behaving like a robot, not like a man. Become aware. Go back and watch, relive the moments and see that you have been doing the same thing again and again – the same anger, then again the repentance; the same marriage, and again the divorce; the same falling in love, and then getting fed-up. If you can see and watch the repetitiveness of your life, the very understanding that you have been repeating will become a consciousness. Next time you propose to another woman you will feel a sudden surge of energy in you, and you will be able to see and feel: no more repetition. Then things will be different.

Learn through life, otherwise things are not going to be different. Everybody thinks, "This time it is going to be different." You are not different so how is it going to be different this time? And if you observe closely you will see that not only do you repeat, you fall in love again and again with the same type of man or woman, the same type. It has to be so.

I have heard about one man who was divorced eight times. And then he suddenly became aware: "What is happening to me? Is somebody playing a joke or what? – because I always fall in love with the same type of woman again."

Nobody is playing a joke...because you are choosing, and if you remain the same and you have not learned, how can you choose another type of woman? Again the same type of woman will appeal to you. You will again fall in love with the same type of woman, then the same circle will be repeated. Eight or eighty times, it makes no difference. If you remain the same you will do the same; you will again find the same person first appealing, then disgusting.

Learn! Learn through life – and the greatest lesson is that you don't see reality as it is. You project on it, and when you project you are bound to be frustrated sooner or later, because the reality cannot adjust to your projection. How can the reality adjust to your projection? Who are you? You have to adjust to reality, reality has not to adjust to your projection. That's why you are in misery – because you feel every time that something goes wrong. Nothing goes wrong. You start with a dream and the reality doesn't believe in your dream, that's all. How can you force reality to adjust to your dream?

I see a door in the wall – my dream – and then I start walking through it. I am hurt. Not that the wall is there to hurt me; the wall is absolutely unconcerned. If I see a door in the wall I will be hurt, because the wall is not going to concede to my dream.

Reality is vast; it is the whole. You are just a part and you will only become mature when you stop making this absurd effort. And this is what I call sannyas – a man, a woman who has come to realize that, "The reality cannot adjust to my dreams, so I will adjust to reality." Immediately, a revolution happens. You are childish if you go on trying again and again to make reality adjust to your demands, dreams, desires – to you. Who are you? But this fallacious notion comes up.

When a child is born the mother is the only reality. He is in contact only with the mother and every desire is fulfilled: he is hungry and mother gives him milk; he is thirsty and water is given; he is feeling wet, the clothes are changed; he is not feeling warm, a blanket is put over him – everything is fulfilled. And every child is a dreamer, has to be. The child starts feeling as if he is the center of the world – he is here to demand and the world is there to fulfill. If you continue in it you remain a child.

I see people not growing at all. They reach their graves, but in fact they have remained in their cradles, still playing with toys, still dreaming. Then they weep and cry because the reality doesn't bother about them; then they feel frustrated, they feel aggressive, they feel that everywhere something is going wrong and against them – as if the reality is your enemy.

It is neither enemy nor friend – it is neither. If you are aware, it becomes your friend; if you are unaware, it proves to be your enemy. In itself it is neither. Reality has no prejudice about you, as a friend or an enemy. Reality simply exists there in all its purity. It is up to you. If you start fighting with it, it becomes your enemy; if you start adjusting to it, if you start accepting it, if you start flowing with it, not upstream but wherever it leads – if you simply leave yourself to it...this is trust, this is *shraddha*, faith.

Science is conflict, religion is trust. What in fact is science? – it is an effort to make reality according to human dreams. It may seem in the beginning that you are succeeding, but sooner or later the success itself proves to be the greatest failure. Wherever science has succeeded it has come to failure – wherever! It has changed the whole biosphere, and now ecological problems have come up. Whatsoever science has done will have to be undone sooner or later. Wherever it succeeds it proves to be a failure. Man is not getting happier; this century is the most unhappy century in the whole history of man. Never before has man been so unhappy. And man has succeeded so much, but succeeded in something which is basically wrong.

You are forcing, you are aggressive. Science is like a rape on nature. You can rape a woman but that is not a success; that is not a success at all, that is a failure. Only a man who has failed completely will try rape. One who cannot love will try rape, but rape is not love. Love is when the woman opens herself, surrenders, yields, becomes receptive, celebrates, dances; but then it is not aggression.

Religion is like love, science is like rape. The whole of nature is suffering because of this rape, and it is only a childish effort. You will not see an old ancient country being scientific, no. They have come to that point many times, and they have realized many times that it is childish.

In India, five thousand years ago, a war happened. They call it Mahabharata, the Great Indian War. If somebody reads about it and analyzes it deeply, it seems they had again come to invent all the weapons we have invented. They had something like the H-bomb, because the description of the destruction is so vast that it could not have been done otherwise. They destroyed the whole country – not only the whole country, the whole world. That time, that moment in history, has now almost become a myth because no record exists. The destruction was so vast, so total, that all the records were lost. After that, India has not tried again to be scientific. It was such a failure. It proved to be destructive, nothing else. Now in the West we are again reaching that culmination point.

But remember, the whole effort is wrong because of a basic thing, and the basic thing is that you try to force reality according to your dreams. Who are you and what is your dream? You are here for a few days, the reality exists beginningless. You will disappear from here again and the reality will exist eternally. Who are you? – a dream which exists in reality for seventy years. Seventy years is nothing for reality – and then, a dream within the dream which tries to force reality to fall according to itself. All utopians are foolish, childish.

Those who know have come to know that, "The reality cannot be changed; the only thing that can be changed is me." And if one changes, suddenly one can see: this is the wall and that is the door. Then there is no effort to pass through the wall, one moves through the door. Reality becomes a friend.

In the West humanity now feels man to be a stranger, not at home. If you fight with reality you are bound to feel, someday or other, that you are a stranger – not only a stranger, but that the reality is against you. In the East we have always felt that man is at home; reality is the mother, reality is the womb. We are not strangers, we are not enemies; reality loves us, that's why we are here. Reality creates us because reality loves us, and we are at home.

But you will not feel that 'at homeness' unless you try to learn one basic thing: drop your dreams. You live according to your dreams and you prove to be a fool in the end. This story is just to show this: how projection affects you. Let us try to understand it.

An old man who was born in Yen but grew up in Chu'u decided to return to his native country.

While he was passing through the state of Chin his companions decided to play a joke on him.

Pointing to a city they said to him, "This is the capital of Yen."

It was not, but once the old man started to think, "It is my country, my capital, here I was born," a dream started. He was very emotional about it. He had come back to his town, and it was not his town – but that was not the point. If you think it is, then it is; if you don't think it is, then it is not.

Have you ever observed that you can pass through a graveyard and if you don't know that it is a graveyard you can go singing and laughing? If you know, impossible; if you know it is a graveyard you cannot pass through it alive. You will have to face many difficulties, not because the graveyard creates the difficulties but because of the thought, "This is a graveyard." You project.

I used to live with one of my relatives. In the night he gnashed his teeth many times, so I used to play jokes. Whenever somebody new would be staying, I would tell him, "Don't move through this room at night, it is very dangerous. A man who used to live here died in the first world war. He had been recently married, married to a very beautiful young woman – poor but beautiful, but with only one eye. The man went to war and he never came back. Nobody ever informed the poor woman that he had died. She inquired and inquired; she would go again and again to the post office for a letter. It never came. Then the woman also died, just waiting and waiting and waiting. She still waits here as a ghost, and whenever a new man comes to this house she thinks, 'Maybe, perhaps my husband has come back.' So she comes in the night, just takes the cover off, and looks at the face. She is a beautiful woman with one eye and wears a red sari. So it is good to tell you, because if we don't tell you and it happens, you may get scared. She never harms anybody, she simply looks. And when she feels he is not the man, she throws the cover-sheet angrily and walks out."

As it happened, almost always people would say, "I don't believe it!" And this is the right victim! Whenever someone says, "I don't believe it," he is the right victim. The more forcibly he says that he doesn't believe, the more forcibly he is suppressing a fear.

I would tell him, "That is not the question, whether you believe or not – but it is an experience. We are not forcing any belief on you, you will come to know. I myself never used to believe, but when I saw...what can one do?"

Then by and by the man would start asking, "And er...how to know that the woman is in the room?"

I would tell him, "You will hear a certain noise, as if someone is gnashing his teeth."

The man who used to sleep in that room would do it eight, ten times during the night. A few people do. Something is wrong with their stomachs at this time; they are tense, then they gnash their teeth.

One woman came and I told her the story. She said, "I don't believe it at all" – a very educated woman, she had a Ph.D. from some university and thought herself an atheist.

I said, "That is not the point, this night will prove it."

She said, "But I don't believe!"

I said, "That's very good. We don't force belief, but it is just our duty to make you aware that this is going to happen. It always happens."

At twelve in the night I went to sleep, and just when I had put the light out, she screamed. I went in, I looked at her – she was completely unconscious, she had fainted. The moment she went to her bed and put the light out, the man did his thing exactly at the right moment. It took four or five minutes for her to come to. She would look at the corner of the room, close her eyes and faint again!

The whole night I had to wait on her. In the morning she was still feverish. I said, "There are no ghosts, don't be bothered."

She said, "Now I cannot say. The woman was just standing in the corner gnashing her teeth, one-eyed and wearing a red sari. I have seen her!"

This was a joke in the beginning, and the whole family with whom I lived all knew. But by and by, they also became afraid. They said, "But when it happens to so many people, there must be something in it." Nobody would sleep in that room, not even the man who crunched his teeth. He said, "No, I cannot sleep. Maybe something is there. Maybe because of that woman I crunch my teeth, because the doctors say nothing is wrong. Maybe she forces me, or it is something she is doing."

A time came when if somebody needed something from that room, they would come to me: "Can you go, because nobody else is ready to."

A few years ago I visited the room. They had locked it because, they said, when I left, nobody was ready to enter that room. And sometimes now in the night, even though that man who used to crunch is no more, that sound is heard.

People project; that's why so many ghosts exist. It doesn't depend on reality, it depends on your mind. If you are afraid, you create something through your fear; a counterpart will immediately come into reality. If you love, you create something; a counterpart immediately comes into reality. You live in a shell of your own mind, it covers you like a capsule.

So remember, there is not one world, there are as many worlds as there are minds. If in a home there are five people, there are five worlds. That's why it is so difficult to communicate, because the other lives in his own world and you live in yours. It is difficult to penetrate.

The town was not the town of his childhood, it was not his birthplace. They were playing a joke. They said:

"This is the capital of Yen." The old man composed himself and looked solemn.

Inside the city they pointed out a shrine: "This is the shrine of your quarter – this is the temple; your parents worshipped here, and you were initiated as a Buddhist in this shrine." He breathed a deep sigh.

They pointed out a hut: "This was your father's cottage." Tears welled up. They are creating a world around him.

They pointed out a mound: "This is your father's tomb." He could not help weeping aloud. They have created a world, they have given him a screen, and all his projections have been brought out.

His companions roared with laughter: "We are teasing you – you are still only in Chin. Your town has not yet been reached, we are passing through another town."

The old man was very embarrassed.

When you come to realize, you also will be embarrassed, absolutely embarrassed. Your whole life has been a trick played not by companions but by your own mind. You were thinking it was beautiful and it was not. You were thinking it was ugly and it was not. You were thinking this was to be achieved and it was worthless, and you were thinking this is not of any worth and it was not so. Everything is topsy-turvy, you live in a chaos.

People come to me and they say, "What is the need of a master? Why is a master needed?" A master is needed to bring something beyond the mind into you, something foreign. Otherwise, how will you be brought out of your mind? You cannot bring yourself out of your mind. It will be just like pulling yourself up by the strings of your own shoes. You may try a little jump but again you will be back on the same earth.

Somebody is needed to pull you out, to slap you, to shock you, to shock you so much that your sleep is broken, that your dream is broken. How are you going to do it on your own? And whatsoever you do, your mind will be the doer – and mind is the problem. Your mind is the problem. How can you come out of it? How can you take a jump out of it? Whatsoever you do will be done by it; whatsoever you think is happening will be created by it. And all the interpretations will be given by the mind.

One night, a policeman saw Mulla Nasruddin. It was midnight, the whole city had gone to sleep. Mulla was passing, drunk, playing on a mouth-organ. The policeman stopped Nasruddin and said, "You are drunk again, Nasruddin. You will have to accompany me."

Nasruddin said, "Sure thing! What you wanna sing?"

"You will have to accompany me," he had said, but when a drunken man listens he interprets in his own way.

Once Mulla was caught and brought to the police station. He was very angry and annoyed. He was shouting, "Why have you brought me here? What do you think I am?" – and many things, as drunken people do.

Then the sergeant who was at the desk said, "You have been brought here for drinking."

Mulla said, "Then it is okay – when do we start?" A drunken man has his own interpretation...so he said, "Then it is okay, beautiful; when do we start?"

Your mind will interpret, and who will be a check on it? Who will tell you that this is your own mind again playing a trick? And your mind is so old, so ancient – thousands of lives! It is so deep-rooted; who will shake you out of it? Somebody who is not asleep like you is needed. That is the meaning of a master, nothing else. But your mind says: I can do it on my own, no need. Then you have already chosen the master – your mind is your master.

There are only two possibilities: either your mind is your master, or you choose someone who is awakened. With the mind as your master you are not going to grow at all. You are listening to the wrong source. Just because it is yours doesn't make any difference. Illness is also yours, but you go to a doctor and you leave it to him.

Krishnamurti has been saying that there is no need for a master. He is right – and absolutely wrong also. He is right because when you become awakened, you also know that there was no need, you were dreaming. When you become alert dreaming stops, and then you can't feel what the need was. "It was just a dream, I could have shaken myself out of it." But it is an afterthought. Even Krishnamurti needed Annie Besant and Leadbeater. He had his own masters. It is an afterthought. When a thing happens, then you can always feel, "I could have done it." But when it has not happened you cannot even think about it, because your thinking will also be a part of your dream.

A master is needed when you are asleep. When you become awakened, you also will think a master was not needed. Then for you, of course, the master is not needed. But then many will be deluded because many egoists will surround you, as you will find. You cannot find anywhere else such a mass of egoists as you will find near Krishnamurti, because the moment the egoist hears that no master is needed he feels very happy. He says, "Right!" He always thinks he is the ultimate; no need to surrender to anybody – because ego resists surrender. And this man says that no master is needed, so egoists feel very happy. Around Krishnamurti you will find all sorts of egoists, because it seems very good, very convenient – no need to surrender.

That is what the ego asks, that's what the ego always insists on – no surrender. Because once you surrender and a foreign element enters you.... That is the meaning of a master: you say, "Now I will not listen to my mind. I have listened enough and I have reached nowhere. I will not listen. Now I will listen to you." Something foreign has entered, something that was never in you before. A new element enters into you, and this new element becomes a crystallizing center.

Now, the mind will say, "Do this!" – but you cannot listen to the mind, you have to listen to the master. The mind will go on saying things for many years, but if you go on listening to the master, by and by the mind will feel tired. Now you don't listen to it, you don't feed it; the mind feels starved, it goes on shrinking. A moment comes when it falls dead. In that very moment you become awakened.

What did these people do to this poor old man? They helped to create an illusion. The illusion was there, and it must have been very real because tears welled up.

They pointed out a mound: "This is your father's tomb." He could not help weeping aloud.

Your father will die someday – everybody has to die – and you will weep and you will cry. Are you certain he was your father or has somebody played a joke? How can you be certain that he was your father? That is the difference between belief and faith. A woman knows who the mother is – that is faith; and a father simply believes that he is the father but he doesn't know. There is no way of knowing it. Fatherhood is a belief, motherhood is a faith. Faith depends on knowing, belief depends on just believing. There is no basis to it. How do you know your father is real and not a joke played on you? But if he dies, whether it is a joke or not makes no difference. Tears well up; you cry and you shout. And if somebody comes and says, "Don't be bothered much, he was not your father," suddenly there will be a change. Then your father is not dead. You live in your mind.

I have heard that a house was on fire and the owner was crying and weeping. He was going mad. Then somebody said, "Why are you weeping and crying? I was present just yesterday and your son has sold the property. It is no longer yours."

The man said, "Is it really so?" Tears simply disappeared and he was enjoying the whole scene just like a spectator.

Then somebody came and said, "Yes, it was talked about, there was talk of selling it, but nothing has been decided. Why are you laughing and enjoying? It is your property."

Again tears welled up. He started beating his chest and he said, "I cannot live anymore! This is my whole life, my whole life's effort."

And then the son came and he said, "Don't be bothered, everything is okay. The money has been given and the man is not aware at all. He lives in another town, he is not aware. The moment the house caught fire, I ran to the other town. Everything is finished; I have taken the money." Again the father began laughing and enjoying.

This is your world, this is how you are behaving – just thoughts; just thoughts and then you cry and weep, just thoughts and then you laugh and enjoy, just thoughts and you are happy, just thoughts and you are miserable. Somebody tells you, "You are beautiful" and you are so happy; somebody says, "You look ugly" and you are so unhappy. Just words! What are you doing? Become a little more alert, otherwise you will be very embarrassed.

When death comes everybody is embarrassed: the whole life has gone to the dogs. As far as I know, at the moment of death there is less a fear and more an embarrassment. The whole thing is gone! You were thinking that your wife would go with you, because she always said, "I cannot live without you" – and she is already planning to get remarried.

Mulla Nasruddin's wife was dying and she said, "Nasruddin, you must remember at least one thing. I know you will get married again, no point in denying it; don't try to deceive me. I know you will get married, but you have to promise me one thing: don't give my clothes to any other woman."

Nasruddin said, "Never! I will never give them away – and anyway, they will not suit Fatima, she is too thin."

Already, everything is decided! And you believed, and you wasted your life for children who don't belong to you, for a wife, for a husband, for money, for prestige. You destroyed your whole life, the whole opportunity.

One feels embarrassed at death. You may feel afraid of death right now, but when death comes nothing can be done – one accepts it. But then the whole life seems to be absurd, meaningless.

The old man was very embarrassed.

When he reached Yen and really saw the capital, and the shrine of his quarter, and his father's cottage and tomb, he did not feel it so deeply.

He learned something, he really learned something. He became a little more mature. What do these tears signify if they can come just by a projection? What is the meaning of all this feeling, emotion? And it was just a mound, not his father's tomb, and he was crying. Now the real tomb is there, but what is the difference between a real tomb and an unreal tomb? They are both mounds – somebody may be playing a trick. And even if nobody is playing a trick, what difference does it make? It was not his home, somebody played a trick; he felt so emotional and sentimental. This may be his home, but what is the difference? – he learned.

This is the message of this story: learn through experience. By and by, all sentimentality stops, drops. And remember one thing: sentimentality, not sensitivity, belongs to the mind. Sensitivity doesn't belong to the mind, sentimentality belongs to the mind. A man who is aware is absolutely sensitive, but not sentimental. There is a vast difference, an absolute difference.

What is sensitivity? Sensitivity is not a projection. Sentimentality is a projection. If this old man had really been an awakened one from the beginning he would not have bothered to go to the old town where he had been born, because that is sentimentality. What difference does it make where you were born? You are the one who is never born. He would not have been bothered about where his father lived, and where his father's tomb was. What difference does it make? The body comes from the earth and goes back to the earth – dust unto dust. The body is not your father.

If the man had been aware you could not have played any trick on him. In the first place he would not bother, and even if passing through the town, somebody had said, "This is your father's tomb," he would have said, "It is okay, everybody dies." He would not have felt embarrassed. There would have been no problem. Sentimentality will always feel embarrassed.

A man of awareness is sensitive. 'Sensitive' means, if somebody is dying he will serve; if somebody is dying and needs him, he will care. If somebody is dying he will share whatsoever he can share. There is no point in crying and weeping, because you don't help that way.

One man is weeping because he is hungry, and you sit by his side and you also weep because you feel very much for that man – this is sentimentality. Your weeping will not become bread for him, he will remain hungry. Instead of one man weeping in the world, now two men are weeping. You have doubled crying and weeping. It is not going to help. Do something!

A sensitive man will do something. A sentimental man will weep and cry, but a sentimental man will always be thought to be sensitive. A sensitive man will not look as though he is sensitive, because he will be doing something. If someone is hungry he will try to find something for him to eat; if he is thirsty, he will go and fetch water. You will not see tears welling up, and you will not see him beating his chest, rolling on the ground saying, "This man is hungry!" You will not be able to see he is sensitive because sensitivity is subtle. He cares – the difference is subtle and delicate.

A buddha will not weep because you are in misery, he will help – he will help you to come out of your misery. If you are in misery, a sentimental man becomes miserable himself. He will cry and weep and you will always feel that he loves you very much. This is not love. He is as ill as you are. If he really cared he would do something. He would try to change, try to transform you.

It happened: There was one woman whose only child had died. Buddha was in the town at that moment. The woman had only one child and her husband was already dead. Gautami was her name. So she started crying and weeping and she would not allow the neighbors to take the dead body, to burn it. She clung, she would not allow, and she carried the dead child all over the town asking people to help, to give some medicine. People said, "Now nothing can be done, the child is dead," but she would not listen.

Then somebody suggested, "Go to Buddha – he is an awakened man, he can do a miracle. You go to him!" So she ran there, and what did Buddha do? Not a tear came to his eyes.

The woman must have felt that he is very hard, he has no heart. She said, "Don't you have any heart? My child is dead, do something! – just touch him and he will become alive. You are enlightened, you are a god, you can do anything; just have mercy on me!"

Buddha said, "I will do something, but you do one thing first. Leave the dead child here and you go into the town. The town is not very big, only three hundred people. Go and knock on every door and just ask them for one thing, because for the miracle I will need a few mustard seeds. But a condition has to be fulfilled: the child will come back, but you have to bring mustard seeds from a house where nobody has ever died."

In her misery the woman could not see the point. When you are miserable your eyes are filled with so many tears that you cannot see, you cannot think clearly. A dying man believes anything. A man who is drowning in a river even clings to a straw. So if a Buddha says to go....

She ran from one home to another, she knocked at every door. People said, "Woman, have you gone mad? Mustard seeds we have – we can give them to you, the crop has just come – but we cannot fulfill the condition because many people have died in this house."

She ran all over the town. Running all over the town, knocking at doors and asking, but in every family somebody had died. There was no family where life had not been destroyed by death.

By and by her tears dried; she started to understand what Buddha meant. By the time she had completed the circuit of the whole town she was a different woman. She went to Buddha and Buddha asked, "Have you brought the mustard seeds?"

She started laughing and she said, "You played a trick! Now initiate me into sannyas. I have come to understand that life is death. My child has died, and you were really compassionate. Even if you had done a miracle and the child had become alive, it would not have led anywhere – the child would have had to die again. It would not have been a real miracle and it would have deceived me further. You have made me aware that whosoever is born is going to die. The child has died, the child's father has died; I also am going to die sooner or later. Initiate me – teach me that which never dies, teach me the deathless."

And she said, "Forgive me, because I was unconscious. I said something to you which was not true; I said to you that you are hard, you are like a rock, that your heart is not a heart. But I know I was wrong." Not a single tear came to Buddha. He is not sentimental, he is sensitive.

When you are sensitive, only then can you help. If you are sentimental you create more mess. When a man understands he becomes more and more sensitive. He helps, he cares, and he will never feel embarrassed. A sentimental man will always feel embarrassed, because something is wrong. You also know when you are behaving in a foolish way – you also know.

When he reached Yen and really saw the capital, and the shrine of his quarter, and his father's cottage and tomb, he did not feel it so deeply.

He has learned a little...and if this learning goes on and on and on, a moment comes when you see the reality as it is. Then there is no misery because the whole mind has been dropped. Then you are face to face with the real. There is no happiness, no unhappiness, because both are projections of the mind. And when both disappear there is peace, when both disappear there is a bliss. Don't misunderstand me – bliss doesn't mean happiness; bliss means the absence of both happiness and unhappiness. Happiness will be disturbed by unhappiness, unhappiness will be disturbed by happiness. They are polarities – the wheel is moving.

Bliss is never disturbed; it is silence, it is peace, it is a tranquility – absolute peace. You have come to understand; now nothing disturbs. Now you move in the world with no-mind, you move in the world with no projection. And then everything is beautiful. Not your beauty of course, because your beauty carries ugliness in it. Now everything is beautiful, but this beauty transcends both your beauty and your ugliness. All dualities are transcended.

Try to learn from every experience – that is the only meditation. Don't allow any experience to just go down the drain. Learn something. Learning will remain with you. The experience will go, but learning will remain with you. And when an accumulation of understanding comes to a certain degree, there is an explosion. It is just like when water is heated up to a hundred degrees: the water disappears and becomes a totally different thing. The quality changes, it evaporates. Ordinarily water flows downwards, but when it evaporates it starts moving upwards, the dimension has changed.

You are like water. If you don't learn you will go on moving downwards. Learn! Learning is a heat, a seasoning, a maturity, a fire. Learn more and you create more fire within you; and then comes the moment of a hundred degrees, and a jump. Suddenly, the downward dimension disappears – you are moving upwards. You are moving higher and higher and higher; you have become a cloud.

This is possible only through experience, when experience becomes learning and learning becomes understanding. Understanding is the essence. It is not a memory, it is just the very essence of all that you have known. You cannot explain your understanding to anybody, no. It is not knowledge, it cannot be given.

A master has to create situations for you to learn, to understand, to gather a momentum, a fire.

You must have seen pictures of the pyramids. They were made by very very secret schools in Egypt. The word 'pyramid' means 'fire within', and the pyramid is made in such a way that it accumulates energy. Just now scientists have become aware that the shape of a pyramid is a great accumulator of energy. Just the shape, just the triangular shape accumulates energy. They became aware of the phenomenon by accident. One scientist was working in the pyramid of Giza. While he was working a dog entered, and he unknowingly closed the door and went away for a holiday. When he came after three weeks the dog was found dead, but the body was mummified, automatically. The dog was dead but the body was not deteriorating at all.

Then he tried many experiments on cats, mice, and he was surprised: something miraculous was happening in Giza. A body dies, it has to deteriorate.... Then he tried a small experiment: he made a small model pyramid and put a mouse in it, and the mouse died and was mummified. The body didn't deteriorate.

Now they have made a patent in Germany – they have made a cardboard pyramid for razor blades. You shave your beard and put the razor in the pyramid; the next day it is automatically sharpened again and one single razor can do for a whole lifetime.

The word 'pyramid' means 'fire within'. The whole human body is like a pyramid. If you move deeper you will come to understand that near the navel an energy shape exists which is triangular. And near the navel, just inside the triangle, in the middle, there exists a fire. It is a very very tiny flame right now. If you learn more, and your learning becomes understanding – you carry the essence of it – you will feel a heat growing near the navel. In Japan they call it *hara*. The heat grows, and as the heat grows near the navel you start changing. A moment comes when you feel a burning fire near the navel; it becomes almost intolerable. And then suddenly everything changes. At one hundred degrees your body becomes totally different.

The flow of the body is no longer downwards. Sex disappears, because sex is the downward flow. Suddenly the energy is going upwards. And then the energy reaches to the topmost peak of your being, the *sahasrar,* from where it enters into the divine. So learn more, don't move unawares. Awareness is fire. When Heraclitus says that fire is the root of all existence, he is right. He knows something – fire is the root of all existence. Not the fire that you see; that fire is just one of the forms.

Understanding is like fire: it burns you completely – you as you are right now, the ego, the mind. It gives you a different dimension: you become a cloud and you move in the sky. You have gained wings.

Don't allow any experience to go by without your learning something through it. Each single moment is valuable; learn something. When tomorrow comes and the sun rises, you should not be the same – you must have learned. These twenty-four hours are valuable; you must learn.

And by learning I don't mean that you should know more; you should understand more. Even an ignorant person can be a very understanding person – ignorant in the sense that he is not educated, he doesn't know much. And a very educated person, an 'Oxford man', can be absolutely non-understanding, but he knows. Can you feel the difference? Knowledge comes through memory, through mind. Understanding comes through experience, through existential experience, not through memory.

Enough for today.

Discourse 10

Making A Nuisance

When Teng Yin Feng was about to die he said to the people around him, "I have seen monks die sitting and lying, but have any died standing?" "Yes, some," they replied. "How about upside down?" asked Teng. "No, never such a thing," they said. So Teng died standing on his head and his clothes also rose up, close to his body. It was decided to carry him to the burning ground, but he still stood there without moving. People from far and near gazed with astonishment at the scene. His younger sister, a nun, happened to be there. She grumbled at him, "When you were alive you took no notice of laws and customs; and even now you're dead you're making a nuisance of yourself." She then prodded her brother with her finger, and he fell down with a bang. Then they went off to the crematorium.

Death is the root of all fear, and if there is fear, you cannot live. With fear there is no life. If there is fear you are already dead. This is the vicious circle: you are afraid of death, and because of fear you cannot live, you are already dead. Then you become more afraid, and the fear creeps into your very center; you become just a trembling.

As I see you, you are just a trembling. If you dig deeply you will always find the fear of death. This fear is the root of all fears. In any fear, whatsoever the form of the fear, somewhere the fear of death is hidden. Why are people so afraid of death? Is death really a phenomenon to be afraid of?

The first thing to remember is that you don't know death. You have not known it, so how can you be afraid of something that you don't know? That's impossible. You can be afraid of something you know, but of something that is totally unknown, absolutely unknown, how can you be afraid? Fear needs an object to be afraid of.

You cannot really be afraid of death, you must be afraid of something else. That something else is an unfulfilled life. You have not been able to live, you have not been able to achieve a fulfillment, you have not been able to overflow, you have not been able to celebrate. Your life has been an emptiness, a hollowness, a nothing.

Death is coming near and you have not been able to live yet – this creates the fear. Death is coming near and you will be no more. The opportunity is being taken away. Every moment you are losing life and you have not lived yet – this creates the fear. Death is approaching – that is not the fear. The fear is that you have not lived yet and death is knocking at the door; the time to leave has come and you are yet unfulfilled.

If you have lived you have a fulfillment, a contentment, a deep gratitude. You have flowered; there is nothing more to achieve. Then you are not afraid of death; rather, you welcome it. You have achieved: now death comes like a deep sleep after the day's labor – a whole day of achievement, of fulfillment, of reaching, of meeting, of encountering, of flowering, and then death comes like a deep sleep. You welcome it. When the tree has flowered, death is welcome; when the tree is still struggling to flower, there is fear.

If you are afraid of death, that is simply one indication that your life has been a wastage. It has been like a desert, nothing has flowered in it. It has been like a pond, closed in itself, not moving anywhere. It has not been like a river – flowing, dancing, running towards the ultimate.

When a river reaches to the ocean there is a death. When a pond dries, becomes more and more dirty, evaporates, that too is death. But both are so absolutely different. When a river reaches to the ocean it is a fulfillment, because there the river will die and will become something greater. It is a jump, a jump from the finite to the infinite: the river losing itself, its identity, and becoming the ocean. Nothing is lost and everything is gained.

But a pond drying up, not reaching anywhere – no ocean anywhere, just drying in itself – is also dying. You are like a pond. That's why there is the fear of death. Be like a river, and then there is no fear of death.

Death itself is like a sleep. Sleep is a temporary death, so if a person becomes very afraid of death he is bound to become afraid of sleep too. In the West, insomnia has now become a common phenomenon; almost everybody is suffering from it. It is not only because of mental tensions that this insomnia exists; deeper than the tensions is fear, the fear of death. You cannot let go.

I know a person who is so afraid of death that he cannot sleep, because he is afraid that he may die in his sleep. He tries to remain awake – he talks, reads, listens to music, but he is afraid of going into sleep. And if you are afraid for many many days it becomes a habit; unknowingly you create a barrier against sleep.

In the West people are afraid of death, and if you are afraid, how can you go into sleep? Sleep is like death. So logically they are right – if you are afraid of death, you should also be afraid of sleep. They are similar phenomena: sleep is a temporary death. After the day's labor, the work, you are exhausted. You need a death so that you can be reborn, so that in the morning you are again rejuvenated, fresh, young. And in sleep, death is exactly what happens.

Have you observed the fact that in sleep you are not the same person at all? You don't remember who you are, you don't remember whether you are rich or poor, you don't remember your own face, you don't remember who your father is and who your mother is; you don't remember anything that you have learned, anything that has been cultivated in you. You drop everything at the door and you go to sleep. That's why it is so refreshing, because you get rid of yourself. You are like a burden – you leave it at the door and you fall into sleep. Sleep opens a different dimension, where no identity, no ego, nothing of this world exists. That's why it is so fresh, so refreshing. In the morning you come back to life; a new day starts, a new life.

The fear of death will automatically create a fear of sleep and a fear of love, because love also is like death. You die in it. That's why people cannot love. They talk about it, they fantasize, they imagine, but they never fall in love. Even if they try, they try to manipulate the phenomenon, not allow it, because love also is like death.

Four things are similar: death, love, sleep and meditation. Their qualities are similar, and the basic similarity is that you have to dissolve. And people are afraid of all of them: if you are afraid of death you will be afraid of sleep, of love, of meditation.

Many come to me and they say, "How to love?" It is not a question of how, and when you ask how you are trying to manipulate. You would like to remain in control, so whenever you want you can push the button on or off. You would like to remain the master of the whole thing.

But nobody can be in possession of love. Love possesses you, you cannot possess it. Love controls you, you cannot control it. Love means you are no longer there, something else has come. That's why love is so rejuvenating. Even if an old man falls in love, suddenly you will see that his face has become younger, his eyes are no longer old; his body may be old, but his total being suddenly becomes young. Why does it happen? – for this very reason: you can allow a let-go; you move to the original source of energy where rebirth is possible. You touch the deathless core. You only touch the deathless core when you are ready to die, that is the paradox. You touch the deepest core when you are ready to die. If you cling to the surface and you are afraid, afraid to let go, then you remain on the surface, and the surface is the body.

People who are afraid of love are not afraid of sex. Love is dangerous; sex is not dangerous, it can be manipulated. There are now many manuals on how to do it. You can manipulate it – sex can become a technique. Love can never become a technique. If in sex you try to remain in control, then even sex will not help to reach the ultimate. It will go to a certain point and you will drop back, because somewhere it also needs a let-go.

That's why orgasm is becoming more and more difficult. Ejaculation is not orgasm, to give birth to children is not orgasmic. Orgasm is the involvement of the total body: mind, body, soul, all together. You vibrate, your whole being vibrates, from the toes to the head. You are no longer in control; existence has taken possession of you and you don't know who you are. It is like a madness, it is like a sleep, it is like meditation, it is like death.

So even in sex you let go up to a point, but you don't allow totality, because if you allow totality then the ego cannot exist. And this is the problem: you are afraid of death because you are not capable of living totally.

Love, meditation, sleep – nothing is total. In your activity also you are not total, because if you were total, there too a moment would come when you would be lost. Losing yourself has become the problem; you cannot lose yourself, you cannot relax – you have to do something. You go into the garden and dig a hole, but you are not total. If you really were total while digging the hole you would forget yourself completely; the self-consciousness would disappear.

You are self-conscious but not conscious of your self; you are aware but there is an ego. You are aware of the total – the trees, the sun's rays, the breezes blowing, the birds singing, your activity, the digging of the hole, the mud coming out – you are aware of everything except your self. If you became conscious of your self, in that moment an orgasmic feeling would happen. It is like deep love, it is like sleep, it is like death. You will come out of it totally different and new.

If you don't move into a let-go, life cannot happen to you. It happens through that passage when you are not. When you are not standing in the way then life happens to you, then you feel fulfilled. When you are fulfilled there is no fear of death. When there is no fear of death you become more and more capable of let-go.

And if you have really known what life is, who bothers about death? If you have really known what life is and celebrated it, then death is not the end; then death is the culmination, the peak, the highest let-go. Then love is nothing, a sexual orgasm is nothing, sleep is nothing. If you have lived life rightly, fulfilled, then death is the greatest bliss because it is the greatest let-go. The more intense and total the let-go, the more the bliss. This is the rule, this is the law.

So what to do? If you want to live, allow death also. They are like two wings. It is not a thing somewhere in the end, it is a process: the day you were born you began dying. It is not life here and death there, life now and death then, no. You cannot divide them; they are together, they have to be. Life is death. Life and death are two wings: the day you are born, that same day you start to die. It is a process. You inhale, it is life; you exhale, it is death. In the morning you get up – it is life; in the evening you go to bed – it is death. You work, act – it is life; then you relax – it is death. It is continuous, every moment it is there. And if you avoid death you will also be avoiding life. If you don't want to exhale deeply how can you inhale deeply? If you don't want to relax, how can you act deeply? – you won't have any energy.

If you are afraid of sleep, in the morning you will not wake up fresh and you will feel sleepy the whole day. Then everything gets mixed up. You are neither alive nor dead, but just dragging on.

And this is a bad situation – just dragging on. Either be alive or be dead, but don't drag on in either case. Either be dead totally and you will attain to a greater life, or live totally and you will attain to a greater death, because they are two aspects of the same coin. Once you can see that life implies death, that every act of being alive is also an act of dying, you have seen the total.

Then life is not serious, then it is fun. It becomes serious because of the fear of death. You cannot laugh loudly because of the fear of death; you cannot enjoy because of the fear of death; you cannot do *anything,* because of the fear of death. Death is always around the corner like a black shadow following you. It doesn't allow you to do anything. Then you become serious and you start thinking: how to attain the deathless? Then you start searching for how to become immortal, how to find the secret, the elixir.

These are all nonsense searches, it is not true seeking. Nowhere does there exist something chemical, alchemical, like elixir, ambrosia – no. The secret is in seeing life and death as a single process. You cannot find the secret anywhere. The philosopher's stone exists nowhere; it exists in this fact that life and death are together. They are one process, a unitary phenomenon. Then you are not afraid. Then rather, on the contrary, you are thankful to death, because life becomes possible only because of death. Through death life becomes possible; through dying everything is renewed.

So death is not against life, it is not the opposite, it is not the enemy. It is through death that life becomes possible: you are alive because you can die. If you cannot die you will not be alive at all. You don't know what you are asking for if you ask for deathlessness. Then you will be like a rock; then you cannot be alive.

Look at the flower that bloomed this morning. Just near the flower there is a rock. By the evening the flower will be gone but the rock will be there, because the flower is more alive and the rock is not so alive. The flower is dead by the evening. What do you want? – to be a rock-like phenomenon or a flower-like phenomenon? Why does the flower die so soon? – because it is so alive, so intensely alive, that death comes quickly, it doesn't linger on. The flower was not dragging; it lived the moment, it lived totally – it danced under the sky, it enjoyed the sun, the breeze. For a moment it was eternity. The flower laughed, the flower sang, the flower did whatsoever was to be done, and by the evening the flower was ready to die – and without a single tear in her eyes, without weeping and crying.

Look at a dying flower: the petals have already fallen on the ground, but you can never say that it is ugly. It is beautiful in death also. Then look at a man dying: he becomes ugly. Why? – because of the fear. Fear makes you ugly. If you are too afraid you will become more and more ugly. The flower is fulfilled; now the time to rest has come and the flower is going to rest, and when the rest is over the flower will come back.

Again and again...life is an eternal recurrence. Death is just a rest. You need not be worried about it, you simply live. And if you live then you are not serious. If you are afraid of death then you are serious. To be sincere is one thing, to be serious is another. A man who loves life is sincere, authentic, but never serious. Life is not like an illness. If you are looking at death and are obsessed with death, then life is just serious – then you will become a long face. You may move to the monasteries, to the temples, go to the Himalayas, but you will remain a long face. It is fear that has taken you to the monastery.

Remember, an authentic religious person is not fear-oriented, he is love-oriented. A really authentic religious person becomes religious to enjoy life more, to enjoy it deeply and totally. He is not scared. A really religious man looks at life as a game: it is not business, it is a game. Hindus call it *leela,* a play – not even a game but a play. There is a difference between a game and play. Children play, but you even make a game out of play. Then it becomes business-like, then even in playing you are seeking victory, success, gain, profit.

Life is a play. There is nothing to be achieved out of it, it itself is the goal; there is nowhere to reach, it itself is the ultimate. Life is not moving to achieve some goal, it is not going anywhere. It is just like children playing: you cannot ask them, "For what are you playing? What is the purpose?" They will laugh at your foolishness. They will say, "We are simply playing. It is so beautiful!" Profit is not their concern, and profit should also not be your concern, but play.

Life is a moment to celebrate, to enjoy. Make it fun, a celebration, and then you will enter the temple. The temple is not for the long-faced, it has never been for them. Look at life: do you see sadness anywhere? Have you ever seen a tree depressed? Have you seen a bird anxiety-ridden? Have you seen an animal neurotic? No, life is not that, not at all. Only man has gone wrong somewhere, and he has gone wrong somewhere because he thinks himself to be very wise, very clever.

Your cleverness is your disease. Don't be too wise. Always remember to stop; don't go to the extreme. A little foolishness and a little wisdom is good, and the right combination makes you a buddha – a little foolishness and a little wisdom. Don't be just wise or else you will be a long face; don't be just a fool or else you will become suicidal.. A little foolishness, enough to enjoy life, and a little wisdom to avoid the errors, that will do.

But one has to know the right combination, and the right combination is always different for each individual. My right combination cannot be your right combination; nobody is a model for anybody else. You have to find your own balance, because everybody is so unique. But always remember not to destroy foolishness completely, because in certain moments to be foolish is to be wise.

Everybody should remain open. In certain moments you should be like children, in certain moments you should simply forget the business of life, purposelessly just enjoying the moment, doing foolish things: dancing and singing, collecting and playing with pebbles on the shore. And nobody inside you says, "What foolishness are you doing? – this time can be devoted to making money. At this time you could be in the office or in the shop and your bank balance could be growing. What are you doing? Are you a child?"

If the child in you is completely lost, then you can never be religious. Religion is for children. That's why Jesus insists: Only those who are like children will be able to enter into the kingdom of my God. But what does being a child mean? Observe a child: he is wise. He is a fool also, but when it is needed he can be wise, very wise.

I was staying with a family for a few days and a small boy in the family was reading a book. On the book cover there was a picture of Atlas supporting the earth, so I asked the child, "Do you know who this Atlas is?"

He said, "Yes, he is a great giant who supports the whole world."

So I said to him, "Correct, but who supports Atlas?"

He thought for a moment and then he said, "I think he must have married a rich wife."

They can be wise and they are fools. When a child is wise, the wisdom has the freshness of a dewdrop in the morning; it is not stale. Your wisdom is stale, contaminated. You have collected it, you have borrowed it; you have taken it from others, it is not your own. What do you know that is your own? You have collected from many sources. That is knowledge, not wisdom.

Wisdom is a response, a fresh response to the moment; knowledge is an old, rotten, collected thing. You don't respond to the moment; you bring the past, the memory into it and you react through it. Wisdom is response, knowledge is reaction. You already have the answer, but a ready-made answer before the question has been raised is not wisdom. A child is wise because he has no knowledge. He has to look around, he has to feel, he has to think, he has to respond – he does not know.

It is said – it is a Christian myth – that when Jesus went to the sea, the sea turned into red wine. Christian theologians have been trying to explain it: how can the sea turn into red wine? They have had much difficulty, puzzled, and no answer has yet been found. But a small child found the answer, and that small child was Lord Byron, who became very famous later on as a great poet. He was a small child in school and the question was asked: Why and how did the sea turn into red wine when Jesus reached it? The answer was fixed, ready-made; it had been taught already. All the other children started writing their answers, only Byron waited with closed eyes. The teacher came many times, but he was so meditative that she thought it better not to disturb him, he was thinking so much.

And of what can a child think? – because thinking is always of the known. If you know, you can think; if you don't know, what can you think? What was he doing? Thinking is possible only if you know something; then you can think. But if you don't know, you don't know. The child was sitting silently, but he looked so beautiful. Then in the end he simply wrote a single sentence, and the sentence was, "Seeing that my Lord had come, the sea became shy and turned red." When Jesus had come – my Lord had come – the sea, seeing that my Lord had come, became shy like a girl. The beloved had come, and that shyness was on the face of the sea. Only a child can answer that way because he does not know the answer. But this is beautiful – all the theologians are just foolish before this child. He has said the right thing; he has explained the whole thing.

A certain wisdom exists when you are innocent. But innocence is ignorance, and of course a certain foolishness exists when you are innocent, when you are ignorant. A child is beautiful because he is both – innocent, wise in his innocence, and a fool, foolish in his innocence. And a child is the right proportion for you. Remember, you will have to attain to a second childhood before you can enter into the kingdom of God.

A second childhood is even more beautiful than the first, because in the first you were not aware. In the second you will be fully aware. This is how Zen masters behave – you will find them sometimes just foolish, and in certain moments you will find them so wise that you cannot believe how this foolishness can exist with such a wise man. And you in your knowledge are also foolish, but your foolishness is contaminated, it is not innocent. When foolishness is innocent it has a wisdom of its own, and when foolishness is contaminated by knowledge it is simply idiocy; it has no wisdom.

I have heard that Albert Einstein was staying with a very knowledgeable woman who knew much. In the night they were sitting near the window and the woman said, "Look outside, Dr. Einstein. This star, this Venus, is so beautiful; it looks like a beautiful woman."

Einstein said, "My dear lady, it is not Venus, it is Jupiter."

The lady said, "Dr. Einstein, you are simply amazing! – you can even judge the sex of a planet from so far away!" She said, "Venus? – Venus is feminine, Jupiter is masculine. You are amazing! How can you judge the sex of a star from so far away?" And the woman was very knowledgeable, a professor in some university, but foolish in her knowledge.

And whenever you are foolish through your knowledgeability you are idiotic, simply idiotic. Be foolish like a child: if you don't know, you don't know – don't pretend. A child can simply say, "I don't know." Can you say so simply that you don't know? It is so difficult to say, "I don't know," because when you say it the 'I' drops. And unless you can say that you don't know, you will never be wise. Only through ignorance does the ego drop, and when there is no ego you have attained to a second childhood.

You will not be able to understand this Zen master if you can't see this quality of a wise fool, of foolishness in one's wisdom – a man who takes life as fun. When he takes life as fun he also takes death as fun. Nothing is a problem to him; he accepts everything, he is playful. Now try to understand this beautiful story.

When Teng Yin Feng was about to die – he was a master, a very well-known master – *he said to the people around him, "I have seen monks die sitting and lying, but have any died standing?"*

"Yes, some," they replied.

"How about upside down?" asked Teng.

"No, never such a thing," they said.

Death is coming near, death is going to knock at the door, and the master says, "How shall I receive it? The guest is coming; how shall I be the host, how shall I receive it?"

You die; a master *receives* death. You die clinging to life, not ready to die. You have to be snatched away, and that's why your whole being becomes ugly. A master prepares; he is even asking for the posture: "What posture shall I die in?"...because death should be received in a unique way. It doesn't come every day, it is a rare guest. One should prepare, one should be ready.

And what type of master was this Teng to say, *"I have seen monks die sitting and lying..."?* Ordinarily, people die lying on their backs, not even sitting. Only a few people, those who die in meditation, who die meditatively, die sitting. Otherwise, ninety-nine percent of the people die on a bed. He asked:

"...but have any died standing?"
"Yes, some," they replied.

A few people, a few rare persons have died standing. They too die standing because they are very meditative. There are certain techniques which can only be done standing. For example, Jaina techniques, Mahavira's techniques, all have to be done standing. He meditated standing for years; he would sit only when tired, otherwise he would stand.

A certain silence immediately comes to you if you stand quietly. Try it in the corner of your room: just stand silently in the corner, not doing anything. Suddenly the energy also stands inside you. Sitting, you will feel many disturbances in the mind, because sitting is a posture of a thinker. Standing, the energy flows like a pillar and is distributed equally all over the body. Standing is beautiful.

There are a few techniques to meditate just standing. Try it, because some of you will find it very very beautiful. If you can stand for one hour, it is just wonderful. Just by standing and not doing anything, not moving, you will find that something settles within you, becomes silent. A centering happens, and you will feel yourself like a pillar of energy; the body disappears.

So a few meditators have died standing....

"How about upside down?" asked Teng.

Standing in a *shirshasan,* a headstand posture...nobody has ever died like that! You cannot even sleep in that posture; dying must be very difficult, because the blood circulates towards the head. So nobody has ever tried this. Teng is the only one who has not only tried it, he did it. It is an absolutely impossible posture for dying because you cannot even sleep in it.

For sleep, a certain phenomenon is needed in the body: the blood should not be circulating towards the head. That's why we use pillows, to make the head a little higher than the body so the blood is not flowing towards the head. If the blood is flowing towards the head, the head continues thinking. The more civilized you become, the more the size of your pillows increases; then you need one, two, three pillows. A great thinker has to use five, six, seven pillows, because the blood circulation has to be stopped. That's why, after eating, sleep becomes easier, because the blood circulates towards the stomach. The body now has a more basic function to perform, and that is to digest the food. Thinking cannot be allowed; thinking is a luxury.

When you have eaten too much then you cannot think, and when you are starving you cannot think. That's why many religions have used fasting as a meditation, because if you fast you cannot think. The body needs energy for more basic functions; energy cannot be given to the head – it is a luxury. That's why animals don't think, they have not come to that standard of life yet.

The more rich a country, the more thinking there is; the poorer a country, the less thinking there is, because you cannot afford energy for thinking. If you fast you will feel that in the night it is difficult to sleep, very difficult, because with nothing to digest the whole energy moves towards the head. The movement of energy towards the head has to be stopped, only then you can sleep. It is difficult to sleep standing in an upside-down posture.

"How about upside down?" asked Teng.
"No, never such a thing," they said.

"We have never heard of it, what are you talking about? A person standing on his head and dying...?"

So Teng died standing on his head, and his clothes also rose up close to his body.

That is possible. Until a few years ago it would have simply been a myth, but now there are scientific explanations for it. It is possible because the body is electricity, it is nothing but bio-electricity. When somebody dies the body becomes a pillar of energy, and that pillar leaves the body. If it is very magnetic energy, as it has to be with a master; the clothes will just be magnetized.

Not only did Teng die upside down, but his clothes rose with his body, they clung to the body. If you rub your clothes on your body you will feel a certain electricity can be created in the clothes. The body is electric, and when the body dies the electricity leaves the body, it is pulled upwards. Just with that flow those clothes might have risen. There is no need to think about it as a myth or a story – it is possible.

So Teng died standing on his head...

Is death so easy that you can die upside down? Yes, death is easy if you have lived. Then you can choose the right moment to die. You must have heard about many saints making a prediction that they will be dying on a certain day, at a certain time. People think that they know how to read the future. That is nonsense, nobody can read the future. Future means that which remains invisible. Then what do they do?

If I say to you, "After seven days pass I will be dying in the morning at six o'clock sharp, so don't miss it," then what will you think? You will think, "How is it possible?" To the mind, the only possibility seems to be that somehow I know the future. That is not the truth – nobody knows the future. But a man who has lived totally can decide when to die. He is not predicting, he is simply saying that he has decided to die on a certain day at six o'clock in the morning.

If you have lived – and when I say lived, I mean totally – then you know what life energy is. You come to know all the nooks and crannies of life energy; then you know all its tides, when it comes to flow and when it ebbs, where there is a peak and where there is a valley. Then you know all its nuances. If you have lived totally you know yourself totally. Then you can decide when to die, there is no problem. It is as simple as saying, "I will leave this room at six o'clock." What is the problem? – at six o'clock you leave the room! But you have to know yourself, the room, and where the door is.

You are not aware of who you are; you are not aware of what you are. You are aware of only a very minute fragment of your being – that is your mind – and that too, not fully. Nine-tenths of your being remains a dark continent; it is yet an Africa, you never enter into it. In your inner being the geography is not yet completely measured, mapped; you don't have your own map.

Once you know your map, the inner geography, the topography, then when the right moment has come you can simply decide to leave. You can leave this body, because this body is just a house, an abode, it is not you. A master is unidentified with the body, unidentified with the mind; he can decide. So Teng stood on his head and died! Even this impossible posture of standing on one's head can be used. If you know how to live you know how to die, because they are both one.

Another thing to be understood is why he was joking about death. Death is a serious affair and he is making fun of it! Standing on his head, he is making fun of death. He is saying that if you have lived, lived a life of celebration, then you can die celebrating – it is fun. When you know that you are not going to die, that something in you is eternal, then the whole of life becomes fun. It is a great cosmic joke and you can play with it.

In his death, Teng was giving a message to his disciples: Everything is fun, don't be too concerned about anything. Just live the moment while it lasts; live it and enjoy it!

This is my feeling also – that if there is any God, he is not going to ask you: What right things have you done and what bad things have you done? What sins have you committed and what virtues have you followed? – no. If there is any God, he is going to ask: Has your life been a celebration or a sadness? That's the only thing that can be asked. When the whole existence celebrates, why are you standing separate, alone, isolated? And then you feel that you are a stranger. When flowers flower, why do you stand aloof? Why not flower? When birds sing, why do you stand aloof? Why not sing, why not become a participant?

Religion is a participation in the mystique that is all around you, in the mystery that is all around you. It is not an effort to know, it is an effort to be, to be a participant. Then everything is beautiful – life is beautiful and death is beautiful, and you can play a joke.

This Teng was a rare man. The disciples were very afraid: What to do? Never before had there been such a precedent; nobody had died standing on his head. What to do with such a man?

It was decided to carry him to the burning ground, but he still stood there without moving.

If you have been an energy pillar in life, an unmoving pillar, if you have attained anything in life that has become crystallized, then you can even use your death.

There are many versions of this story. In one version the sister came and said, "Why are you making a fool of yourself?" Teng laughed and fell dead.

People from far and near gazed with astonishment at the scene. His younger sister, a nun, happened to be there.

She lived in another monastery, for women. She came not because the brother was dead, she came just to see the foolishness that he was doing. She was like an elder sister to Teng and she could teach him the last lesson.

She grumbled at him, "When you were alive you took no notice of laws and customs, and even now you are dead you're making a nuisance of yourself."

This Teng is one of the rebellious Zen masters. He lived a life without any laws and without any regulations. He lived a life without any enforced discipline. Not that he was not disciplined; he was absolutely disciplined, otherwise how could he have stood on his head and died? He was not only disciplined in life, he was disciplined in his death. You cannot find such an absolute discipline with no enforced discipline. This discipline came from his inside; he followed his own way, he never followed anybody. He had rules, but the rules were not fixed by any outside code, they came out of his own awareness. Of course, he was a nuisance to other people.

It is said of Teng that when he lived with his own master and was himself a disciple, he would sleep long after everybody else was up and the whole monastery was working. It would be nine o'clock in the morning and he would still be sleeping. Once the master came and he said, "Teng, what are you doing? This is a monastery – one has to get up in the *brahmamuhurt,* at five o'clock."

It is reported that Teng said, "Of course I always get up in the morning, I always get up in the brahmamuhurt!"

The master said, "What are you saying? It is nine o'clock; four hours ago the sun has risen!"

Teng said, "Whenever the Brahma within me wants to get up, then I get up. That is the brahmamuhurt, the moment of God. When the God within me wants to get up, who am I to make rules? – I get up immediately, I never lose a single moment. Whenever the God within me wants to get up, I jump out of the bed; whenever he wants to go to bed, I jump into bed. Who am I, Master, to create a disturbance?"

And the master said, "You are right – you have found the right brahmamuhurt."

It is said about him that he would never eat according to the rules – because in a Buddhist monastery you have to follow rules, everything is fixed. That has a beauty of its own, and for some people that fixed routine suits very well. But don't try to follow Teng; you may not be a Teng.

Remember, for some people, almost fifty percent, a routine helps, because whenever something becomes routine you need not worry about it, it takes care of itself. If it is five o'clock you have to get up. You need not decide it every day, because to decide every day will create more anxiety and thinking. If it is six o'clock you have to go to the meditation, so you go; it is seven o'clock so you go for breakfast. At breakfast, fixed things are given every day so you need not think about what is going to be given. You need not even desire because there is no point – the breakfast is fixed, it is always the same. And this way the routine continues.

By and by, it becomes a robot-like thing around you; you are completely free of decisions. You can do other things – you can meditate, you can become aware; you need not be worried about the petty things around you. To fifty percent of the people this suits perfectly; to fifty percent this never suits. To fix themselves into a routine becomes a worry and an anxiety for them; they are not made that way.

One has to feel oneself, one has to feel how one is made and never follow anything else. First just feel yourself. And there are only two possibilities: either you can live a life of spontaneity, or you can live a life of discipline. Both are good, because the basic thing is to become alert and aware.

Teng never followed any rules. Whenever he felt hungry he would eat, even though it might be midnight; whenever he was not hungry he would not eat, although many days would pass. It was not fasting, because fasting has to be forced. It was not a fast; he was not feeling hungry so it was okay, he would not eat. Many nights he would not sleep if he was not feeling sleepy; if he was feeling to, for days together he would sleep.

That's why the sister said:

"When you were alive you took no notice of laws and customs; and even now you are dead you are making a nuisance of yourself."

The sister was also enlightened; otherwise she would have been crying and weeping. She is not crying and weeping; on the contrary, she is giving right advice to this dying man – a fool who was always a nuisance, now even in death. The sister is a totally different type.

This has been my feeling: that women are the type who will need an outer discipline. In that fifty percent of people who would need discipline, about forty percent will always be women. There are reasons for it. The whole of nature has made women to follow a certain law. That's why every twenty-eight days the period comes. The body follows a routine; if there is something wrong, only then is that discipline broken. Otherwise, it is absolutely fixed.

A woman's body follows laws – it has to because she is going to give birth to a child; she is going to become a mother, and a child cannot be left with somebody who moves in an individual way. A woman has a collective unconscious, not an individual unconscious. She has to, because a purpose has to be fulfilled through her. The child will come in nine months, and if a woman is healthy everything will be a routine. If you can make a routine, everything will become healthy. So the sister belongs to the opposite polarity.

From the very beginning you will feel that a girl behaves differently than a boy. A girl is more graceful, more rounded, more obedient, not rebellious. A boy from the very beginning is a trouble-maker, rebellious. If you say, "Don't do this," then he is bound to do it. A boy is totally different. Even in the womb a mother can feel whether the child is going to be a boy or a girl, because the boy starts kicking in the womb. You can feel the girl remain absolutely silent and relaxed, but the boy starts kicking. Even in the womb the male energy is different from the female energy.

This sister must have been always telling him, "You are wrong." But he was true to himself even in his death. He was true to himself when he was alive and he is true to himself when he is dead. He had remained a true, authentic man – true to his own being, not following anything, just following his own life-energy wherever it leads. But the sister was also true to herself: even when the brother was dead she was not weeping and crying. The last advice that could be given she was giving. She said, "You were a nuisance in your life. You created trouble for others because you never followed any laws and customs. And now, even in your death, you are a nuisance to yourself."

She then prodded her brother with her finger and he fell down with a bang. Then they went off to the crematorium.

Both of them knew that there is no death. It is said that when the brother fell down with a bang, the sister just went back to her monastery.

If you take life easily, if you enjoy life, if your life by and by becomes a fulfillment, the same will be your death. What are we doing? We are not enjoying life, we are only preparing to enjoy it – and life is here and now, no preparation is needed. I see people always preparing: they are preparing to live a great life somewhere in the future. They will be afraid of death, because in the future death is waiting. And your life is also in the future: you are making a house, purchasing a car, and this and that, accumulating things – just getting ready to live. You will never be ready, and by the time you are ready, death will knock at your door. That's the fear, that "Death may come before I am ready."

A man of understanding lives life here and now; every moment he lives it. For him there is no death because there is no future life. He exhausts the moment, he lives it totally, he enjoys it, he thanks God for it, he is grateful. Where is the fear of death if at this moment you are alive? Here, at this moment, you are alive – where is the fear of death? Don't try to get ready to die, just live. And I tell you: everybody, as he is, is ready to live this very moment.

Don't miss this moment and don't ask for long preparations; that way you will never be ready. And the mind gets a habitual form: always thinking of tomorrow, tomorrow, it becomes fixed. By the time you have accumulated wealth the mind will again be telling you: Tomorrow, tomorrow. 'Tomorrow' is the disease of the mind.

A new life comes into existence when you live now. A new life is a 'now' life. Then where is the fear? Who is worried about death? Then you can play a joke in the end. And if you live you start feeling what life is. It is felt only through living, there is no other way to feel it. It is just like swimming: you swim and you learn. Swimming comes through swimming, life is felt through living.

You postpone; you don't feel life, you feel death all around. Through postponing you will feel death, through living you will feel life. If you feel life, it is eternal. It has no death to it, it never dies; it goes on and on and on, and each moment is eternity.

Remember it as deeply as possible: don't postpone, don't move into tomorrow. Here, now, is all that you need. Enjoy it, and the more you enjoy the more will be given to you. That is what Jesus meant when he said: Knock and the door shall be opened unto you. Ask and it shall be given. This very moment the door is there. Ask, knock, live! – don't postpone.

This is the whole message of all those who have become awakened: Today is enough, tomorrow will take care of itself. And tomorrow never comes, it is always today. If you know the knack of living here and now, you will be able to live every moment that comes. Even at the moment of death you will be able to live. This is what this Teng did: he lived the moment of death. And if you can live the moment of death, how can you die? Then you change your death also into life.

Just the opposite is happening to you right now: you are changing your life into death because of postponement. Tomorrow – always getting ready, ready, ready; and when the moment comes your mind is still getting ready. Drop all postponements, knock at the moment, and you will be as beautiful as the lilies in the field that Jesus talks about: not even Solomon at the peak of his glory was so beautiful.

You are beautiful, why are you wasting yourself? You are divine, why are you wasting yourself? You are the ultimate, why are you getting lost in tomorrows, in future preparations, in the mind? Why are you wasting your life energy in the desert of time? Be here and now, and this 'now and here' becomes the door. And the door is always waiting for you. Just knock. Just for the knocking, it opens.

Enough for today.

NOTES

1. p.2, from "One Note of Zen" from "Zen Flesh, Zen Bones," page 66, by Paul Reps, Charles E. Tuttle Co., Inc., Tokyo © copyright 1957.

2. p.26, from "Zen Buddhism," page 42, © copyright 1959 Peter Pauper Press, Inc., New York. Reprinted with permission.

3. p.52, from "The Three Types of Religious Method" from "The Cat's Yawn" by Sokei-an, First Zen Insititute of America, New York, 1947.

4. p.74, from "Zen Flesh, Zen Bones," supra, note 1, at page 42.

5. p.101, from "The Practice of Zen" by Chang Chen-chi, Harper & Brothers, New York, 1959.

6. p.132, from "Wisdom of the East Series, The Book of Lieh-Tzu," page 52, translated by A. C. Graham, John Murray Publishers Ltd., London.

7. p.155, from "Zen: Poems, Prayers, Sermons, Anecdotes, Interviews," page 133, © copyright 1965 Lucien Stryk and Takashi Ikemoto, Doubleday, a division of Bantam Doubleday Dell Publishing Groups, Inc.

8. p.178, "Zen Buddhism," supra, note 2, at pages 13-14.

9. p.202, "Wisdom of the East Series, The Book of Lieh-Tzu," supra, note 6, at page 73.

10. p.230, from "Oriental Humor" by R. H. Blyth, Hokuseido Press, Tokyo, 1959.

About The Author

Most of us live out our lives in the world of time, in memories of the past and anticipation of the future. Only rarely do we touch the timeless dimension of the present – in moments of sudden beauty, or sudden danger, in meeting with a lover or with the surprise of the unexpected. Very few people step out of the world of time and mind, its ambitions and competitiveness, and begin to live in the world of the timeless. And of those who do, only a few have attempted to share their experience. Lao Tzu, Gautam Buddha, Bodhidharma...or more recently, George Gurdjieff, Ramana Maharshi, J. Krishnamurti – they are thought by their contemporaries to be eccentrics or madmen; after their death they are called "philosophers." And in time they become legends – not flesh-and-blood human beings, but perhaps mythological representations of our collective wish to grow beyond the smallness and trivia, the meaninglessness of our everyday lives.

Osho is one who has discovered the door to living his life in the timeless dimension of the present. He has called himself a "true existentialist", and has devoted his life to provoking others to seek this same door, to step out of the world of past and future and discover for themselves the world of eternity.

Osho was born in Kuchwada, Madhya Pradesh, India, on December 11, 1931. From his earliest childhood, his was a rebellious and independent spirit, insisting on experiencing the truth for himself rather than acquiring knowledge and beliefs given by others.

After his enlightenment at the age of twenty-one, Osho completed his academic studies and spent several years teaching philosophy at the University of Jabalpur. Meanwhile, he traveled throughout India giving talks, challenging orthodox religious leaders in public debate, questioning traditional beliefs, and meeting people from all walks of life. He read extensively, everything he could find to broaden his understanding of the belief systems and psychology of contemporary man. By the late 1960s Osho had begun to develop his unique dynamic meditation techniques. Modern man, he says, is so burdened with the outmoded traditions of the past and the anxieties of modern-day living that he must go through a deep cleansing process before he can hope to discover the thought-less, relaxed state of meditation.

In the early 1970s, the first Westerners began to hear of Osho. By 1974 a commune had been established around him in Poona, India, and the trickle of visitors from the West was soon to become a flood. In the course of his work, Osho has spoken on virtually every aspect of the development of human consciousness. He has distilled the essence of what is significant to the spiritual quest of contemporary man, based not on intellectual understanding but tested against his own existential experience.

He belongs to no tradition – "I am the beginning of a totally new religious consciousness," he says. "Please don't connect me with the past – it is not even worth remembering."

His talks to disciples and seekers from all over the world have been published in more than six hundred volumes, and translated into over thirty languages. And he says, "My message is not a doctrine, not a philosophy. My message is a certain alchemy, a science of transformation, so only those who are willing to die as they are and be born again into something so new that they cannot even imagine it right now...only those few courageous people will be ready to listen, because listening is going to be risky.

"Listening, you have taken the first step towards being reborn. So it is not a philosophy that you can just make an overcoat of and go bragging about. It is not a doctrine where you can find consolation for harassing questions. No, my message is not some verbal communication. It is far more risky. It is nothing less than death and rebirth."

Osho left his body on January 19, 1990. His huge commune in India continues to be the largest spiritual growth center in the world attracting thousands of international visitors who come to participate in its meditation, therapy, bodywork and creative programs, or just to experience being in a buddhafield.

Suggested Further Reading

Heartbeat of the Absolute

Discourses on the Ishavasya Upanishad

In these discourses Osho gave during a Mount Abu meditation camp, sutras from ancient Hindu scriptures are transmuted into stunning insights that can open the reader's eyes to his own inner reality. Osho speaks on issues that touch the heart of every intelligent individual – on love, possessiveness, God as another name for existence, our investment in forgetting the phenomenon of death, karma, the nature of the mind, and meditation. In addition, he gives practical suggestions about how to prepare for meditation and how to derive the most from meditation techniques.

No Water No Moon

Osho breathes new life into many familiar Zen stories.

"I found *No Water No Moon* one of the most refreshing, cleansing and delightful books I could imagine," wrote the renowned violinist Yehudi Menuhin. "It is a book which will never cease to be a comforting companion."

Finger Pointing to the Moon

Discourses on the Adhyatma Upanishad

These seventeen talks were given at a meditation camp at Mount Abu, Rajasthan. In this beautiful series on the seeds of wisdom, the Upanishads, Osho says, "This Upanishad is a direct encounter with spirituality. There are no doctrines in it; there are only experiences of the fulfilled ones.... In it there is no discussion of that which is born out of curiosity or inquisitiveness, no; in it there are hints to those who are full of longing for liberation, from those who have already attained liberation...."

The Heart Sutra

Discourses on Gautam Buddha's Prajnaparamita Hridayam Sutra highlight both Osho's and Buddha's essential teachings: the merging of negative and positive, the non-existence of the ego and the buddha-nature of mankind. In addition, Osho speaks on the seven *chakras* and the corresponding facets in man – the physical, psychosomatic, psychological, psycho-spiritual, spiritual, spiritual-transcendental and transcendental.

Journey to the Heart

Discourses on the Sufi way

This is a journey towards the heart, on the path of the Sufis. Here Osho speaks on some of the ancient teaching stories of the Sufi mystics, including those of Bayazid, Bahauddin, Dhun-Nun and Maruf Karkhi. This is the path of love: the lover and the beloved. The search for the beloved, the godliness that is within us all.

"Sufism is *the* religion. Whenever a religion is alive it is because Sufism is alive within it." – *Osho*

Osho Commune International

The Osho Commune International in Poona, India, guided by the vision of the enlightened master Osho, might be described as a laboratory, an experiment in creating the "New Man" – a human being who lives in harmony with himself and his environment, and who is free from all ideologies and belief systems which now divide humanity.

The Commune's Osho Multiversity offers hundreds of workshops, groups and trainings, presented by its nine different faculties:

Osho School for Centering and Zen Martial Arts
Osho School of Creative Arts
Osho International Academy of Healing Arts
Osho Meditation Academy
Osho Institute for Love and Consciousness
Osho School of Mysticism
Osho Institute of Tibetan Pulsing Healing

Osho Center for Transformation
Osho Club Meditation: Creative Leisure

All these programs are designed to help people to find the knack of meditation: the passive witnessing of thoughts, emotions, and actions, without judgment or identification. Unlike many traditional Eastern disciplines, meditation at Osho Commune is an inseparable part of everyday life – working, relating or just being. The result is that people do not renounce the world but bring to it a spirit of awareness and celebration, in a deep reverence for life.

The highlight of the day at the Commune is the meeting of the White Robe Brotherhood. This two-hour celebration of music, dance and silence, with a discourse from Osho, is unique – a complete meditation in itself where thousands of seekers, in Osho's words, "dissolve into a sea of consciousness."

For Further Information

MANY OF OSHO'S BOOKS have been translated and published in a variety of languages worldwide. For information about Osho, His meditations, books, tapes and the address of an Osho meditation/information center near you, contact:

Osho International
24 St James's Street, St James's,
London SW1A 1HA, UK

Osho Commune International
17 Koregaon Park
Poona 411001, India

Chidvilas Inc.
P.O. Box 3849, Sedona
AZ 86340, U.S.A.